SAFe® 4.5 Distilled

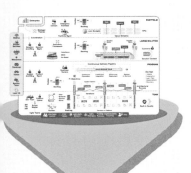

SAFe® 4.5

SAFe®
DISTILLED

**APPLYING THE
SCALED AGILE FRAMEWORK®
FOR LEAN ENTERPRISES**

**Richard Knaster
Dean Leffingwell**

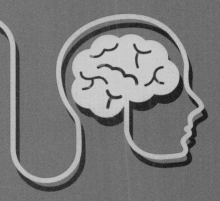

✦Addison-Wesley

Boston • Columbus • New York • San Francisco • Amsterdam • Cape Town • Dubai
London • Madrid • Milan • Munich • Paris • Montreal • Toronto • Delhi • Mexico City
São Paulo • Sydney • Hong Kong • Seoul • Singapore • Taipei • Tokyo

For information about buying this title in bulk quantities, or for special sales opportunities (which may include electronic versions; custom cover designs; and content particular to your business, training goals, marketing focus, or branding interests), please contact our corporate sales department at corpsales@pearsoned.com or (800) 382-3419.

For government sales inquiries, please contact governmentsales@pearsoned.com.

For questions about sales outside the U.S., please contact intlcs@pearson.com.

Visit us on the Web: informit.com/aw

Library of Congress Control Number: 2018941639

ISBN-13: 978-0-13-517049-6

ISBN-10: 0-13-517049-4

1   18

From Richard

Dedicated to my Mom, Sandra Knaster, to whom I am forever grateful for her unconditional love and support. Thanks, Mom!

From Dean

Dedicated to my mother, Louise Hallock, for a lifetime of doing so well that which only a mother can do. Thanks, Mom!

Contents

Preface

When the Scaled Agile Framework (SAFe) was introduced to the public in 2011, we passionately believed that it had the potential to change the way the largest enterprises in the world would develop software and deliver value.

Today, we can say unequivocally that SAFe has lived up to its promise. Hundreds of the world's largest brands now depend on SAFe to stay competitive in an ever-disruptive marketplace, and as of early 2018, more than 250,000 individuals had enhanced their careers by training and becoming certified in SAFe practices. That's a big responsibility, and one that we take very seriously.

As the demand for SAFe continues to grow, so do our efforts to support it. Through Scaled Agile, Inc.—the company behind the Framework—we are continually creating, refining, and delivering tools, resources, and learning events to help enterprises achieve the best possible results with SAFe:

- *The SAFe website.* A freely available knowledge base of proven, integrated principles and practices for Lean, Agile, and DevOps (scaledagileframework.com).

- *Learning and Certific*ation. A comprehensive role-based curriculum for successfully implementing SAFe that includes eight courses and certifications and growing (scaledagile.com/learning).

- *SAFe Community Platform.* Continuous learning, tools, and connections for SAFe professionals with communities of practice for each role, as well as videos, toolkits, and resources for professional development (scaledagile.com/community).

- *Scaled Agile Partner Network.* Worldwide SAFe expertise and support through 170-plus partners (scaledagile.com/find-a-partner).

- *A Global and Regional SAFe Summits.* Annual SAFe Summit conferences are held in the United States and Europe (safesummit.com).

The success of SAFe is a direct result of practicing what we preach. We run our entire business—not just product development—with SAFe. Our walls are plastered with Kanban boards, sticky notes, objectives, and backlogs, and we plan, iterate, and deliver as we prescribe in SAFe. But most importantly, we have hard-wired ourselves to embrace a *learning* mindset. We never assume that we have all the answers, and we do our best to listen to our detractors as much as our enthusiasts. Indeed, we find motivations in both!

Development of SAFe was and is driven by fast feedback and a relentless pursuit of the best possible version of the Framework along with the highest-quality training, certification, and customer experience. And, of course, future versions of the Framework are always in development.

We're grateful to the thousands of forward-thinking individuals who have been instrumental in proving and realizing SAFe's potential: the enterprise adopters and practitioners who are doing the heavy lifting in applying the Framework in enterprises, and the partners, consultants, and trainers who support them.

It's a wonderful thing we've all built together, and we are inspired to continuously evolve SAFe to provide value to the industry—better systems, better business outcomes, and better daily lives for the people who build the world's most important new systems.

Why SAFe?

Digital technologies provide unlimited choices for today's consumer. It's possible to buy anything, from anyone, instantaneously. Businesses that fail to adapt to this new reality do so at their peril. Despite this need for adaptability, many enterprises remain entrenched in legacy processes and outdated organizational hierarchies that impede their ability to rapidly detect and respond to signals from the marketplace.

Organizations must embrace a more fluid business model to compete effectively—a model that quickly allows for new technologies to be assessed, tested, analyzed, and acted upon. This 'fail fast, succeed faster' mentality requires a fundamental shift in work culture and behavior.

Agile was a major step toward enabling that shift, providing a rapid feedback loop between the drivers of business requirements and developers transforming them into solutions. However, Agile was developed for small teams and, by itself, does not scale to the needs of the larger enterprise. So how do employees in an enterprise running 10, 20, or even hundreds of teams align with each other, the customer, and the greater vision of the business?

More than 70% of the *Fortune* 100 and a growing number of the Global 2000 have found the answer in SAFe. The Framework marries the iterative development practices of Agile with the mindset of Lean manufacturing, where the aim is to use fewer resources and eliminate waste while maximizing customer value. With SAFe, organizations are able to create efficiencies and link strategy to execution. This has proved to be a powerful advantage that enables businesses to leverage digital disruption to their advantage.

As case studies on the SAFe website (scaledagileframework.com) show, many enterprises—large and small—are getting outstanding business results from adopting SAFe. These results typically include

- 30–75% faster time-to-market

- 25–75% increase in productivity

- 20–50% improvements in quality

- 10–50% increased employee engagement

As you can imagine, with results like those, SAFe is spreading rapidly around the world. Two leading surveys cite SAFe as the preferred method for scaling Agile, and the 2017 Gartner Research Circle survey "Agile in the Enterprise" describes a steady growth of organizations adopting an enterprise Agile framework; of those frameworks, SAFe is the most commonly adopted and considered.

About This Book

"SAFe® 4.5 Distilled *is the book we've all been waiting for. It breaks down the complexity of the Framework into easily digestible explanations and actionable guidance. A must-have resource for beginners as well as seasoned practitioners.*"

   —Lee Cunningham, Senior Director, Enterprise Agile Strategy
   at CollabNet VersionOne

The SAFe knowledge base at http://www.scaledagileframework.com/ is an invaluable resource for people who build software and systems, but navigating the guidance can be daunting for the uninitiated. SAFe is a robust framework supported by hundreds of web pages. Where do you start? In which order should you read the articles? Which information is really important to you and when?

We get it. There's a Wikipedia aspect to the SAFe body of knowledge that takes time to parse. Our recent publication, *SAFe® 4.5 Reference Guide*, is a handy companion, but it's basically a printed version of the website. It doesn't really tell a story—and that's why we wrote *SAFe® 4.5 Distilled: Applying the Scaled Agile Framework® for Lean Enterprises*.

This book is divided into six parts, each with a specific purpose.

- **Part I: Overview** makes the business case for SAFe and provides an overview of the major elements of the Framework. While we didn't write it to stand alone, it does make a pretty good introduction for those just needing to get a basic understanding of SAFe.

- **Part II: Mindset, Principles, and Leadership** provides the foundational principles that make SAFe effective, including the role of Lean-Agile leaders, the Lean-Agile mindset, and the all-important SAFe principles and values.

- **Part III: Essential SAFe** is the heart of the Framework and is the simplest starting point for implementation. It serves as the basic building block for all other SAFe configurations and describes the most critical elements needed to realize the majority of the Framework's benefits. You'll learn about the primary value delivery mechanisms of SAFe, and how people are organized into Agile teams and Agile Release Trains. You'll also learn how to plan and execute a Program Increment (PI), and how to achieve relentless improvement with the Inspect and Adapt event.

- **Part IV: Large Solution SAFe** is intended to help those building the world's largest, most complex, and most critical systems. Here you will find an overview of the large solution level, discover how to define large and complex solutions, and learn how to execute program increments for Solution Trains.

- **Part V: Portfolio SAFe** describes how to align portfolio execution to the enterprise strategy by organizing Agile development around the flow of value, through one or more value streams. You'll learn how to improve business agility through the principles and practices for portfolio strategy and investment funding, Agile portfolio operations, and Lean governance. In addition, you'll learn how to implement advanced Lean portfolio concepts including Lean budgeting, forecasting, and contracting. You'll also gain insights into potential Agile development capitalization strategies.

- **Part VI: Implementing SAFe** describes how to implement the Framework's principles, practices, and activities. Here you will learn a step-by-step approach to implementation, including how to form a sufficiently powerful guiding coalition, how to design the implementation, how to launch Agile Release Trains (ARTs), and how to sustain and continuously improve the benefits of your SAFe Lean-Agile adoption.

We sincerely hope that you will enjoy reading this book as much as we enjoyed writing it (well, more, actually). Most importantly, we hope that this book will help you build higher-quality software and systems more quickly, to the benefit of your enterprise and your customers.

And as we wrote this book for you, the practitioner, we strongly believe that building such great systems should be fun, too!

—*Richard Knaster and Dean Leffingwell*

Register your copy of *SAFe® 4.5 Distilled* at informit.com for convenient access to downloads, updates, and corrections as they become available. To start the registration process, go to informit.com/register and log in or create an account. Enter the product ISBN (9780135170496) and click Submit. Once the process is complete, you will find any available bonus content under "Registered Products."

Acknowledgments

First and foremost, this is a book about SAFe—and therefore the authors are deeply indebted to all those who have contributed to the development of the Framework. There are more than 100 books and authors who (knowingly or unknowingly) contributed to the bodies of knowledge that underlie SAFe. In addition, there are another 100 or so contributors, reviewers, commenters, editors, graphic designers, and others who make SAFe what it is. But if we were to take time to thank all those who contributed, we wouldn't be able to call this book 'Distilled.' Fortunately, the SAFe Contributors page (scaledagileframework.com/contributors) does the job of acknowledging those contributions, so we needn't repeat that information here.

However, it is most appropriate to thank all those who contributed directly to this work: our Addison-Wesley acquisition editor Greg Doench; production manager Julie Nahil; project manager Dana Wilson; copy editor Jill Hobbs; Scaled Agile, Inc., design director Regina Cleveland; and graphic designers Jeff Long and Kade O'Casey. Last but certainly not least, Alan Sharavsky, copy editor, helped improve the readability of the first edition of this book.

SAFe Distilled Contributors

We would also like to thank everyone who contributed a short story to this book to help clarify SAFe's concepts and make it more interesting and fun.

(In alphabetical order by last name)

Em Campbell-Pretty (SAFe Fellow)

Charlene M. Cuenca (SPCT)

Fabiola Eyholzer (SPC)

Jennifer Fawcett (SAFe Fellow)

Drew Jemilo (SAFe Fellow)

Harry Koehnemann (SAFe Fellow)

Steve Mayner (SAFe Fellow)

Isaac Montgomery (SPCT)

Inbar Oren (SAFe Fellow)

Mark Richards (SAFe Fellow)

Carl Starendal (SPC)

Brian Tucker (SPCT)

Joe Vallone (SPCT)

Eric Willeke (SAFe Fellow)

Yuval Yeret (SPCT)

About the Authors

Richard Knaster, SAFe Fellow, Principal Consultant, Scaled Agile, Inc.

Richard has more than 30 years' experience in software and systems development, in roles ranging from developer to executive, and has been leading large-scale Agile transformations for well over 15 years. Richard actively works on advancing SAFe's Lean-Agile methods as a SAFe Fellow and methodologist. As a principal consultant, he is passionate about helping organizations create a better environment to deliver value, improve quality and flow, and be more engaging and fun. Richard is also co-author of *SAFe® 4.5 Reference Guide.*

Dean Leffingwell, creator of SAFe, Chief Methodologist, Scaled Agile, Inc.

Widely recognized as the one of the world's foremost authorities on Lean-Agile best practices, Dean Leffingwell is an author, serial entrepreneur, and software and systems development methodologist. His two best-selling books, *Agile Software Requirements: Lean Requirements Practices for Teams, Programs, and the Enterprise* and *Scaling Software Agility: Best Practices for Large Enterprises,* form much of the basis of modern thinking on Lean-Agile practices and principles. He currently serves as CEO and Chief Methodologist to Scaled Agile, Inc., which he co-founded in 2011.

Abbreviations Used in This Book

ART   Agile Release Train

BVIR   Big Visible Information Radiator

CapEx   Capital Expenses

CD   Continuous Deployment

CE   Continuous Exploration

CI   Continuous Integration

CoD   Cost of Delay

CoPs   Communities of Practice

DSU   Daily Stand-Up

FW   Firmware

HW   Hardware

I&A   Inspect and Adapt

IP   Innovation and Planning

LACE   Lean Agile Center of Excellence

LPM   Lean Portfolio Management

MBSE   Model-Based Systems Engineering

MMF   Minimal Marketable Feature

MVP   Minimum Viable Product

NFR   Nonfunctional Requirements

OpEx   Operating Expenses

PI   Program Increment

ROI	Return on Investment
RTE	Release Train Engineer
SAFe	Scaled Agile Framework
SBD	Set-Based Design
SPC	SAFe Program Consultant
STE	Solution Train Engineer
SW	Software
UX	User Experience
WIP	Work in Progress
WSJF	Weighted Shortest Job First
XP	Extreme Programming

Part I
Overview

"If you can't describe what you are doing as a process, you don't know what you're doing."

—W. Edwards Deming

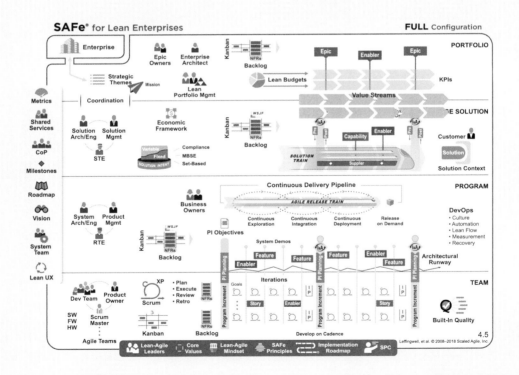

- Chapter 1 – Business Need for SAFe
- Chapter 2 – SAFe Overview

Introduction

In part I, we'll introduce the business need for SAFe and discuss the challenges of software and systems development. We'll also consider how SAFe leverages three main bodies of knowledge—Agile, Lean product development, and systems thinking—to achieve better business outcomes. In addition, this part includes an overview of SAFe that will help you understand the framework and serve as a foundation for your learning journey.

Business Need for SAFe

"Every company is a technology company, no matter what product or service it provides. The companies that embrace this fact are the ones that shape our world."

   —Stephenie Stone, CIO, Americas at M+W Group

Why Do Businesses Need SAFe?

In our fast-paced digital economy, businesses must respond rapidly to advances in technology to maintain a competitive edge. Software and systems are everywhere, driving business innovation and new ways of working, while replacing aging business models.

> "Today, no company can make, deliver or market its product efficiently without technology. While smart phones and the internet used to be cutting edge, these days, new application code release dates and time to market for new technologies are shrinking. This is forcing companies accustomed to a four-year release cycle to adopt to change faster. Businesses must learn how to integrate technology release cycles into their production and service cycles.[1]"

Despite this compelling need to apply technology in their businesses, many enterprises still struggle to develop significant software and systems—the modern fabric of nearly every product, in every industry across the globe.

Companies that understand the urgency to move and adapt faster—and change their ways of working—will succeed. Those that don't will struggle, or simply go out of business. Indeed, the business world is littered with examples: Blockbuster, Kodak, Tower Records, Borders, Palm Computing, Novell, BlackBerry, Polaroid, Nokia (phones), and

---

1. https://www.forbes.com/sites/forbestechcouncil/2017/01/23/why-every-company-is-a-technology-company/#53938fb557ae

Compaq were all iconic market leaders that couldn't adapt to new business models and technology innovations ahead of their competitors.

The lesson is simple: Enterprises must learn how to adapt quickly to changing technology and economic conditions or they will become extinct, no matter their size, smarts, or strength. This holds true even for businesses that don't consider themselves to be information technology (IT) or software companies. Professional services, financial services, healthcare institutions, manufacturers, builders of cyber-physical systems, and government entities are all highly dependent on their ability to produce new technology-based products and services.

The Challenge of System Development

Clearly, our development methods must keep pace with an increasingly complex and interconnected world, which is replete with innovations in mobile technologies, big data, social media, and the Internet of Things (IoT). But organizations must also maintain their existing systems, defend against cyber-attacks, and guard against theft of digital information and intellectual property. Systems are bigger, more extensive, more complex, and more integrated, and their impact on the global economy is enormous. Moreover, the failure of a critical system often has unacceptable social and economic consequences.

Due to this complexity, the size of an enterprise's technology group and the range of technical skills needed is constantly expanding. Although outsourcing can help overcome some of these challenges, it can also present additional risks and complexities, such as delayed communication, dependency on external providers, and loss of internal capabilities. Likewise, outsourcing can also present difficulties in maintaining solution quality and regulatory compliance.

Despite these challenges, many companies still use traditional, 'waterfall' development methods, which rely on linear, sequential phases and phase-gate approvals. This way of working was created more than 40 years ago, when the rate of innovation was slower and the development tools and processes were less complex.

If the enterprise's processes and systems are still based on traditional, sequential ways of thinking and working, even teams that have adopted Agile methods will be unable to deliver value quickly. Moreover, the organization will still struggle to scale its people, processes, and technology to keep up with the digital economy.

Figure 1-1 shows common development problems that many industries experience.

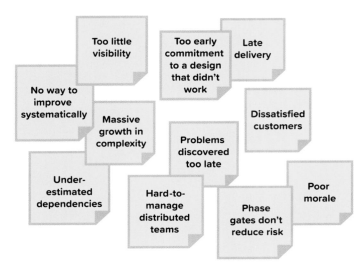

Figure 1-1. Common development problems from retrospectives across many industries

Faced with these difficult challenges, what can be done? Perhaps our best insight comes from W. Edwards Deming, the renowned author and management consultant, who has taught us that the source of most such problems is not poor people performance. *Rather, the problems lie with the system in which people work.*

To achieve broader change, the entire development value stream—from idea to market release—must become more nimble, leaner, and responsive to change. Unfortunately, the organizational structures, processes, and cultures of most businesses were developed more than a century ago. They were built for control and stability, not for innovation, speed, and agility. Small incremental changes to how businesses manage, strategize, and execute are often insufficient to ensure that those firms remain competitive. True transformation to leaner and more agile approaches requires sweeping changes that have a positive, long-lasting impact on the entire enterprise.

Applying New Bodies of Knowledge

Considering the many challenges businesses face in developing large-scale solutions, and the systemic nature of the problems, it simply makes sense to apply all the tools and contemporary knowledge we have available. Fortunately, the last few decades have provided three bodies of knowledge that we can use to address these challenges: *Agile development, systems thinking,* and *Lean product development.* These bodies of knowledge inform the values, principles, and practices of the Scaled Agile Framework (SAFe). Each is described in the following sections.

Agile Development

"We are uncovering better ways of developing software by doing it, and helping others do it."
—Agile Manifesto

In the late 1990s, a number of thought leaders working independently pioneered Agile development. Jim Highsmith, Kent Beck, Martin Fowler, Ken Schwaber, Brian Marick, and many others were experimenting with alternatives to the document-driven, heavyweight processes of that era. Looking for common ground, 17 of them came together at a meeting in Snowbird, Utah. The attendees included independent experts, as well as some of the creators of the lighter-weight software development frameworks, including Extreme Programming (XP), Scrum, and Dynamic System Development Method (DSDM).

What emerged was the *Manifesto for Agile Software Development,* which ignited an industry-wide movement and unified several philosophies and practices behind a common belief system. The manifesto unleashed a dramatic and entirely new way of thinking and working for software developers, one that unlocks the intrinsic motivation of those who do the work.

The importance of this breakthrough cannot be overstated. SAFe is founded on the culture and innovative team-based methods that Agile embraces. Indeed, the manifesto is a critical part of the *SAFe Lean-Agile mindset,* which is further described in chapter 3, 'Lean-Agile Mindset.'

Systems Thinking

"A system must be managed. It will not manage itself. Left to themselves, components become selfish, independent profit centers and thus destroy the system .... The secret is cooperation between components toward the aim of the organization."
—W. Edwards Deming

The second body of knowledge that informs SAFe is *systems thinking,* which is probably best represented by the influential work of Deming. A holistic approach to solution development, this philosophy views a system as an interrelated set of elements.

Systems thinking also acknowledges two distinct systems that must be considered: the system being built for the customer's benefit and the system that constitutes the organization that builds it. The path to better outcomes requires constant focus on the systems thinking principles that apply to both.

Fundamental to the design and implementation of SAFe is the understanding that individuals—the teams, programs, and business units—are all part of the product development system. Systems thinking is further described in Principle #2, Apply Systems Thinking, which can be found in chapter 4, 'SAFe Principles.'

Lean Product Development

"All we are doing is looking at the timeline from when the customer gives us an order to when we receive the cash, and we are reducing the timeline by eliminating the non-value-added wastes."
  —Taiichi Ohno, father of the Toyota Production System

The third body of knowledge, Lean product development, is a hybrid of Lean thinking and product development flow. Lean thinking primarily originates from *Total Quality Management,* and the *Toyota Production System*, and they are a remarkably rich source of Lean guidance. In the preceding quote, Toyota's Taiichi Ohno distills Lean to its very essence: the continuous evaluation of existing processes to eliminate waste and delays. This relentless improvement mindset enables the enterprise to achieve the goal of Lean: delivering the maximum customer value in the shortest sustainable lead time with the highest possible quality to customers and society. Indeed, this is a very worthy goal. In the last few decades, thought leaders such as Allen Ward, Michael Kennedy, Don Reinertsen, Eric Ries, and others have applied the science of Lean to product development. Today, an extensive body of knowledge—Lean product development—can be used by enterprises to dramatically improve their products and solutions. Highlights of Lean product development include the following:

- Understand the full value stream—the sequence of steps used to take a concept from idea to market. Focus on removing waste and delays.

- Develop and manage a sustainable flow of value. Cadence and synchronization, reducing batch size, managing queue lengths, and visualizing and limiting Work in Process (WIP) are keys to achieving flow.

- Respect for people and culture. Lean recognizes that people do all the work. Respecting people—while embracing the cultural changes that support newer and leaner habits—is essential to Lean.

- Accelerate innovation by releasing a Minimum Viable Product (MVP) to get fast feedback with the least investment.

- Embrace kaizen, a culture of continuous improvement. All members of the organization dedicate themselves to relentless improvement.

- Engage in Lean-Agile leadership. Responsibility for implementation and continuous improvement of Lean-Agile development rests with management. Only leaders can change the system by first being trained in—and then becoming trainers of—these leaner ways of thinking and working.

Improving System Development Outcomes

By applying and integrating these three bodies of knowledge, SAFe has evolved as a proven approach for developing complex systems and software. It helps enterprises answer the following types of questions:

- How do we align the company around shared business and technical goals and organize teams around value so that our programs deliver effectively, without the delays and bureaucracy inherent in a hierarchy?

- How do we deliver new value on a predictable schedule so that the rest of the business can plan and execute? How do we manage and minimize dependencies between teams, programs, and value streams?

- How do we scale Agile practices from the team to the larger business objectives?

- How do we improve the quality of our solutions to delight our customers?

- How can we change our culture so that it tolerates failure, rewards risk-taking, and creates an engaging environment that fosters collaboration, innovation, and relentless improvement?

By adopting SAFe—and applying its values, principles, and practices—individuals and enterprises can address these questions and realize greater business results.

That is the subject and purpose of this book.

The Business Benefits of SAFe

"The products we're developing are bigger than one Agile team. For the teams to interact and plan together, we really needed SAFe as the foundation. It brings the practices and methodologies to coordinate multiple teams working on the same product at the same time."

—Mike Eason, CIO, Commercial Banking, Capital One

Now in its fourth major revision, SAFe 4.5 is improving business outcomes for companies of all sizes around the world. It has helped enterprises produce dramatic increases in time-to-market, employee engagement, quality, customer satisfaction, and improved economic outcomes. It also helps create cultures that are more productive, rewarding, and fun.

Figure 1-2 highlights these benefits. These and other benefits are further described in case studies at ScaledAgileFramework.com/case-studies/.

| 10–50% happier, more motivated employees | 30–75% faster time-to-market |
| 20–50% increase in productivity | 25–75% defect reduction |

Figure 1-2. Business results from customer case studies

The following sections highlight these and other benefits.

Quality

SAFe's *built-in quality* practices increase customer satisfaction and provide faster, more predictable value delivery. They also improve the ability to innovate. Companies that apply SAFe typically experience rapid and compelling increases in solution quality:

- "95% decrease in defects" —Telstra
- "5× reduction in deployment impact" —CSG International
- "55% defect reduction rate" — SK Hynix

- "44% decrease in post-release defects" —Mitchell International
- "50% warranty expense decrease" —John Deere
- "20–25% increase in client satisfaction" —SEI Investments

Productivity

Productivity is a critical, personal need for team members. Everyone feels better when they're contributing more—and when they're doing less wasteful work. When productivity increases, system development economics improves, as does employee engagement:

- "Productivity has increased by at least 20–25%." —Discount Tire
- "Team productivity is up by 20–50%." —BMC Software
- "A single defect gets fixed only once now." —TomTom

Employee Engagement

"Fostering a more engaged workforce will help your organization achieve its mission, execute its strategy, and generate positive business results."[2] According to the Hay Group the combination of high employee engagement and enablement results in a 40% increase in employee performance, an 18% increase in customer satisfaction rates, and more than four times higher rates of financial success.[3] Clearly, employee engagement is directly linked to business performance, and SAFe helps improve employee engagement:

- "Employee happiness rating went from 47–67% in 10 weeks." —A medical systems company
- "Improved productivity and morale" —Valpak
- "Overall happier teams" —Elekta

Faster Time-to-Market

SAFe helps businesses deliver value to the market more quickly, thereby helping companies gain first-mover advantages and the higher margins afforded to market leaders. SAFe enterprises typically see a 30–75% (up to 3 times!) improvement in time-to-market:

---

2. SHRM Foundation Executive Briefing, "Employee Engagement: Your Competitive Advantage"; https://www.shrm.org/resourcesandtools/business-solutions/documents/engagement%20briefing-final.pdf

3. http://atrium.haygroup.com/nz/our-products/employee-effectiveness-benefits.aspx

Together, the team and program levels form an organizational structure called the Agile Release Train (ART). The ART brings multiple Agile teams, key stakeholders, and other resources together to pursue an ongoing solution mission.

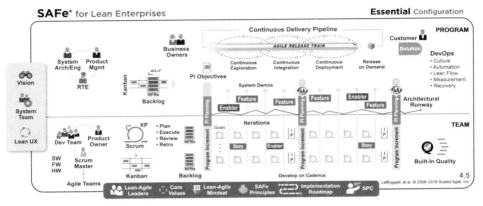

Figure 2-2. Essential SAFe configuration

Highlights of Essential SAFe

The Essential SAFe configuration provides the fundamental elements of the Framework:

- The ART aligns management, teams, and stakeholders to a common mission through a shared vision, roadmap, and program backlog.

- ARTs deliver the features (user functionality) and the enablers (technical infrastructure) needed to provide value on a sustainable basis.

- Team iterations are synchronized and use the same duration and the same start and end dates.

- Each ART delivers valuable and tested system-level increments every two weeks.

- Program Increments (PIs) provide longer, fixed timeboxes for planning, execution, and inspecting and adapting.

- ARTs use large scale, face-to-face PI planning to assure collaboration, alignment, and rapid adaptation.

- ARTs build and maintain a continuous delivery pipeline to regularly develop and release small increments of value. This enables teams to release solutions at any time the market demands.

- ARTs provide common and consistent approaches to system architecture and user experience (UX).

- DevOps—which is a mindset, a culture, and a set of technical practices—provides communication, integration, automation, and close cooperation among all the people needed to plan, develop, test, deploy, release, and maintain a solution.

The following roles help align multiple teams to a common mission and vision, with the necessary coordination and governance:

- *System Architect/Engineer.* The System Architect/Engineer is an individual or a small cross-disciplinary team that applies systems thinking. The people filling this role define the overall architecture for the system, identify new nonfunctional requirements (NFRs), determine the critical elements and subsystems, and identify the interfaces and collaborations among them.

- *Product Management.* Product Management provides the internal voice of the customer, working with Product Owners and customers to understand and communicate their needs, define system features, and participate in validation. Product Management is responsible for the program backlog and prioritizing features and enablers using an economic approach.

- *Release Train Engineer (RTE).* The RTE is a servant leader and the chief Scrum Master for the ART. The person filling this role helps improve the flow of value in the program using mechanisms such as the program Kanban, Inspect and Adapt (I&A) events, PI planning, and more.

- *Business Owners.* Business Owners are a small group of stakeholders who have the primary business and technical responsibility for governance, compliance, and return on investment for a solution developed by an ART. They are key stakeholders who must evaluate fitness for use and actively participate in certain ART events.

- *Customer.* Customers are the ultimate deciders of value and are an integral part of the Lean-Agile development process and value stream. They have specific responsibilities in SAFe.

Three major activities help coordinate the ART: PI planning, system demo, and the I&A event. They are briefly described in the next section and represent three of the ten essential elements of SAFe.

The Ten Essential Elements

Essential SAFe identifies 10 critical elements—applied in all SAFe configurations—that are necessary for successful Lean and Agile development. If enterprises incorporate these elements when creating new solutions, they will be well on their way to realizing SAFe's full benefits.

1. *Lean-Agile Principles.* Nine essential principles inform SAFe practices, and if these practices do not apply directly to a particular context, the underlying principles guide teams to make sure that they are moving on a continuous path to the shortest sustainable lead time.

2. *Real Agile Teams and Trains.* Properly formed and operating Agile teams and trains have everything and everyone needed to produce a working, tested increment of the solution. Fully cross-functional, self-organizing, and self-managing, ARTs allow value to flow more quickly, with a minimum of overhead. Product Management, System Architects/Engineers, and RTEs offer content and technical authority and streamline the development process. Product Owners and Scrum Masters help the development teams meet their objectives. The customer plays a critical role throughout the development process.

3. *Cadence and Synchronization.* Cadence provides a rhythmic pattern of events that is the heartbeat of the development process. It ensures that various team, program, and large solution events are held on a regular schedule to make them routine (e.g., daily stand-up, PI planning, system demo, I&A event, solution demo). Synchronization allows multiple perspectives to be understood and resolved simultaneously. For example, it brings the distinct assets of a system together to assess solution-level feasibility.

4. *Program Increment (PI) Planning.* The cornerstone of the PI, there is no event more powerful in SAFe than PI planning. This event serves as the heartbeat for the ART, aligning all the teams on the ART to a shared mission and vision.

5. *DevOps and Releasability.* SAFe's 'CALMeR' approach to DevOps provides the *culture, automation, Lean-flow, measurement,* and *recovery* capabilities that enable an enterprise to bridge the gap between development and operations. Releasability focuses on the business's capacity to deliver value to its customers more often and according to market demand. Together, DevOps and releasability allow an organization to achieve better economic results through more frequent releases and faster validation of hypotheses.

6. *System Demo.* The primary measure of the ART's progress is the objective evidence provided by a working solution in the system demo. Every two weeks, the full system—the integrated work of all teams on the train for that iteration—is demoed to stakeholders, who then provide the feedback the train needs to stay on course and take corrective action.

7. *Inspect and Adapt (I&A).* The I&A is a significant event held every PI. A regular time to reflect, collect data, and solve problems, the I&A event assembles teams and stakeholders to assess the solution. It's a scheduled opportunity to define the improvements needed to increase the velocity, quality, and reliability of the next PI.

8. *Innovation and Planning (IP) Iteration.* The IP iteration occurs at least once every PI and serves multiple purposes. It acts as an estimating buffer for meeting PI objectives and dedicates time for innovation, continuing education, and PI planning and I&A events. It's like extra fuel in the tank: Without it, the train may start straining under the 'tyranny of the urgent' iteration.

9. *Architectural Runway.* The architectural runway consists of the existing code, components, and technical infrastructure necessary to support implementation of high priority, near-term features without excessive delay and redesign, which accelerates value delivery.

10. *Lean-Agile Leadership.* For SAFe to be effective, the enterprise's executives, and managers must take leadership responsibility for Lean-Agile adoption and success. Therefore, leadership must be trained in—and become trainers of—these leaner ways of thinking and operating. The SAFe transformation achieves its full benefits only when leaders are *actively participating* and taking *responsibility* for the implementation.

Portfolio SAFe

The Portfolio SAFe configuration (Figure 2-3) aligns the execution of the portfolio's initiatives with the enterprise strategy, organizing Agile development around the flow of value through one or more value streams.

The portfolio configuration defines strategy and investment funding for the value streams and their solutions in the portfolio. It also provides Agile portfolio operations and Lean governance for the people and resources needed to deliver solutions. Lean budgeting and Agile governance practices help assure that investments will provide the benefits the enterprise needs to meet its strategic objectives.

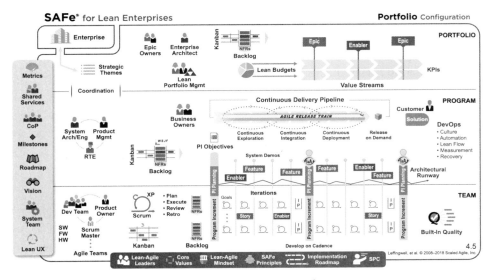

Figure 2-3. Portfolio SAFe configuration

Portfolio SAFe Highlights

This configuration builds on Essential SAFe by adding the following portfolio-level concerns:

- *Lean Budgets.* Lean budgeting allows fast and empowered decision-making, with appropriate financial control and accountability.

- *Value Streams.* Each value stream is an ongoing, repeatable series of steps (e.g., system definition, development, deployment, and release) that continuously builds and deploys solutions. Each has funding for the people and resources needed to deliver value to the business or customer.

- *Portfolio Kanban.* This Kanban makes upcoming portfolio work visible and supports Work-in-Process (WIP) limits to assure that demand matches the value stream capacity.

The following roles and functions provide the accountability and governance of portfolio investments:

- *Lean Portfolio Management (LPM).* The LPM function has the highest level of decision-making and financial accountability for a SAFe portfolio. It's responsible for three primary areas: strategy and investment funding, Agile portfolio operations, and Lean governance.

- *Epic Owners.* Epic Owners take responsibility for coordinating epics through the portfolio Kanban system.

- *Enterprise Architect.* The Enterprise Architect is an individual or a small team that works across value streams and programs to deliver the strategic technical direction that can optimize portfolio outcomes. The Enterprise Architect often acts as an Epic Owner for enabler epics.

Large Solution SAFe

The Large Solution SAFe configuration (Figure 2-4) is used by those developing the largest and most complex solutions, typically requiring multiple ARTs and suppliers, but without portfolio-level considerations. Large solutions are common in industries such as aerospace and defense, automotive, and government, where the large solution—not portfolio governance—is the primary concern.

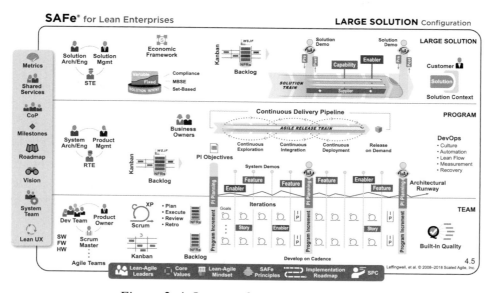

Figure 2-4. Large solution configuration

Large Solution Highlights

This configuration builds on Essential SAFe by adding the following large solution–level concerns:

- *Solution Train.* The Solution Train is the critical organizational element at the large solution level. It aligns the people and the work with a common solution vision, mission, and backlog.

- *Supplier.* Suppliers develop components, subsystems, or services needed by a Solution Train.

- *Economic Framework.* The economic framework provides financial boundaries for the Solution Train's decision-making.

- *Solution Intent.* Solution intent is a repository for current and future solution behaviors that supports system definition, communication, verification, validation, and compliance. It also extends built-in quality practices with system engineering disciplines, including set-based design (SBD), Model-Based Systems Engineering (MBSE), and compliance.

- *Solution Context.* The solution context describes how the system will interface and be packaged and deployed in its operating environment.

- *Solution Kanban.* The solution Kanban facilitates the flow of capabilities and enablers for the solution.

The following roles help align multiple ARTs and suppliers to a shared mission and vision, with the necessary coordination and governance:

- *Solution Architect/Engineer.* The Solution Architect/Engineer is an individual or small team that defines the technical and architectural vision for the solution under development.

- *Solution Management.* Solution Management has the content authority for the large solution level and works with customers to understand their needs. These individuals create the solution vision, backlog, and roadmap, as well as define the requirements (capabilities and enablers), and guide the work through the solution Kanban.

- *Solution Train Engineer (STE).* The STE is a servant leader and coach who facilitates and directs the work of all ARTs and suppliers.

Three critical activities help coordinate Solution Trains, which are composed of multiple ARTs and suppliers:

1. *Pre- and Post-PI Planning.* Pre- and post-PI planning events allow Solution Trains to build a unified plan across ARTs and suppliers for the next PI.

2. *Solution Demo.* In the solution demo, the results of all the development efforts from multiple ARTs—along with the contributions from suppliers—are integrated, evaluated, and made visible to customers and other stakeholders.

3. *Inspect and Adapt (I&A).* The Solution Train I&A event is held at the end of each PI; it is where the current state of the solution is demoed and evaluated by the Solution Train. Representatives of multiple ARTs and suppliers then reflect and identify improvement backlog items in a structured problem-solving workshop.

Full SAFe

The Full SAFe configuration (Figure 2-5) is the most comprehensive version of the Framework. It supports enterprises that build and maintain large, integrated solutions that employ hundreds of people or more and includes all levels of SAFe: team, program, large solution, and portfolio. The largest enterprises may require multiple instances of various SAFe configurations.

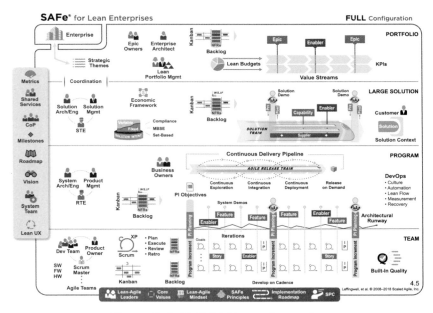

Figure 2-5. Full SAFe configuration

Full SAFe Highlights

This configuration builds on Essential SAFe by adding the portfolio and large solution levels. It also has the following aims:

- Allows organizations to combine multiple and varied SAFe configurations

- Provides the most comprehensive and robust configuration to meet the needs of the largest enterprises

SAFe's configurable framework provides just enough guidance to meet the needs of any product, service, or organization. An enterprise can start simply, and grow as its needs evolve over time.

Each of these four configurations is supported by a 'spanning palette' and 'foundation' elements that support the Framework's flexibility, as shown in Figures 2-6 and 2-7, and is described in the following sections.

The Spanning Palette

The spanning palette contains various roles and artifacts that may apply to a specific team, program, large solution, or portfolio context. An essential feature of SAFe's flexibility, it permits organizations to select only those elements they need for their configuration.

Figure 2-6 illustrates two versions of the spanning palette: The figure on the left appears only with Essential SAFe, while the one on the right supports all other configurations. However, since SAFe is a framework, enterprises can apply any of the elements from the larger spanning palette to Essential SAFe.

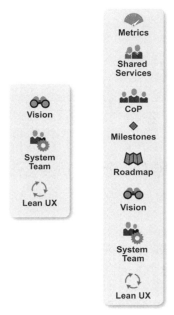

Figure 2-6. Spanning palette

Following is a brief description of each spanning palette element:

- *Metrics.* The primary measure of progress in SAFe is objective evidence of working solutions that is assessed throughout the process and more formally at every PI. SAFe also defines other intermediate- and long-term measures that teams, trains, and portfolios can use to evaluate progress.

- *Shared Services.* Shared services represent specialty roles that are typically required but cannot be dedicated full time to any specific train.

- *Community of Practice (CoP).* A CoP is an informal group of team members and other experts who share practical knowledge in one or more relevant domains in the context of a program or enterprise.

- *Milestones.* Three types of milestones—fixed-date, program increment, and learning milestones—represent significant planned and specific goals or events.

- *Roadmap.* The roadmap communicates the planned deliverables and milestones over a time line.

- *Vision.* The vision describes a future view of the proposed solution, reflecting customer and stakeholder needs, including the features and capabilities suggested to address them.

- *System Team.* The System Team helps build the Agile development environment, including continuous integration and test automation, and other technologies used by Agile teams in a continuous delivery pipeline.

- *Lean UX.* Lean UX applies Lean principles to user experience design. Through constant measurement and learning loops (build–measure–learn), it employs an iterative, hypothesis-driven approach to product development. SAFe utilizes Lean UX at scale, with the right combination of centralized and decentralized UX design and implementation.

The Foundation

As illustrated in Figure 2-7, The SAFe foundation contains the supporting principles, values, mindset, implementation guidance, and leadership roles needed to successfully deliver value at scale. Each foundation element is described next.

Figure 2-7. SAFe foundation

- *Lean-Agile Leaders.* Management has the ultimate responsibility for business outcomes. As a result, leaders must be trained in—and become trainers of—these leaner ways of thinking and operating. Lifelong learners and teachers, Lean-Agile leaders understand, apply, embrace, and teach Lean and Agile principles and practices.

- *Core Values.* Four core values—alignment, built-in quality, transparency, and program execution—define the larger value system of SAFe. (These values are described in the next section.)

- *Lean-Agile Mindset.* The Lean-Agile mindset is the combination of beliefs, assumptions, and actions of SAFe leaders and practitioners who embrace the concepts of the Agile Manifesto and Lean thinking.

- *SAFe Principles.* These nine fundamental truths, beliefs, and economic tenets inspire and inform the roles and practices that make SAFe effective. The principles are described further in chapter 4, 'SAFe Principles.'

- *SAFe Implementation Roadmap.* Implementing the changes necessary to become a Lean enterprise requires a substantial shift in practices and thinking for most companies. SAFe provides an implementation roadmap to guide the journey, which is described in part VI, 'Implementing SAFe.'

- *SAFe Program Consultants (SPCs).* SPCs are change agents who combine their technical knowledge of SAFe with an intrinsic motivation to improve their company's software and systems development processes.

Core Values

SAFe's core values define its essential ideals and beliefs. They help people understand what to focus on and how to determine whether their organization is on the right path to fulfill its business goals.

1. *Alignment.* When management and teams align with a common mission, all the energy flows toward helping the customer. Everyone is "on the same page," working toward the same goals. Alignment occurs when everyone in the portfolio, and every team member on every ART, understands the strategy and the part they play in delivering it.

2. *Built-in Quality.* The economic impact of poor quality is simply unacceptable at scale. Built-in quality practices increase customer satisfaction and provide faster, more predictable value delivery. They also increase the ability to innovate and take risks. Without built-in quality, businesses cannot achieve the Lean

goal of 'maximum value in the shortest sustainable lead time.' These practices also ensure that each solution element, at every increment, meets quality standards throughout the process.

3. *Transparency.* You can't manage a secret. Transparency builds trust, which is essential for performance, innovation, risk-taking, and relentless improvement. After all, large-scale solution development is hard; things don't always work out as planned. Creating an environment where the *facts are always friendly* is the key to building trust and improving performance. It enables fast, decentralized decision-making and increases employee empowerment and engagement.

4. *Program Execution.* SAFe delivers value in the shortest sustainable lead time with the highest possible quality by creating stable, long-lived teams-of-Agile-teams, known as an ART. The ART is basically an Agile program, which is a virtual organization designed to span functional silos, eliminate unnecessary handoffs and steps, and accelerate value delivery by adopting SAFe's Lean-Agile principles and practices. Fully cross-functional, self-organizing, and self-managing, ARTs allow value to flow more quickly, with a minimum of overhead.

Summary

The type and extent of software and solution development initiatives within the larger enterprise vary widely. There can be no one-size-fits-all approach for every context. Along with the flexible spanning palette, SAFe's four out-of-the-box configurations—Essential SAFe, Portfolio SAFe, Large Solution SAFe, and Full SAFe—provide the adaptability needed to address most solution development challenges. This helps SAFe enterprises deliver the world's most important systems in the shortest sustainable lead time with the best possible quality and value.

Part II
Mindset, Principles, and Leadership

"The foundation for any successful change is the right mindset, principles, and leadership."

> —The SAFe authors

- Chapter 3 – Lean-Agile Mindset
- Chapter 4 – SAFe Principles
- Chapter 5 – Lean-Agile Leaders

Introduction to Part II

In part II, we introduce perhaps the most important elements of SAFe: the Lean-Agile mindset, principles, and Lean-Agile leadership. Ultimately, transforming an organization requires a new way of thinking. Only when we change our thinking and change ourselves does it become possible to change those around us—and perhaps even the entire world. If you want your enterprise to adapt and change, then you must do the same—you need to embody the change and adapt to a new way of thinking, behaving, and leading.

Lean-Agile Mindset

"It is not enough that management commit themselves to quality and productivity, they must know what it is they must do. Such a responsibility cannot be delegated."

"People are already doing their best. The problem is with the system. Only management can change the system."

    —W. Edwards Deming

Overview

Deming's quotes remind us of a basic premise of SAFe: Management is ultimately responsible for the success of the business and, therefore, any significant change to its way of working. There is no question that moving to a Lean-Agile paradigm will be a huge change. Not only are the practices different, but the belief system, core values, culture, and philosophies are different as well.

To begin this journey of change and instill new habits into the culture, leaders and managers need to learn and adopt a 'Lean-Agile mindset,' as shown in Figure 3-1.

The two primary aspects of a Lean-Agile mindset are:

1. *Thinking Lean.* Organized around six concepts, the SAFe 'House of Lean' is shown in Figure 3-1. The roof represents the goal of delivering value. The pillars support this through the concepts of respect for people and culture, flow, innovation, and relentless improvement. Lean leadership provides the foundation on which everything else stands.

2. *Embracing Agility.* SAFe rests entirely on the skills, aptitude, and capabilities of Agile teams and their leaders. Although there's no single definition of Agile,

the manifesto provides the value system and principles that introduced Agile methods into mainstream software development. We must *enhance* it, not abandon it, as we scale.

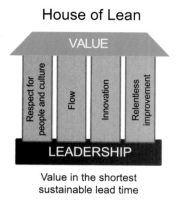

House of Lean | **Agile Manifesto**

Individuals and interactions over processes and tools

Working software over comprehensive documentation

Customer collaboration over contract negotiation

Responding to change over following a plan

That is, while there is value in the items on the right, we value the items on the left more.

Figure 3-1. The aspects of a Lean-Agile mindset

Thinking Lean and embracing agility combine to make up the Lean-Agile mindset. This new management approach improves workplace culture by providing the concepts and beliefs that leaders need to guide a successful business transformation. In turn, this helps individuals and enterprises achieve their goals.

Thinking Lean

Lean was originally developed to streamline manufacturing.[1] However, the principles and practices of Lean thinking are now deeply embedded and extensive in software, product, and systems development. For example, Alen Ward,[2] Don Reinertsen,[3] Mary and Tom Poppendieck,[4] Dean Leffingwell,[5] and others have reframed Lean thinking in the product

1. James P. Womack, Daniel T. Jones, and Daniel Roos, *The Machine That Changed the World: The Story of Lean Production—Toyota's Secret Weapon in The Global Car Wars That Is Revolutionizing World Industry* (Free Press, 2007).
2. Allen Ward and Dunward Sobeck, *Lean Product and Process Development* (Lean Enterprise Institute, 2004).
3. Donald G. Reinersten, *The Principles of Product Development Flow: Second Generation Lean Product Development* (Celeritas, 2009).
4. Mary Poppendieck and Tom Poppendieck, *Implementing Lean Software Development: From Concept to Cash* (Addison-Wesley, 2001).
5. Dean Leffingwell, *Agile Software Requirements: Lean Requirements Practices for Teams, Programs, and the Enterprise* (Addison-Wesley, 2011).

development context. Combined with these ideas, we developed the SAFe House of Lean (described next), which was inspired by the Toyota 'House of Lean' and others.

Goal: Value

The 'roof' of the house represents value and the goal is to deliver the *maximum value in the shortest sustainable lead time*, while providing the highest possible quality to customers and society. High morale, emotional and physical safety, and customer delight are also goals with economic benefits.

Pillar 1: Respect for People and Culture

By itself, a Lean-Agile approach cannot implement or perform any real work. Indeed, people do all the work. Respect for people and culture is a basic tenet of Lean. SAFe enables people to evolve their own practices and improvements. Management challenges them to change and may guide them. However, individuals and teams learn problem-solving and reflection skills and are accountable for making the appropriate improvements.

To evolve into a Lean organization, the enterprise's culture will need to change substantially. Respect for people and culture should also be extended to relationships with suppliers, partners, customers, and the broader community; all of those parties are vital to the long-term success of the enterprise. When there's real urgency for change, culture improves naturally. First, understand and implement SAFe values and principles. Second, deliver winning results. Cultural change will surely follow.

GLOBALLY DISTRIBUTED TEAMS AND RESPECT FOR PEOPLE

Steve Mayner, SAFe Fellow and SPCT at Scaled Agile, Inc., shares an experience he had with respect for people:

"Respect for people is often put to the test when globally distributed organizations form their ARTs [Agile Release Trains] and begin considering how to build high-performing teams-of-teams that are not collocated. The two most common mistakes I've seen are underestimating the level of technological infrastructure needed to enable face-to-face communications, and a bias toward scheduling based on the time zone of the corporate headquarters. At a recent ART launch, the company made tremendous commitments to overcoming these barriers and invested heavily in the video and audio support needed to make participants in all five countries be fully represented on the train. They also adjusted the start times so that all locations shared the scheduling sacrifice needed to have all ART members participating simultaneously. The gratitude of these teams was powerfully expressed in the PI Planning retro!"

Pillar 2: Flow

The secret to successfully implementing SAFe is to establish *a continuous flow of incremental value delivery* based on continuous fast feedback and adjustment. Continuous flow enables quicker value delivery, effective built-in quality practices, constant improvement, and evidence-based governance.

The principles of flow are an important part of the Lean-Agile mindset:

- Understanding the full value stream
- Visualizing and limiting Work in Process (WIP)
- Reducing batch sizes
- Managing queue lengths

Additionally, a Lean organization focuses intensely on reducing delays and eliminating waste.

Pillar 3: Innovation

Flow builds a solid foundation for value delivery. But without innovation, both the product and the process will rapidly decline. To foster innovation, Lean-Agile leaders must do the following:

- Understand and implement the Japanese concept of 'Gemba,' which advises management to 'get out of the office' and into the workplace. The workplace is where actual value is produced and products are created and used. As Toyota's Taiichi Ohno has said, "No useful improvement was ever invented at a desk."

- Provide a regular time and space for people to be creative. Time for innovation must be purposeful and become part of the regular development rhythm. SAFe's Innovation and Planning (IP) iteration provides one such opportunity.

- Avoid the trap of focusing solely on the 'tyranny of the urgent' iteration. Innovation cannot occur with 100% utilization and constant firefighting.

- Apply innovation accounting[6] to establish early, nonfinancial, actionable metrics that provide fast feedback on the important elements of the solution's new concepts, features, and its associated business model.

- Validate innovations with customers and then 'pivot without mercy or guilt' when the hypothesis needs to change.

---

6. Eric Ries, *The Lean Startup: How Today's Entrepreneurs Use Continuous Innovation to Create Radically Successful Businesses* (Crown Business, 2011).

Pillar 4: Relentless Improvement

The fourth pillar is relentless improvement. It guides the business to become a learning organization through continuous reflection and adaptation. A 'constant sense of competitive danger' drives the aggressive pursuit of improvement opportunities. Leaders and teams systematically do the following:

- Optimize the whole, not just the parts, of the organization and the development process.
- Consider facts carefully and then act quickly.
- Apply Lean tools and techniques to determine the root cause of problems and apply effective countermeasures quickly.
- Reflect at key milestones to openly identify and address process shortcomings at all levels.

Foundation: Leadership

The foundation of Lean is leadership, the starting point of team success. The enterprise's managers, leaders, and executives are responsible for the adoption and success of the Lean-Agile paradigm. To be successful, leaders must be trained in these new and innovative ways of thinking and exhibit the principles and behaviors of Lean-Agile leadership.

Embracing Agility

The right half of the Lean-Agile mindset is, of course, Agile. In chapter 1, 'Business Need for SAFe,' we introduced the Agile Manifesto, the foundation for cross-functional, self-organizing, self-managing teams. The second half of this chapter is devoted to this critical element of SAFe.

SELF-MANAGING AND SELF-ORGANIZING

The manifesto and the methods that support it rely on self-managing, self-organizing teams. To traditional management, this can be disturbing, so some explanation is warranted. A self-organizing, self-managing team is a group of people who work together to achieve a goal or objective with minimal direction. They have authority and autonomy to plan and execute their work, make decisions, and adapt to changing conditions. They determine when and how to do the work, and who will do it. Self-managing teams monitor their own progress, solve problems together, and continuously improve their process. All of this occurs with subtle or no management control. The teams, however, are aligned with management and the business via common goals, solution architecture, user experience guidelines, and enterprise standards.

The Values of the Agile Manifesto

Figure 3-2 illustrates the Agile Manifesto and is followed by a description of its four values.

The values of the Agile Manifesto

We are uncovering better ways of developing software by doing it and helping others do it.

Through this work we have come to value:

Individuals and interactions over processes and tools

Working software over comprehensive documentation

Customer collaboration over contract negotiation

Responding to change over following a plan

That is, while there is value in the items on the right, we value the items on the left more.

Figure 3-2. Manifesto for Agile Software Development

We Are Uncovering Better Ways

The first phrase of the manifesto deserves emphasis: *"We are uncovering better ways of developing software by doing it and helping others do it."*

We interpret this as describing an ongoing journey of discovery to increasingly embrace Agile behaviors, a journey with no end. SAFe is not a fixed, frozen-in-time framework. As soon as we uncover better ways of working, we adapt the framework, as evidenced by more than five major releases as of this writing.

Where We Find Value

We'll discuss the values shortly, but the final phrase of the manifesto is also important and sometimes overlooked: *"That is, while there is value in the items on the right, we value the items on the left more."*

Some people may misinterpret the value statements as a binary decision between two choices (for example, working software versus comprehensive documentation), but that's not the intended meaning. Both items have value; however, the item on the left has more value (for example, working software). The Agile Manifesto is not rigid or dogmatic. Instead, it embraces the need to balance the values based on the context.

Individuals and Interactions over Processes and Tools

Concerning process, Deming notes, "If you can't describe what you are doing as a process, then you don't know what you are doing." So, Agile processes in frameworks like Scrum, Kanban, and SAFe do matter. However, a process is only a means to an end. When you're captive to a process that isn't working, then you may know what you're doing, but 'what you are doing' may not be working. So, *favor individuals and interactions,* then modify processes accordingly.

In a distributed environment, tools are critically important to assist with communication and collaboration (for example, video conferencing, text messaging, ALM[7] tools, and wikis). This is especially true at scale. However, tools should not replace face-to-face communication.

Working Software over Comprehensive Documentation

Documentation is important and has value (for example, user help, system models, regulatory/compliance documentation). But creating documents for the sake of complying with potentially outdated corporate governance models has negative value. As part of a change program, governance, as reflected in part by documentation standards, needs to be updated to reflect the Lean-Agile way of working.

One form of documentation, software requirement specifications, is particularly tricky, and one might assume that the authors of the manifesto were concerned about their over-constrained effect. Too often, requirement specifications cause Big Design Up Front (BDUF) and project delays consistent with waterfall thinking. They frequently constrain development to overly complicated specifications—early, 'fixed point' solutions—that are often impractical to implement.

Rather than create detailed documentation too early—especially the wrong kind—it's more valuable to show customers working software to get their feedback. Therefore, favor *working software.* And document only what's necessary.

Customer Collaboration over Contract Negotiation

Customers are the ultimate deciders of value, so their close collaboration is essential in the development process. To convey the rights, responsibilities, and economic concerns of each party, contracts are often necessary—but recognize that contracts can

---

7. ALM: application life-cycle management

over-regulate what to do and how to do it. No matter how well they're written, they don't replace regular communication, collaboration, and trust. Instead, contracts should be win–win propositions. Win–lose contracts usually result in poor economic outcomes and distrust, creating short-term relationships instead of long-term business partnerships. Instead, favor *customer collaboration*. An approach to more agile contracts is highlighted in chapter 17, 'Lean Governance.'

Responding to Change over Following a Plan

Change is a reality that the development process must reflect. The strength of Lean-Agile development is in how it embraces change. As the system evolves, so does the understanding of the problem and the solution domain. Business stakeholder knowledge also improves over time, and customer needs evolve as well. Indeed, those changes in understanding add value to our system.

Of course, the manifesto phrase "over following a plan" indicates that *there is in fact a plan*. Planning is an important part of Agile development. Indeed, Agile teams and programs plan more often and more continuously than their counterparts using a waterfall process. However, plans must adapt as new learning occurs, new information becomes visible, and the situation changes. Worse, evaluating success by measuring conformance to a plan drives the wrong behaviors (e.g., following a plan in the face of evidence that the plan is not working).

> Martin Fowler[8] reports that, "in the latter part of the Snowbird meeting, and in the following couple of months, we worked on identifying the twelve principles." Fowler goes on to say, "The manifesto is a rallying cry: it says what we stand for and also what we are opposed to. Several items were worded to clearly make a distinction between our views and that of many others in the software industry. I hope the manifesto will make clear what is and isn't agile."

Agile Manifesto Principles

The Agile Manifesto has 12 principles that support its values.[9] Listed here, these principles take those values a step further and specifically describe what it means to be Agile:

---

8. http://martinfowler.com/articles/agileStory.html (July 9, 2006).
9. http://agilemanifesto.org/principles.html

1. Our highest priority is to satisfy the customer through early and continuous delivery of valuable software.

2. Welcome changing requirements, even late in development. Agile processes harness change for the customer's competitive advantage.

3. Deliver working software frequently, from a couple of weeks to a couple of months, with a preference for the shorter time scale.

4. Business people and developers must work together daily throughout the project.

5. Build projects around motivated individuals. Give them the environment and support they need, and trust them to get the job done.

6. The most efficient and effective method of conveying information to and within a development team is face-to-face conversation.

7. Working software is the primary measure of progress.

8. Agile processes promote sustainable development. The sponsors, developers, and users should be able to maintain a constant pace indefinitely.

9. Continuous attention to technical excellence and good design enhances agility.

10. Simplicity—the art of maximizing the amount of work not done—is essential.

11. The best architectures, requirements, and designs emerge from self-organizing teams.

12. At regular intervals, the team reflects on how to become more effective and then tunes and adjusts its behavior accordingly.

Most of these are self-explanatory. They need no elaboration, except for a discussion of applying the Agile Manifesto at scale, which is covered next.

The combination of values and principles in the manifesto creates a framework for what the Snowbird attendees believed was the essence of Agile. The industry is the better for the extraordinary business and personal benefits conferred by this new way of thinking and working. We are grateful for it.

Applying the Agile Manifesto at Scale

The brief document that launched this massive movement is more than 17 years old. Since then, not one word has changed. So, it's fair to ask, given all the advancements in the last 17 years: Is the Agile Manifesto still relevant? Or should it be treated like a historical document that has long since served its purpose?

What's more, Agile was defined for small, potentially fast-moving software-only teams. And that raises another valid question: Does the Agile Manifesto scale? Does it meet the needs of enterprises developing the biggest and most complex software and systems? Does it serve the needs of systems that require hundreds of people to build them and have unacceptably high costs of failure?

Rather than judge Agile's ability to remain relevant on our own, what better way to assess the manifesto's practicality than by asking the people actively engaged in building these new systems? Specifically, we routinely ask SAFe students to do the exercise described in Figure 3-3 in class.

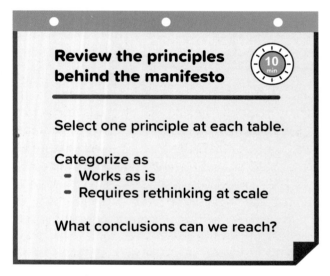

Figure 3-3. Agile Manifesto class exercise

The typical response is that principles 1, 3, 4, 7, 8, 9, 10, and 12 'work as-is.' The conclusion is that most Agile principles scale without requiring any rethinking, and indeed, *most need even more emphasis* when applied at scale. The other principles typically foster a little more discussion, as highlighted here:

1. *Principle #2—Welcome changing requirements, even late in development. Agile processes harness change for the customer's competitive advantage.* The comments here are, 'It just depends.' This reaction doesn't reflect indecision on the part of the class participants. Instead, it recognizes that the cost of change

SAFe Principles

"The impression that 'our problems are different' is a common disease that afflicts management the world over. They are different, to be sure, but the principles that will help to improve the quality of product and service are universal in nature."

—W. Edwards Deming

Why Focus on Principles?

SAFe is based on Lean-Agile principles—the core beliefs, fundamental truths, and economic values that drive effective roles and practices. It is based on principles because they are enduring. No matter the situation, they stand the test of time and can be applied universally. Principles inform SAFe practices—the specific activity, action, or way of accomplishing something. But a practice that works in one situation may not necessarily apply or work in another. Therefore, before an enterprise can apply SAFe practices, it requires an understanding of the underlying principles. This chapter describes the nine SAFe Lean-Agile principles, illustrated in Figure 4-1.

#1 - Take an economic view

#2 - Apply systems thinking

#3 - Assume variability; preserve options

#4 - Build incrementally with fast, integrated learning cycles

#5 - Base milestones on objective evaluation of working systems

#6 - Visualize and limit WIP, reduce batch sizes, and manage queue lengths

#7 - Apply cadence, synchronize with cross-domain planning

#8 - Unlock the intrinsic motivation of knowledge workers

#9 - Decentralize decision-making

Figure 4-1. SAFe principles

Principle #1: Take an Economic View

"While you may ignore economics, it won't ignore you."
—Don Reinertsen, *Principles of Product Development Flow*

Achieving the goal of Lean—the *shortest sustainable lead time, with the best quality and value to people and society*—requires understanding the economics of building systems. Without that, even a technically competent system may cost too much to develop, take too long to deliver, or have manufacturing or operating costs that cannot be sustained. Leadership, management, and knowledge workers must grasp the economic impact of their actions. Therefore, SAFe's first Lean-Agile principle is to *take an economic view*, which is founded on two basic concepts:

- Deliver incrementally, early, and often.
- Sequence jobs for maximum benefit.

Each of these is described in the next sections.

Deliver Incrementally, Early, and Often

The primary benefit of SAFe, and the Agile economic imperative, is to develop and deliver solutions iteratively and incrementally. Each increment (represented by the little boxes in Figure 4-2) reduces risk and uncertainty and produces value on its own. This is in sharp contrast to the waterfall development approach, illustrated at the top of this figure.

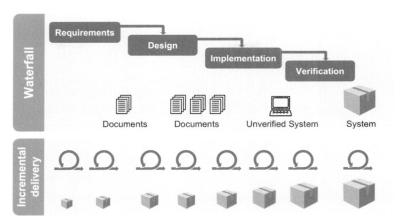

Figure 4-2. Moving to early and continuous delivery of value

With SAFe, each increment delivers value to the customer much earlier, as shown in Figure 4-3.

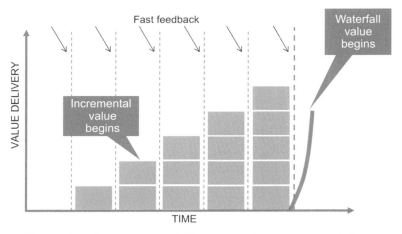

Figure 4-3. Incremental delivery accelerates value delivery

Moreover, the value of each increment persists over time, and the accumulated value delivers substantial benefits even early in the solution life cycle. By comparison, *all* the value for waterfall delivery must wait until the end, when all the features are complete. (And that's only if they're delivered on time!) Also, new features or solutions delivered to market early are typically *more* valuable than those delivered later. This means that a solution delivered early—even with a set of minimal marketable features—provides more economic value than a theoretically more complete product delivered later. Early and often is just better economically—that is the Agile economic imperative.

Sequence Jobs for Maximum Benefit

In chapter 1, 'Business Need for SAFe,' we mentioned the critical role that Reinertsen's *Principles of Product Development Flow* plays in providing some of the foundation for SAFe. After all, SAFe is a *flow-based* system, designed to provide a continuous flow of value to the customer. This is a critical difference from traditional systems development, which favors large, infrequent releases. In turn, this perspective requires a far different approach to prioritizing work. In a flow-based system, work must be reprioritized continuously, depending on the economic and technical facts known at that time. Understanding how to *sequence jobs* is critical to achieving the best economic outcomes.

Reinertsen describes an algorithm for job sequencing called Weighted Shortest Job First (WSJF). WSJF is calculated by dividing the Cost of Delay (CoD) for a job (i.e., the value not achieved while waiting) by the duration of the job, as shown in Figure 4-4.

$$\text{WSJF} = \frac{\text{Cost of Delay}}{\text{Job Duration (Job size)}}$$

Figure 4-4. A formula for WSJF

The job with the highest WSJF is the next most important job, as it delivers the most value in the least amount of time. WSJF can be applied at any level of SAFe. To better understand WSJF, refer to Reinersten's original work[1] and the SAFe article[2] by that name.

Calculating the Cost of Delay

In SAFe, *jobs* are the epics, features, and capabilities that deliver value. SAFe describes three parameters that contribute to the CoD:

---

1. Donald Reinertsen, *The Principles of Product Development Flow: Second Generation Lean Product Development* (Celeritas Publishing, 2009).

2. http://dev.scaledagileframework.com/wsjf/

- *User and/or business value.* This represents the value to the user and/or customer of the particular job. Do people prefer this over that? What is the revenue or business impact?

- *Time criticality.* This captures the time-sensitivity of the job. Does the timing of delivery matter? Is there a fixed deadline? Will the customers wait or move to another solution?

- *Risk reduction and/or opportunity enablement.* This value represents some of the critical intangibles. What else does this item do for our business? Does it reduce the risk of this delivery or of one in the future? Will this feature create new business opportunities?

The sum of these elements is the total CoD for the job, as shown in Figure 4-5.

To establish the CoD, it isn't necessary to determine the absolute monetary value for each parameter. That can be hard to do and can create significant overhead. But Agile teams know how to estimate work relatively, and this technique applies well to the CoD parameters. In other words, teams just compare jobs to each other and rank each CoD parameter relative to other jobs in the backlog.

$$\text{Cost of Delay} = \frac{\text{User - Business}}{\text{Value}} + \frac{\text{Time}}{\text{Criticality}} + \frac{\text{Risk Reduction and/or}}{\text{Opportunity Enablement}}$$

Figure 4-5. The parameters of the cost of delay in SAFe

Duration

Next, teams need to estimate the denominator of WSJF, job *duration*, which can also be challenging. Before development starts, it can be difficult to predict what level of resources might be available when it comes time to do the job, so duration cannot always be predicted in advance. Fortunately, all other things being equal, bigger jobs take longer to do, so *job size* is usually a good proxy for duration. To quickly establish the *job size*, relative estimating can be used here, too. Agile teams get pretty good at estimating relative job size.

Despite this recommendation, job size does *not* always make a good proxy for the duration of the WSJF. For example, sometimes the duration is not directly proportional to the job size. A small job may have multiple dependencies on other work that cause it to take longer than a bigger job, or a large item might potentially be completed in a shorter timeframe than a larger one due to high resource availability. In these cases, the job duration is the appropriate denominator of WSJF.

Calculate Weighted Shortest Job First

With that data, we can then compare jobs to each other with a straightforward calculation using the worksheet illustrated in Figure 4-6.

Feature	User- business value	Time criticality	RR | OE value	CoD	Job size	WSJF
		+	+	=	÷	=
		+	+	=	÷	=
		+	+	=	÷	=

· Scale for each parameter: 1, 2, 3, 5, 8, 13, 20
· Note: Do one column at a time; start by picking the smallest item and giving it a "1."
· There must be at least one "1" in each column!
· The highest priority is the highest WSJF.

Figure 4-6. An example spreadsheet for calculating WSJF

Teams enter the job name and the job's individual parameters relative to other jobs, then calculate the result. The jobs with the highest WSJF have the highest priority. This simple, fast, and effective prioritization technique allows stakeholders for ARTs (Agile Resource Trains) and Solution Trains to pick the most important job to work on next, without a lot of delay or overhead.

Supporting Economic Principles

Delivering incrementally and sequencing jobs are two essential methods that achieve better business outcomes. However, Reinertsen describes several additional economic principles as well:

- Do not consider money already spent (ignore sunk costs).
- Understand the economic trade-off parameters.
- Make economic choices continuously.
- Use decision rules to decentralize economic control.

Principle #2: Apply Systems Thinking

"A system must be managed. It will not manage itself. Left to themselves, components become selfish, independent profit centers and thus destroy the system . . .. The secret is cooperation between components toward the aim of the organization."

—W. Edwards Deming

Chapter 1, 'Business Need for SAFe,' briefly introduced systems thinking as one of SAFe's three foundational bodies of knowledge. Systems thinking takes a holistic approach to solution development. It incorporates all aspects of a system and its environment into its design, development, deployment, and maintenance. Figure 4-7 illustrates the primary aspects of systems thinking. Understanding them helps leaders and teams navigate the complexity of solution development, the organization, and the larger picture of total time-to-market.

The solution itself is a system.

The enterprise building the system is a system too.

Optimize the full value stream.

A system must be managed.

System Arch/Eng

Lean-Agile Leaders

Figure 4-7. Aspects of systems thinking

The Solution Is a System

Solution SAFe guides the development and deployment of complex software and systems. The result of those efforts is the *solution*, referring to the output of each value stream. Applications, satellites, medical devices, and websites are all examples of solutions. When it comes to such systems, Deming's guidance that "a system must be managed" leads to several critical insights.

- Team members must understand clearly what the boundaries of the system are, what the system is, and how it interacts with the environment and systems around it.

- Optimizing a component does not optimize the whole system. Components can become selfish and hog the resources—computing power, memory, electrical power, whatever—that other elements need.

- For the system to behave well as a system, intended behavior and some higher-level understanding of its architecture (how the components work together to accomplish the aim of the system) must be understood. Intentional design is fundamental to systems thinking.

- The value of a system passes through its interconnections. Those interfaces—and the dependencies they create—are critical to providing ultimate value. Continuous attention to those interfaces and interactions is vital.

- A system can evolve no faster than its slowest integration point. The faster the full system can be integrated and evaluated, the faster the system knowledge grows.

The Enterprise Building the System Is a System, Too

The people, management, and processes of the organization that builds the solution also form a system—an idea that is the second concept behind systems thinking. The understanding that *systems must be managed* applies here as well. Otherwise, the components of the organization building the system will optimize locally and become selfish, limiting the rate and quality of the overall value delivery. In addition to the rules given earlier, this leads to another set of insights:

- Building complex systems is a social endeavor. Therefore, leaders must create an environment in which people can collaborate on better ways to build systems.

- Suppliers and customers are integral to the value stream. The enterprise must treat them as partners, building a long-term foundation of trust.

- Optimizing a component does not optimize the system here, either. Locally optimizing teams or functional departments does not optimize the flow of value through the enterprise.

- Value crosses organizational boundaries. Accelerating value delivery requires eliminating functional silos and creating cross-functional organizations, such as an ART.

Understand and Optimize the Full Value Stream

 A SAFe portfolio is a collection of value streams, each delivering one or more solutions to the market. As illustrated in Figure 4-8, each development value stream consists of the sequence of steps necessary to implement a new capability, integrated and deployed via a new or existing system.

Figure 4-8. The solution development value stream

This third belief behind systems thinking—understand and optimize the full value stream—is the only way to reduce the total time it takes to go from "concept to cash."[3] Systems thinking mandates that leaders and practitioners comprehend and continuously enhance the full value stream, especially as it crosses technical and organizational boundaries.

Value stream mapping[4] provides a systematic way to view all the steps required to produce value and address this challenge. Doing so reveals that the steps adding actual value—creating code and components, deployment, validation and so on—consume only a small portion of the total time to market. It then becomes obvious to focus on eliminating or reducing delays between steps to improve cycle time.

Only Management Can Change the System

"Everyone is already doing their best; the problems are with the system . . . only management can change the system."
  —W. Edwards Deming

This Deming quote prepares us for a final set of insights: Systems thinking requires a new approach to management as well. Managers must be systematic problem solvers. They must take the long view, proactively eliminate impediments, and lead the organizational changes necessary to improve the systems that limit performance.

---

3. Mary Poppendieck and Tom Poppendieck, *Implementing Lean Software Development* (Addison-Wesley, 2006).
4. Karen Martin, and Mike Osterling. *Value Stream Mapping* (McGraw-Hill, 2014).

Understanding these systems-thinking principles help leaders and teams comprehend *what* they are doing, *why* they are doing it, and *how* they are affecting those around them. In turn, this leads to a leaner and smarter enterprise, one that can better navigate the organization and solution development complexities, leading to better business outcomes. In chapter 5, 'Lean-Agile Leaders,' we'll cover this topic in greater detail.

Principle #3: Assume Variability; Preserve Options

"Generate alternative system-level designs and subsystem concepts. Rather than try to pick an early winner, aggressively eliminate alternatives. The designs that survive are your most robust alternatives."

—Allen C. Ward, *Lean Product and Process Development*

Solution development can be described as the "process of converting uncertainty to knowledge."[5] Development happens amid tremendous variability. Technology and market uncertainty are always present. But variability is inherently neither bad nor good, as it drives both risk and opportunity. Rather, it's the type and timing of variability that determine economic value.

On the one hand, attempting to eliminate variability too soon causes poor economic outcomes and a risk-adverse culture that cannot innovate. On the other hand, teams must resolve unnecessary variability resulting from routine work—for example, automated code deployment that eliminates error-prone manual processes. What's left, then, is the remaining, inherent variability of technology uncertainty.

Set-Based Design

Understanding that variability is ever-present drives teams to develop more effective development practices. One example is *set-based design*. Traditional development practices tend to drive teams to select a single design option quickly and then modify that design until it eventually meets the system intent. "This can be an effective approach, unless of course one picks the wrong starting point; then subsequent iterations to refine that solution can be very time-consuming and lead to a suboptimal design."[6]

---

5. Dantar Oosterwal, *The Lean Machine* (Amacom, 2010).

6. Marco Lansiti, "Shooting the Rapids: Managing Product Development in Turbulent Environments" (*California Management Review* 38, 1995).

This strategy can be described as a 'point-based' approach, as shown at the top of Figure 4-9. Here, a single option chosen up front often results in significant rework and delays due to problems that are typically discovered at the end. What's more, the later those problems are found, the costlier they are to fix. And the bigger and more technically innovative the system is, the higher the odds are that you will choose the wrong starting point!

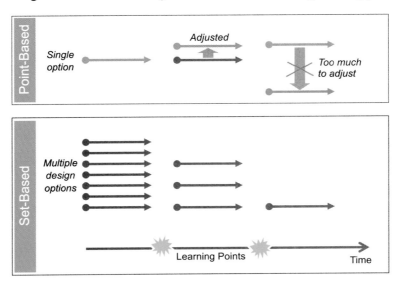

Figure 4-9. Point-based versus set-based design

A better approach is *set-based design*, shown at the bottom of Figure 4-9. Set-based design manages risk better by considering multiple design options at the start. From there, teams continuously weigh economic and technical trade-offs—as identified from objective evidence presented at integration *learning points*. They then eliminate the weaker options over time. Based on the knowledge they've gained to that point, they decide on a final design. This process keeps design options open for as long as possible, converges as necessary, and produces more optimal technical and economic outcomes.

Principle #4: Build Incrementally with Fast, Integrated Learning Cycles

"The epiphany of integration points is that they control product development and are the leverage points to improve the system. When the timing of integration points slips, the project is in trouble."

—Dantar P. Oosterwal

This principle of both Lean and Agile development is pivotal to describing the mechanism for a new approach to systems building.

In traditional, phase-gated development, investment costs begin immediately, accumulating until a solution is delivered. Often, little to no actual value is delivered until all the committed features are available or the program runs out of time or money. Moreover, during development, it's difficult to get meaningful feedback because the process isn't designed for that. Likewise, the system isn't set up for delivery of incremental capabilities. So, the risk remains in the program until the deadline, and even into deployment and initial use.

This process often reduces trust between the teams building the solution and the customer. In response, customers and teams try even harder to define the requirements and select 'the best' design up front, often implementing more rigorous phase gates. Unfortunately, each of these solutions actually *compounds* the underlying problem.

The principles of taking an economic view, applying systems thinking, and relying on set-based design inform us that a better approach is to *build incrementally, with fast integrated learning cycles*. This leads to the next set of insights.

Integration Points Create Knowledge from Uncertainty

By focusing development on *integration points*, the Lean-Agile team gains knowledge quickly and incrementally. The knowledge gained from integration points establishes continuous technical feasibility. In addition, many integration points can serve as Minimum Viable Products (MVPs) or prototypes to release in the market for the purposes of product testing, establishing usability, and gaining objective customer feedback. Where necessary, these fast feedback points allow teams to 'pivot' to an alternative course of action, one that should better serve the needs of the intended customers.

Integration Points Occur by Intent

The development process and the solution architecture are designed, in part, to focus on cadence-based integration points. Each point creates a 'pull event,' which pulls the various solution elements into an integrated whole, even though it addresses only a portion of the system intent. Integration points pull the stakeholders together as well, creating a routine synchronization that helps assure everyone that the evolving solution addresses the real and current business needs, as opposed to the assumptions established at the beginning. Each integration point delivers its value by converting uncertainty into knowledge.

Figure 4-10 illustrates how integration points reinforce Shewhart's[7] basic 'Plan–Do–Check–Adjust' (PDCA) scientific learning process. As previously described, these integration points serve as the primary mechanism for controlling the variability of solution development. Like science, the system advances one cycle at a time.

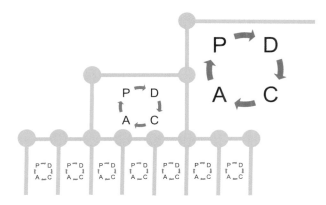

Figure 4-10. Nested, harmonized integration points occur by intent using a fixed cadence

Moreover, *the more frequent the integration points, the faster the learning.* In complex systems, local integration points assure that each element, component, or capability is meeting its responsibilities to the overall solution intent. Local integration points for features or components must then be integrated at the next higher system level. The larger the system, the greater the number of integration levels. The highest, least-frequent integration point (for example, a solution in SAFe) provides the only true measure of solution progress. When the timing of integration points slips, it's a sure sign of problems, and probably a delayed schedule. Even then, this early warning system helps facilitate recovery by changing the technical approach, scope, cost, or delivery schedule.

Principle #5: Base Milestones on Objective Evaluation of Working Systems

"There was, in fact, no correlation between exiting phase gates on time and project success . . . the data suggested the inverse might be true."

—Dantar P. Oosterwal, *The Lean Machine*

---

7. Walter Andrew Shewhart, *Statistical Method from the Viewpoint of Quality Control* (New York: Dover, 1939).

The Problem with Phase-Gate Milestones

Building today's large-scale systems requires substantial financial investment. Stakeholders need to collaborate to ensure that the proposed return on investment will occur *throughout the development process*, versus just hoping that everything will be okay in the end.

Many companies rely on a sequential, phase-gated development process to assess progress and control of investments, relying on review and approval of completed milestones as shown in Figure 4-11. But this model has an inherent flaw: In most cases, a working solution isn't available at the gates that demonstrates the actual progress or solution viability. As a result, true progress isn't known until the end, when the solution is integrated and tested. Figure 4-11 also shows that late discovery of problems is a significant and common weakness of the phase-gate approach.

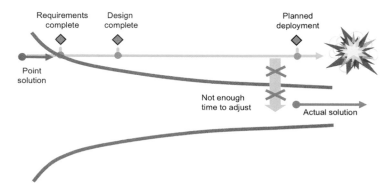

Figure 4-11. The problem with one-pass, phase-gate milestones

Milestones Provide Objective Evidence

Unlike phase-gated development, SAFe iteration and Program Increment (PI) milestones include all the steps in the process that produce an increment of value: requirements, design, development, and testing. Milestones are reviewed routinely, on a fixed cadence, as illustrated in Figure 4-12.

The larger PI milestones provide objective evidence of the viability of the full solution in process. They also help the team assess the overall progress against the nearer-term objectives and the road map and provide the opportunity to fully evaluate the solutions and to Inspect and Adapt (I&A) the development process itself.

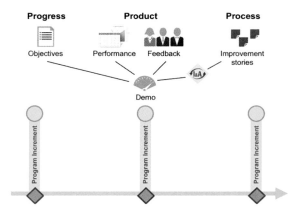

Figure 4-12. Iteration and PI milestones replace phase-gate milestones

Principle #6: Visualize and Limit WIP, Reduce Batch Sizes, and Manage Queue Lengths

"Operating a product development process near full utilization is an economic disaster."

—Donald Reinertsen

To achieve the shortest sustainable lead time, Lean enterprises strive for a state of continuous flow, which allows them to move new system capabilities quickly from concept to deployment. This requires sufficient resources to be able to respond to unforeseen events. In addition to resource capacity, there are three primary keys to implementing flow:

1. Visualize and limit Work in Process (WIP).

2. Reduce the batch sizes of work.

3. Manage queue lengths.

Visualize and Limit WIP

Having too much work in the system causes multitasking and frequent context switching. It overloads the people doing the work and reduces focus, productivity, and throughput. The results: increased wait times for new functionality and unhappy people. To solve these problems, the first step is to make the current WIP visible to all stakeholders. The simple Kanban board in Figure 4-13 provides one example of how to do this.

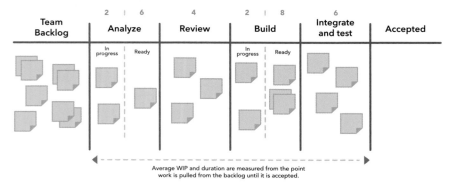

Figure 4-13. Example Kanban board

Kanban boards show the total amount of work at each development step and help identify bottlenecks. In some cases, merely visualizing the current work allows developers to address the systemic problems of too much work *starting* and not enough *finishing*. The next step is to establish WIP limits, thereby balancing the work against the available capacity. When any step reaches its WIP limit, no new work is started until the bottleneck is addressed. Flow increases measurably.

Reduce Batch Size

Another way to improve flow is to decrease the batch sizes of the work. Small batches flow through the system faster and with more predictable completion times, which in turn fosters faster learning and value delivery. As Figure 4-14 illustrates, the economically optimal batch size depends upon both the holding cost (the cost of inventory and of delaying feedback and value) and the transaction cost (the cost of planning, implementing, and testing the batch).

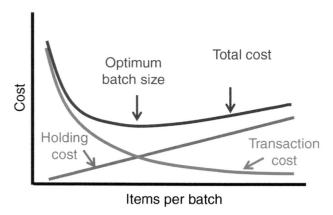

Figure 4-14. Total cost is the sum of the transaction and holding costs

To improve the economics of handling smaller batches and increase throughput and reliability, it's essential to reduce the transaction costs associated with any batch. This typically involves increasing investment in infrastructure and test automation, including practices such as continuous integration, test-driven development, and DevOps.

Manage Queue Lengths

The last insight to improve flow is to manage and reduce the lengths of the work queue. Long queues of work are just bad. They create all sorts of undesirable results:

- *Longer cycle times.* There's a longer wait for new items entering the queue.

- *Increased risk.* The items in the queue, such as requirements, decay over time.

- *Increased variability.* Each item has some variability, and the more items, the more total variability.

- *Lower motivation.* A really large queue of work lowers the sense of urgency.

In contrast, reducing queue length decreases delays, reduces waste, and increases quality and predictability of outcomes.

Decreasing Wait Times

Little's law—the fundamental law of queuing theory—tells us that the *average wait time is equal to the average queue length divided by the average processing rate.* (While this may sound complicated, even the line at Starbucks teaches us that the longer the queue, the longer the wait.) It also tells us that there are only two options to decrease wait times: reduce the length of the queue or increase the processing rate. Increasing the processing rate—doing things faster—is indeed beneficial, but improvements in processing rates may reach their limits before they truly impact quality. So, the *fastest* way to reduce wait times is to reduce the *length of the queue*. Keeping backlogs short and largely uncommitted facilitates accomplishing this goal. Visualizing the backlog also helps immensely. By combining the three elements of *visualizing and limiting WIP*, *reducing batch sizes*, and *managing queues*, measurable improvements in throughput, quality, customer satisfaction, and employee engagement are possible.

Principle #7: Apply Cadence; Synchronize with Cross-Domain Planning

"Cadence and synchronization limit the accumulation of variance."

—Donald Reinertsen

Solution development is an inherently uncertain process. This uncertainty conflicts with the business's need to manage investment, track progress, and plan and commit to a longer-term course of action. The Lean-Agile approach strives to balance this inherent *variability* with the *certainty* needed to enable the business to plan and operate effectively. When it comes to R&D, it's a balancing act, to be sure. The primary way to achieve this feat is to use *cadence* and *synchronization*, supported by *cross-domain planning.*

- *Cadence* transforms unpredictable events into predictable ones. It makes routine that which can be routine. Cadence provides a rhythmic pattern—the dependable heartbeat of the development process.

- *Synchronization* causes multiple events to happen at the same time. It allows multiple development perspectives to be understood, resolved, and integrated simultaneously, which limits deviation from the plan to a single time interval.

Figure 4-15 highlights many of the benefits of cadence and synchronization.

Cadence	Synchronization
• Makes waiting times for new work predictable	• Facilitates cross-functional trade-offs of people and scope
• Supports regular planning and cross-functional coordination	• Aligns all stakeholders
• Limits batch sizes to a single interval	• Provides for routine dependency management
• Controls injection of new work	• Supports integration and assessment of full system
• Provides scheduled integration points	• Provides feedback from multiple perspectives

Figure 4-15. Benefits of cadence and synchronization

Applying Cadence in SAFe

The SAFe 'develop on cadence' mantra illustrates how critical cadence is to the development process. The following are examples:

- Agile teams use a fixed cadence for iterations (typically 2 weeks); ARTs and Solution Trains apply a fixed cadence for PIs (8 to 12 weeks).
- Event calendars are established well in advance. This includes PI planning, system demos, Inspect and Adapt (I&A) events, and team-level events.
- System and solution integration are frequent and programmatic.

However, Reinertsen notes that 'delivering on cadence' is another matter entirely, and one that requires scope or capacity margin. Programs need to be careful about planning to meet date-based commitments, which requires some scope or capacity margin (buffer)—something that you'll see in many elements of the SAFe planning and commitment processes.

Applying Synchronization in SAFe

SAFe applies cadence-based synchronization routinely. The following are examples:

- To support communication, coordination, and system integration, teams align their iterations to the same schedule.
- Routine events such as Scrum of Scrums (SoS) and Product Owner (PO) Sync help manage dependencies.
- ARTs in a Solution Train use the same schedule for PIs.
- System and solution demos integrate components of the system to routinely assess overall viability.
- Regular, cross-functional planning aligns the development teams, business, customers, and suppliers to a common mission and context.

Taken together, cadence and synchronization—and the associated activities—help reduce uncertainty and manage the variability inherent in solution development.

Synchronize with Cross-Domain Planning

"Future product development tasks can't be pre-determined. Distribute planning and control to those who can understand and react to the end results."

— Michael Kennedy, *Product Development for the Lean Enterprise*[8]

As Kennedy notes, and as decentralized decision-making (Principle #9) implies, centralized planning for significant solution initiatives is problematic. Simply put, the complexity is too great, and the facts change too quickly for a centralized planning function to be effective. In its place, SAFe provides for routine, *cross-domain*, face-to-face planning. This kind of planning is the glue that holds the entire process together. The most obvious example is PI planning, in which teams and stakeholders from different functional areas gather to plan the work for an upcoming PI. This event is essential to SAFe: If you aren't doing PI planning, then you aren't doing SAFe. PI planning (and pre- and post-planning for Solution Trains) serves three primary purposes:

1. *Assesses the current state of the solution.* An integrated, solution-level demonstration provides an objective assessment of the current state. This typically occurs just before the planning event.

2. *Realigns all stakeholders to a common technical and business vision.* Based on the current state, business and technology leaders reset the mission, with the minimum number of constraints (Principle #8 and Principle #9). This aligns all stakeholders to a common vision, both near- and long-term.

3. *Plans and commits teams to the next PI.* Based on the new knowledge, the teams plan what they can accomplish in the upcoming timebox. Sharing the planning and control empowers teams to create the best possible plans to achieve the best possible solution within the given constraints.

With synchronized cross-domain planning, the business has a current ongoing plan that leads to the appropriate actions. Also, the development of large-scale systems is fundamentally a social activity. This planning event provides a continuous opportunity to create and improve the social network that builds the solution. This is such an important topic that chapter 7, 'Planning a Program Increment,' is devoted entirely to the value and mechanisms of PI planning.

---

8. Michael Kennedy, *Product Development for the Lean Enterprise* (Oaklea Press, 2003).

Principle #8: Unlock the Intrinsic Motivation of Knowledge Workers

"Knowledge workers are people who know more about the work they perform than their bosses."

—Peter Drucker[9]

Drucker's definition of a knowledge worker is a wake-up call for many people in business today. After all, how can managers seriously attempt to supervise, outthink, and coordinate the technical work of a large number of people who know more about the system than they do? Simply put, they can't. Instead, it's far more beneficial for management to focus on *unlocking the intrinsic motivation of knowledge workers*. Tips for accomplishing this include the following:

- Leverage systems thinking.
- Understand the role of compensation.
- Create an environment of mutual influence.
- Provide autonomy, mastery, and purpose.

Leverage Systems Thinking

Leveraging systems thinking allows knowledge workers to communicate across functional boundaries, make decisions based on economics, and receive fast feedback about the viability of their solutions. They can participate in continuous, incremental learning and mastery, and they can contribute to a more productive and fulfilling solution development process.

Understand the Role of Compensation

Many organizations still embrace outdated assumptions about human potential and individual work performance. Despite mounting evidence that short-term incentives and pay-for-performance plans don't work and often do harm, they continue to apply these and similar measures. Authors as varied as Pink[10] and Drucker[11] have highlighted the

---

9. Peter F. Drucker, *The Essential Drucker* (Harper-Collins, 2001).
10. Daniel Pink, *Drive: The Surprising Truth about What Motivates Us* (Riverhead Books, 2011).
11. Peter F. Drucker, *The Essential Drucker* (Harper-Collins, 2001).

core paradox of compensation for knowledge workers: If you don't pay people enough, people won't be motivated. But after a certain point, *money no longer motivates.* In fact, specific monetary incentives can have the opposite effect on knowledge workers.

Lean-Agile leaders understand that neither money nor the reverse—threats, intimidation, or fear—inspires ideation, innovation, and deep workplace engagement. Specifically, incentive-based practices, based on individual objectives, cause internal competition and can destroy the cooperation needed to achieve the larger aim. These ill-guided efforts should be eliminated.

Create an Environment of Mutual Influence

"To effectively lead, the workers must be heard and respected."
—Peter Drucker

An environment of mutual influence fosters motivation and empowerment. Leaders create an environment of mutual influence by giving honest feedback supportively, showing willingness to become more vulnerable, and encouraging others to do the following:[12]

- Disagree when appropriate.
- Advocate for the positions they believe in.
- Make their needs clear and push to achieve them.
- Enter into joint problem solving with management and peers.
- Negotiate, compromise, agree, and commit.

Provide Autonomy, Mastery, and Purpose

"It appears that the performance of the task provides its own intrinsic reward . . . this drive . . . may be as basic as the others. . ."
—Daniel Pink, *Drive: The Surprising Truth About What Motivates Us*

Daniel Pink's work, and the work of many others, helps us understand that there are three primary factors in establishing deep workplace engagement: *autonomy, mastery,* and *purpose.*

---

12. David L. Bradford and Allen Cohen, *Managing for Excellence: The Leadership Guide to Developing High Performance in Contemporary Organizations* (John Wiley and Sons, 1997).

them with new behaviors. For most leaders, that usually involves taking *Leading SAFe*, a two-day class for leaders that has proved effective in helping management gain the knowledge needed to lead the change.

Emphasize Lifelong Learning

The bodies of knowledge that inform SAFe—Agile development, systems thinking, and Lean product development—are documented in hundreds of books, many distilling a lifetime of expertise into a few hundred pages. While the SAFe bibliography contains more than 100 references, a recommended reading list[2] is provided on the SAFe website. This list focuses on the books most relevant to the values and principles that describe SAFe and changes as new works become available. We encourage leaders, SPCs, and knowledge workers to read as many as they can on their learning journey.

Leaders can also facilitate ongoing learning in the following ways:

- Sponsoring and participating in book clubs

- Hosting lunch-and-learns

- Benchmarking with other companies

- Supporting outside conferences and educational opportunities

Develop People

In the book *Managing for Excellence*,[3] Bradford and Cohen describe three different leadership styles:

- Leader as expert

- Leader as conductor

- Leader as developer of people

All three styles can play a role in being an effective leader—there is no one, perfect leadership style. Depending on the situation and context, each can be effective and may work well when a leader knows when to apply them. Each is described next.

---

2. http://www.scaledagileframework.com/recommended-reading/
3. David L. Bradford and Allan R. Cohen, *Managing for Excellence* (Wiley Publishing,1997).

Leader as Expert

The 'leader as expert' is technically proficient in their domain. In this style, the leader defines tasks and selects courses of action. This approach can make sense when the leader knows more about the work than their reports. Figure 5-1 highlights some of the characteristics and challenges of this model.

Characteristics	Challenges
• Technician or master craftsman • Promoted because they were best at their job • Problem solver, the one people go to for answers • Understands the domain and the technology • Work is when people leave them alone	• Limits learning and growth of direct reports • Focuses on technical problem to the detriment of human factors • Leader's knowledge becomes outdated

Figure 5-1. Leader as expert

Most people became managers based on their technical or scientific expertise, so the leader as expert is common in the high-tech world. Promoted into management, these leaders' competence ensured that solutions were technically and economically viable. That makes sense. Who wants a manager who doesn't know what they are talking about?

However, as Figure 5-1 illustrates, there's also a potential disadvantage of this leadership style. The leader as expert may view productive work only as when 'people leave me alone,' or perceive that 'my role is to define a technical course of action for others.' That limits the growth and empowerment of the direct reports.

Leader as Conductor

'Leader as conductors' do not provide the technical solution. Instead, they orchestrate the activities of the organization to achieve its objectives. This, too, is a sensible leadership method. This leader may have influence beyond the local team, may better understand the organization and its politics, and can let others focus on the technical tasks. It's especially effective when coordination is essential for maximum performance. However, this style has challenges, too, as Figure 5-2 illustrates.

Characteristics	Challenges
• The central decision maker, nerve center, coordinator	• Narrows the focus of direct reports to their own areas
• Orchestrates all individual parts of the organization into a harmonious whole	• Pushes conflict upward, looking for the boss to fix it
• Subtle and indirect manipulation to their solution	• Uses systems and procedures to control work
• Manages across individuals, teams, and departments	• Works harder and harder without realizing full potential
• Work is coordinating others	

Figure 5-2. Leader as conductor

And this style has a significant disadvantage: If this leader's work *is to coordinate others*, how do the direct reports gain their own experience in coordinating and managing?

Leader as Developer of People

The goal of the 'leader as developer of people' is to help individuals and teams realize their fullest potential. In other words, the leader's *work is to develop other's knowledge, skills, and experience.* The behaviors and benefits of this style appear in Figure 5-3.

Behaviors	Benefits
• Creates a team jointly responsible for success	• Increased direct report ownership and responsibility
• Asks, "How can each problem be solved in a way that further develops my people's commitment and capabilities?"	• Increased employee engagement and motivation
	• Allows leader to spend more time managing laterally and upward
• Work toward developing others' abilities	• There is no limit to the power of getting things done

Figure 5-3. Leader as developer of people

This leadership style is generally favored by knowledge workers, who typically need a high degree of personal growth, as well as collaboration and coordination with others. These leaders take the following steps:

- Create a team jointly responsible for success
- Let others design the solution and coordinate the activities necessary to bring it to market
- Give credit for successes to the team but shoulder personal responsibility when things go wrong
- Show empathy and support when the team makes mistakes
- Create a learning culture that enables people to continually develop their knowledge and skills and to pursue their passion
- Encourage and help individuals leave their comfort zone to solve challenging problems and take on new opportunities
- Foster an environment that rewards risk-taking and innovation, without fear

This style allows each direct report to reach their own potential. It increases productivity and engagement, maximizing the personal and professional benefits of the management relationship. As Lean-Agile leaders, we have no greater responsibility or opportunity.

Inspire and Align with Mission. Minimize Constraints

"The Principle of Mission: Specify the end state, its purpose, and the minimal possible constraints."[4]
    —Don Reinertsen

This principle defines the primary responsibility of leadership in the Lean enterprise: Define the mission, but reduce the boundaries and conditions for teams to address it.

Leaders should communicate the broad strategic goals but avoid constraining teams with outdated rules or planning methods. The mission simply describes the *what* and the *why*,

---

4. Don Reinertsen, *The Principles of Product Development Flow* (Celeritas Publishing, 2012).

not the *how*. This way, the teams have the autonomy to develop the best solution, as well as the freedom to pivot quickly as new ways arise to meet the mission.

In addition, leaders need to eliminate demotivating policies and procedures, especially those that promote unhealthy competition, encourage favoritism, or cause busywork.

Decentralize Decision-Making

As previously described in chapter 4, 'SAFe Principles,' most Lean experts reach the same conclusion: Decentralized decision-making is critical to flow and delivering value quickly.

Unlock the Intrinsic Motivation of Knowledge Workers

Along with Lean's endorsement of empowered problem solving, the work of Drucker,[5] Daniel Pink,[6] and others leads us to SAFe Lean-Agile Principle #8—*unlock the intrinsic motivation of knowledge workers*. This principle was previously described in chapter 4, 'SAFe Principles.'

Evolve the Development Manager Role

By applying the principles of Lean-Agile development, SAFe emphasizes the values of nearly autonomous, cross-functional teams and ARTs. It supports a leaner management infrastructure, with more empowered teams and faster, local decision-making. It eliminates the need for daily employee instruction and activity management.

Development management, however, is still necessary. Employees need managers to help them with career growth, compensation, and general personnel responsibilities. As a consequence, managers must help build systems by providing the mission and

---

5. Peter Drucker, *The Effective Executive*, rev. ed. (Harper Business, 2006).
6. Daniel Pink, *Drive: The Surprising Truth about What Motivates Us* (Riverhead Books, 2010).

systematically addressing impediments and bottlenecks encountered along the way. And of course, management remains ultimately accountable for results.

Over time, these 'managers as Lean-Agile leaders' will evolve from a command-and-control style to a new servant-leadership approach. That said, they will still have the following responsibilities in the Lean-Agile enterprise:

- Recruiting and retaining talent
- Providing vision and mission alignment
- Supporting built-in quality and Agile software engineering practices
- Coaching Agile teams
- Providing transparency everywhere possible
- Serving as Business Owners

Evolving the role of the development manager is such an important consideration that it can block the move to Lean-Agile development, or hinder it to the point of ineffectiveness. Refer to the 'Lean-Agile Leaders'[7] article on the SAFe website for more information.

Adopt a Servant-Leadership Approach

Servant leadership is a philosophy and set of practices that enriches the lives of individuals, builds better organizations, and ultimately creates a more just and caring world.[8] This philosophy is a critically important aspect of Lean-Agile leadership.

Robert Greenleaf, the author of *The Power of Servant Leadership*, discusses the following characteristics that embody servant leaders:

1. *Listening.* Listen to employees receptively and support them in problem-solving and decision-making.
2. *Empathy.* Understand and empathize with others.

---

7. scaledagileframework.com/lean-agile-leaders/
8. https://www.greenleaf.org/what-is-servant-leadership/

3. *Self-awareness.* Get to know yourself and understand your strengths and weaknesses. Think deeply about your emotions and behavior.

4. *Persuasion.* Use persuasion rather than authority to manage people. Strive to build consensus.

5. *Conceptualization.* Create mission and vision statements. Help your teams understand how their work supports the goals of the company.

6. *Stewardship.* Take responsibility for the actions and performance of your team and be accountable for the role team members play in your organization.

7. *Commitment to the growth of people.* Commit to the personal and professional development of your teams. Build a sense of community within your organization.

Evolve the Partnership with Human Resources Management

Digital transformation requires changing the way that work is performed. So, it's not surprising that Human Resources (HR) practices must also change. SAFe provides guidance on this topic in a white paper entitled 'Agile HR with SAFe: Bringing People Operations into the 21st Century with Lean-Agile Values and Principles.'[9]

The white paper describes six themes that leaders and their HR partners can use to apply contemporary Lean-Agile people solutions in the modern enterprise:

1. Embrace the new talent contract.

2. Foster continuous engagement.

3. Hire for attitude and cultural fit.

4. Move to iterative performance feedback.

5. Take the issue of money off the table.

6. Support meaningful learning and growth.

---

9. http://www.scaledagileframework.com/agile-hr/

HR professionals should become educated and knowledgeable about Lean-Agile values, principles, and practices, including finding opportunities to connect with Agile teams to understand how they operate. It's essential to invite your HR organization to participate in the Lean-Agile Center of Excellence (LACE) and SAFe events, training, and other learning sessions. This helps them bring a Lean-Agile mindset to their role. Even better, they can begin applying Agile practices to the HR context.

An investment in Lean-Agile HR is an investment in your people and your future.

On the Future of Leadership

As we'll see in this book, organizing around value is a fluid process. Value moves, and our organizations must evolve quickly to support those changes. Traditional organizational structures—whether functional or lines of business—may not have the agility needed to compete in the digital economy. Nor can they necessarily provide the business environment in which this next generation of knowledge workers and millennials can thrive.

For a different and distinctive view of leadership, we refer to a *Harvard Business Review* article, 'Leadership in Online Labs,' by Reeves, Malone, and O'Driscoll.[10] Based on their studies from the field of online gaming, the authors present a futuristic view. Their research highlights aspects of gaming that create the right environment for high-performing teams:

- Leaders switch roles naturally. Leadership is a task, not a permanent identity.
- Hyper-transparency of a wide range of information fosters effective leadership and results.
- Use nonmonetary incentives instead of financial rewards.

The authors conclude that perhaps what the industry needs is 'more fluid workforces, self-organized and collaborative work activities, and decentralized, nonhierarchical leadership.' In many ways, this describes Lean-Agile management patterns. Moreover, as one of the gamers noted, "If you want better leadership . . . why not change the game instead of trying to change the leaders?" Fair point.

---

10. https://hbr.org/2008/05/leaderships-online-labs

Summary

In SAFe, leadership leads the change to a successful implementation of Lean-Agile development. These Lean-Agile Leaders 'know the way.' They understand and exhibit Lean-Agile values, principles, and practices, and teach them to others. This creates a persistent foundation for the successful implementation of SAFe and drives the relentless improvement necessary to sustain and improve the business's performance long into the future.

Part III
Essential SAFe

"Simplicity—the art of maximizing the amount of work not done—is essential."

—Agile Manifesto

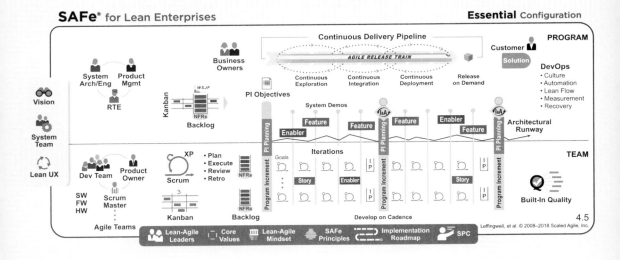

Introduction to Essential SAFe

The Essential SAFe configuration is the heart of the Framework and is the simplest starting point for implementation. It's the basic building block for all other SAFe configurations and describes the most critical elements needed to realize the majority of the Framework's benefits.

The Essential SAFe configuration was briefly introduced in chapter 2, 'SAFe Overview,' where we described its individual elements. However, that chapter didn't explain how Essential SAFe works as an integrated system. In part III, we tell that story by first describing the Agile Release Train, which is a combination of the program and team levels. Then, in the next four chapters, we discuss how the ART plans, iterates, executes, and inspects and adapts.

The Agile Release Train

*"The more alignment you have, the more autonomy you can grant.
The one enables the other."*

—Stephen Bungay, author and strategy consultant

Overview

The Agile Release Train (ART) is a long-lived team of Agile teams, which, along with other stakeholders, develops and delivers solutions incrementally, using a series of fixed-length iterations within a Program Increment (PI) timebox. Each ART is typically a virtual organization (50–125 people) that plans, commits, and executes together. ARTs are organized around the enterprise's significant value streams and exist solely to realize the promise of that value by building solutions that deliver benefit to the end user. The cross-functional ARTs have all the capabilities—software, hardware, firmware, DevOps, and other—needed to define, implement, test, and deploy new system functionality. An ART operates with a goal of achieving a continuous flow of value, as shown in Figure 6-1.

Figure 6-1. The long-lived Agile Release Train

The ART aligns teams to a common mission and program backlog. Each ART operates on a set of common principles, which helps manage the inherent risk and variability of solution development:

- It uses a fixed schedule (typically 8–12 weeks) and delivers value every 2 weeks; teams are synchronized to the same PI length and have common iteration start/end dates and durations (typically 2 weeks).

- Trains are predictable and can reliably estimate how much cargo (new features) can be delivered in a PI.

- Agile teams power the train, build the solution, and embrace the Agile Manifesto and the values and principles of SAFe.

- Most people are dedicated to the train full time.

- Trains dedicate time for innovation and planning activities and the Inspect and Adapt (I&A) event at the end of every PI.

- Trains apply DevOps to deliver value with an automated continuous delivery pipeline and use Lean UX to get fast feedback and reduce waste.

- Trains use cadence and synchronization to help manage the inherent variability of research and development.

- Additionally, in larger value streams, several ARTs collaborate to build larger solution capabilities as part of a Solution Train. In these cases, some ART stakeholders participate in Solution Train events, including the solution demo and pre- and post-PI planning. Solution Trains are discussed in detail in part IV, 'Large Solution SAFe.'

ART Organization

Figure 6-2 shows a traditional organization, where each role works independently in its own functional silo. Although there are valid reasons for organizing functions in this way, value flows poorly within this structure, as many hand-offs and explicit management direction are needed to move value across silos. As a result, progress is slow, and self-organization and self-management aren't possible.

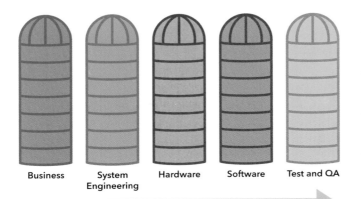

- Value delivery is inhibited by hand-offs and delays

- Political boundaries can prevent cooperation

- Silos encourage geographic distribution of functions

- Communication across silos is difficult

Management challenge: connect the silos

Figure 6-2. Traditional functional organization

ARTs are typically virtual—rather than line management—organizations that have all the people and resources needed to define and deliver value. This alignment approach breaks down the functional silos that traditionally exist before implementing SAFe. As an alternative to that structure, the ART takes a 'systems view' and builds a cross-functional organization, optimized to facilitate the flow of value from business requirements to deployment, as Figure 6-3 illustrates.

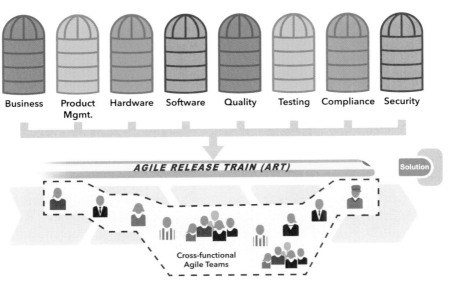

Figure 6-3. Agile Release Trains are fully cross-functional

Likewise, Agile teams within the ART are themselves cross-functional, as shown in Figure 6-4.

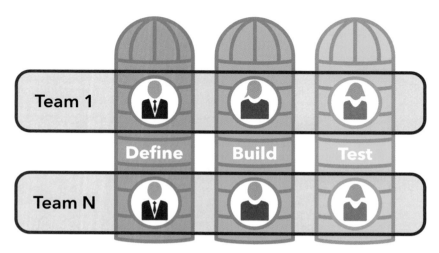

Figure 6-4. Agile teams are also cross-functional

Each Agile team has the skills and people needed (designers, developers, testers, and so on) to effectively deliver a feature or component with a minimum number of dependencies on others. On a collective basis, this fully cross-functional organization—whether physical (direct organizational reporting) or virtual (line of reporting is unchanged)—has everyone and everything it needs to deliver value. It's self-organizing and self-managing (at both the team *and* program levels), which creates a leaner organization where traditional project management is no longer required. The result is a faster flow of value with minimum overhead. That's the main purpose of the ART.

Agile Release Train Roles

In addition to the Agile teams, three primary roles help ensure successful execution of the ART's work, as shown in Figure 6-5:

- A *Release Train Engineer (RTE)* is a servant leader and coach for the ART. RTEs facilitate ART events and processes and assist the teams in delivering value. They communicate with stakeholders, escalate impediments, help manage risk, and drive relentless improvement.

- *Product Management* is responsible for 'what gets built,' as defined by the vision, roadmap, and new features in the program backlog. These managers collaborate with customers and Product Owners to understand and communicate their needs, and they also validate solutions.

- A *System Architect/Engineer* defines the technical and architectural vision for the system, working at a level of abstraction above the teams and components. These individuals define major system elements, subsystems, interfaces, and Nonfunctional Requirements (NFRs).

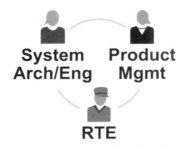

System Arch/Eng **Product Mgmt**

RTE

Figure 6-5. ART leadership

In addition to these three roles, the following roles are integral to the ART:

- *Business Owners* are a small group of stakeholders who have the overall business and technical responsibility for governance, compliance, and return on investment for the ART's solution. They evaluate the solution's business value and fitness for use and actively participate in ART events.

- *Customers* are the ultimate buyers of the solution. Their continuous participation in solution development is essential for success.

- A *System Team* typically assists in building the development environment, including aspects that support continuous integration, test automation, and continuous deployment. They help integrate assets from Agile teams, often perform end-to-end solution testing, and assist with deployment and release.

- *Shared Services* are specialists who cannot devote themselves full-time to a single train. Examples include data security professionals, information architects, database administrators, and technical writers.

Develop on Cadence. Release on Demand

ARTs address a common problem with traditional, team-based Agile development. With such development, teams work on the same solution, but often operate independently, on different schedules and with potentially different objectives and priorities. That makes it extremely difficult to integrate the full system routinely. Although the teams work in short iterations, the result is that the *system itself* may not be sprinting (iterating) at all. In turn, issues and problems are still discovered late in the process, and delivery slippage is a likely result, as shown in Figure 6-6.

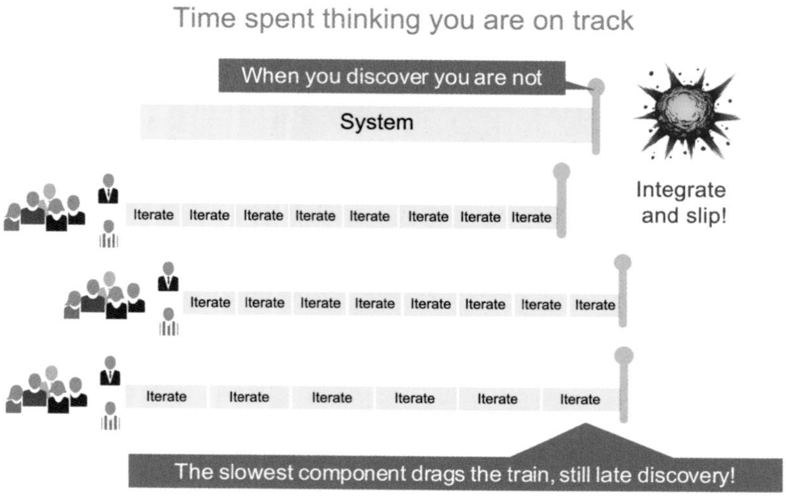

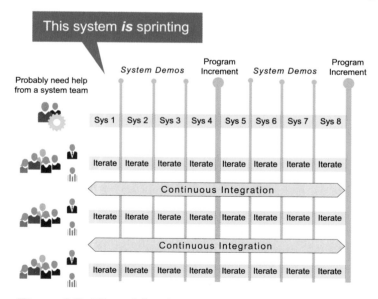

Figure 6-6. Agile teams working independently without alignment

Instead, the ART applies *cadence* and *synchronization* and continuous integration so that the *system is sprinting as a whole*, as shown in Figure 6-7. This pattern assures that the focus is on the evolution and objective assessment of the *full system*. The system demos provide real, objective evidence that the system is, in fact, iterating.

Figure 6-7. Aligned development; this system is sprinting

Separating Development and Release Concerns

More frequent delivery of solutions results in better economic outcomes. Indeed, for many enterprises, *continuous delivery* represents the ideal end state. For others, however, that may impractical or undesirable due to requirements for security, high availability, licensing, risk management, and more. However, the customer's operational or business environment may not support continuous deployment. Therefore, SAFe decouples the development and release cadences to provide needed flexibility. The mantra is 'develop on cadence' and 'release on demand,' as illustrated in the Big Picture. The fixed development cadence provides the reliable heartbeat for ARTs. Releasing, however, is a different concern and is covered in chapter 9, 'Executing the Program Increment.'

Vision

Primarily the responsibility of Product Management, the role of the *vision* is to communicate the intent and direction of the solution. It answers the following types of questions:

- What is the system supposed to do, and which NFRs will it deliver? Which problems will it solve for the user, and for our business?
- Which features will it provide, and for whom?
- How will the solution be different from the current state or differentiate us from competition?

The vision should inspire and motivate people to come along on the journey to the more desirable, future state. Typical formats include rolling wave briefings, vision documents, preliminary data sheets, draft press releases, and more. But no matter how the vision is captured, at the beginning of each PI Planning event, Product Management presents the vision as a proposed set of new *features* that the system will provide to its users. In this way, ART teams and stakeholders can listen, react, and align to a common direction.

Features

Features describe larger system behaviors that fulfill users' needs. Features are sized (or split) so that a single ART can deliver each feature in a single PI—a relationship that drives incremental delivery and fast feedback. Features also conveniently lend themselves to the *Lean UX* implementation process model, which includes a definition of the Minimum Marketable Feature (MMF) and the benefit hypothesis. The MMF helps limit the initial scope and investment, enhances agility, and provides fast feedback. (For more information about Lean UX and MMF, see chapter 9, 'Executing the Program Increment.') Features are typically expressed in plain language in a simple feature and benefit (FAB) matrix.

- *Feature*: a short phrase with a name and context.
- *Benefit hypothesis*: the proposed measurable benefit.

Figure 6-8 shows an example of four proposed features for a network router.

Feature	Benefit Hypothesis
In-service software update	Significantly reduced planned downtime
Hardware VPN acceleration	Improve WAN security with high performance encryption
Traffic congestion management	Improve overall quality of service across different protocols
Route optimization	Improve quality of service due to faster and more reliable connectivity

Figure 6-8. Features and benefits matrix

Accepting Features

Features also include *acceptance criteria*, which are used to further define system behavior and to help assess whether the implementation should deliver the benefits hypothesis. Figure 6-9 shows acceptance criteria for an example enabler feature for a network router.

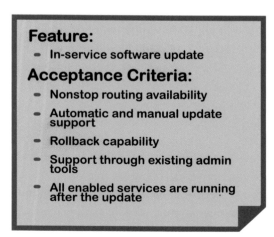

Figure 6-9. Feature acceptance criteria example for a network router

Acceptance criteria reduce implementation risk and enable early validation of the benefit hypothesis. Also, they typically serve as the source of various stories, as well as driving functional tests, developed and automated to support refactoring and regression testing of the feature. Product Management is responsible for accepting features by applying acceptance criteria to determine whether the functionality has been implemented properly and NFRs have been met.

Program Backlog

Features are developed, elaborated, and maintained in the program backlog until they are implemented. Product Management is responsible for identifying, prioritizing, and sequencing features, with development of features then being the primary driver for the ART. Features originate from various stakeholders—customers, Product Management, Business Owners, Product Owners, Architects, and more. They may originate from the local context of the ART, or they may result from splitting larger epics or capabilities.

The program backlog also includes *enabler* features that advance learning and build the architectural runway. Enablers are used to ensure that the solution architecture can continuously support the implementation of near-term features, without excessive redesign and delays.

Estimating and Prioritizing Features

Feature estimation helps forecast availability and supports Weighted Shortest Job First (WSJF) sequencing. Feature estimation occurs in the analysis state of the program Kanban.

During analysis, subject-matter experts engage in research and do preliminary sizing. At this stage, sizing features does not require splitting them into stories or including all the teams in the process. Since implementing the right jobs in the right sequence produces the maximum economic benefit, the WSJF prioritization method is then used to sequence features based on flow economics. (For more on WSJF, see the 'Sequence Jobs for Maximum Benefit' section in chapter 4, 'SAFe Principles.')

Roadmap

Features are implemented every PI. The system advances methodically, one PI at a time. However, planning for only a single PI can be problematic; there must be some sense of the future so that current decisions are made in the right longer-term context. Establishing that context is the job of the *roadmap*, which consists of a series of planned PIs with anticipated features and other milestones. A gaming company example is shown in Figure 6-10.

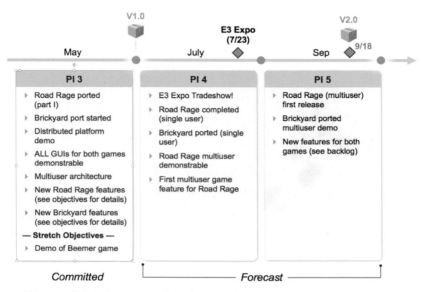

Figure 6-10. An example of a roadmap for a gaming company

The roadmap shows the deliverables for the current committed PI and offers visibility into the next two PIs. Notice that the forecasted PIs in the roadmap are not completely full. This allows room for new features to be added that will naturally arise in the near future. Moreover, the roadmap provides enough detail to run the business, yet offers a short enough timeframe to keep long-term commitments from interfering with the flexibility needed to adapt to changing business priorities. The program roadmap is developed and updated by Product Management as the vision and delivery strategy evolve.

Agile Teams Power the Train

ARTs consist primarily of Agile teams—that is, the people who actually define, build, test, and, where applicable, deploy the systems features and components. SAFe Agile teams apply various Agile practices, combining Scrum, XP, and Kanban.

Each Agile team is cross-functional and has dedicated individual contributors to cover all the activities necessary to build a quality increment of value for an iteration. Teams can deliver software, hardware, or firmware, or any combination of these. Each Agile team does the following:

- Estimates and manages its own work

- Determines the technical design in its area of concern, within architectural and user experience guidelines

- Commits to the work it can accomplish in an iteration and PI timebox

- Implements and tests the functionality, and deploys it to the staging and production environments in collaboration with operations

- Supports and/or builds the automation necessary to implement the continuous delivery pipeline

- Continuously improves the process and deliverables

With this organizational model, instead of projects 'that bring people to the work,' enterprises implement flow by 'bringing work to the people.' This helps create stable, long-lived organizations that grow and retain knowledge and relentlessly improve their ability to deliver solutions.

Agile Team Roles

SAFe teams are mainly structured after the roles in Scrum. Each team consists of the three primary roles that help ensure successful execution, as shown in Figure 6-11.

Figure 6-11. Agile team structure

- *Scrum Master.* The Scrum Master is the servant leader for the team, facilitating meetings, fostering Agile behavior, helping remove impediments, interacting with the larger organization, and maintaining the team's focus. The Scrum Master's primary responsibility is to help build a high-performing and self-managing team.

- *Product Owner.* The Product Owner owns the team backlog, defines user stories, acts as the customer for developer questions, prioritizes the work, and collaborates with Product Management to plan PIs and to deliver the larger scope of value.

- *Dev Team.* The Development (Dev) Team is a subset of the Agile Team; it has three to nine dedicated individual contributors, covering all the roles necessary to build a quality increment of value for an iteration. Developers, testers, engineers, and various specialists create and refine user stories and acceptance criteria; they define, build, test, and deliver stories in support of features.

Team Kanban roles are less rigorously defined, though for convenience and organizational efficiency, most SAFe Kanban teams implement similar Scrum roles.

User Stories and the Team Backlog

User Stories

During PI planning, features are broken down into smaller *user stories.* As defined in XP, user stories are negotiable expressions of intended system behavior. They are not requirements, but rather short, simple descriptions of a small piece of desired functionality told from the user's perspective.

Stories provide just enough information to explain the intent to both business and technical people. They are a 'promise for a conversation' intended to prompt a more thorough discussion of the proposed behavior and impact. Details are deferred until the story is ready to be implemented. Stories are often described in terms of *a user story voice* format, as shown in Figure 6-12.

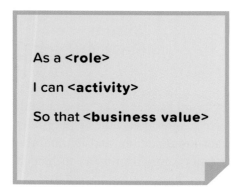

Figure 6-12. User story voice format

The user story voice has three parts:

1. *User role*: the person performing the action.
2. *Activity*: the action the user does with the system.
3. *Business value*: the value the user receives from the action.

Through conversations and acceptance criteria, stories get elaborated as they are implemented, helping to ensure system quality. Acceptance criteria can be captured and automated as acceptance tests, which confirm that the functionality has been implemented properly. Acceptance tests are used for regression testing as the solution evolves. This is a critical element of built-in quality practices.

Although the user story voice is the common case, not every system interacts with a traditional end user. Sometimes the 'user' is a device (for example, a mobile phone) or another system (for example, a transaction server). In this case, the role in the user story can be the device or system. Enabler stories lay the foundation for the development of future user stories. They may express any of the following:

1. *Infrastructure.* These stories are created to build, enhance, and automate the development, testing, and deployment environments.
2. *Architecture.* These stories build the architectural runway, which enables smoother and faster development.
3. *Exploration.* These stories support the research, prototyping, and other activities needed to develop an understanding of customer needs, to explore prospective solutions, and to evaluate alternatives.
4. *Compliance enablers.* These stories help manage specific compliance activities.

Estimating Stories

Agile teams estimate their work with story points, a single number that represents a combination of things:

- *Volume*: How much is there to do?
- *Complexity*: How hard is it?
- *Knowledge*: What's known?
- *Uncertainty*: What's not known?

Stories are sized relative to each other; they are not connected to any specific unit of measure. The size (effort) of each story is estimated relative to the smallest story, which is arbitrarily assigned a size of 1. A modified Fibonacci number sequence (1, 2, 3, 5, 8, 13, 20, 40, 100) is used to reflect the inherent uncertainty in estimating, especially large numbers (for example, 20, 40, 100, and so on). Two good techniques for sizing stories are 'estimating (planning) poker' and 'white elephant sizing.'[1]

The number of story points a team can achieve in an iteration is the team's *velocity*. The team uses its current velocity to estimate the amount of work it can accomplish in an iteration; in other words, the current velocity isn't a measure of team performance. Velocity varies from team to team and also depends on the type of work. The ART's velocity is determined by adding all the team's velocities for the PI, which—again—is used to help plan future work. Teams estimate their work using normalized estimation techniques. This way, features that require the work of multiple teams can be estimated using a 'common currency,' permitting meaningful economic decisions.

Team Backlog

User and enabler stories are maintained in the *team backlog*. Several important concepts underlie this seemingly simple construct:

- It contains all things. If a thing is in there, it might get done. If it isn't, there's no chance it will be implemented.

- It's a list of 'want to do' items. Items may be estimated (preferable) or not, but neither case implies a specific commitment.

- It contains user stories, enablers, and improvement stories from the team's retrospectives.

- It has a single owner—the team's Product Owner. This protects the team from the problem of multiple stakeholders with potentially differing views of what's important.

By having a single source of work for each team, the team backlog helps manage some of the complexity of Agile at scale. Figure 6-13 illustrates a view of the team backlog, with its three primary input sources.

---

1. You can find more information on these techniques on www.tastycupcakes.org, a community-run website that provides Agile games, techniques, and approaches.

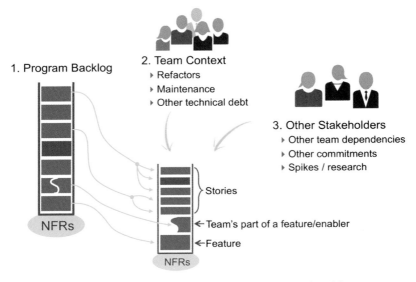

Figure 6-13. Expanded view of the team backlog

Balancing Types of Work with Capacity Allocation

Every team faces the problem of how to balance the backlog of internally facing work—maintenance, refactors, and technical debt—with the new user stories that deliver more immediate business value. Because the Product Owner is always trying to compare the value of dissimilar items—including defects, refactors, and new user stories—work sequencing becomes challenging. To solve this problem, *capacity allocation* is used to determine how much effort should be applied to each type of activity for a given period, as Figure 6-14 illustrates.

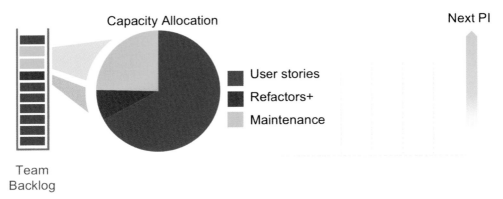

Figure 6-14. Team backlog capacity allocation

Capacity allocation helps avoid a reduction in velocity due to technical debt, while keeping existing customers happy with a stream of new functionality.

Summary

The ART is the fundamental organizational construct in SAFe. Each is organized around the enterprise's significant value streams and exist solely to realize the promise of that value by building solutions that deliver benefit to the end user. This team-of-agile-teams aligns everyone to a common mission by planning, committing, and executing together. ARTs are cross-functional and have all the roles and capabilities needed—software, hardware, firmware, DevOps, and other—needed to define, implement, test, and deploy new system functionality. To manage the variability inherent in solution development, ARTs develop on cadence, but they release based solely on business and market demand.

Planning a Program Increment

*"Future product development tasks can't be predetermined.
Distribute planning and control to those who can understand and
react to the end results."*

   —Michael Kennedy, *Product Development for the Lean Enterprise*

Overview

"There is no magic in SAFe . . . except maybe for PI planning."

   —The authors

No event is more powerful in SAFe than PI planning. It's the cornerstone of the Program Increment (PI), which provides the cadence and rhythm for the Agile Release Train (ART).

When 100 or so people work together at the same time, striving to achieve a common mission, vision, and shared purpose, it's incredible how much alignment and energy their efforts create. Gaining that alignment in just two days can save months of delays caused by waiting on decisions, tracking down the right people, and getting agreement via a flurry of emails.

PI planning is a required critical and cultural milestone for each ART implementation. During this event, the teams come together to define and design the system that best fulfills the ART's vision. Teams commit to near-term PI objectives, and a sense of shared mission, responsibility, cooperation, and collaboration permeates the entire ART. Responsibility for planning moves from a central authority to the teams who do the work. This signals a real change of empowerment and the birth of the social network on which the ART depends so heavily.

Figure 7-1 shows a real-life planning event. Such an event can occur face-to-face in a single location, or in this case, multiple face-to-face locations simultaneously. In this example, teams in the United States are planning at the same time as remote teams in India using video conferencing. Leads from teams in Eastern Europe are attending the U.S. event in person while collaborating with their remote team members in real time. Business Owners based in the United States are sitting at the table in the middle, accessible to everyone. Product Owners are physically located with their teams in India.

Figure 7-1. Distributed PI planning

Whenever possible, attendees include *all* members of the ART. After all, the people on the teams do the work, so only they can design the system, plan, and then commit to that plan. Led by a facilitator, who is usually the Release Train Engineer (RTE), PI planning takes place over two days and occurs within the Innovation and Planning (IP) iteration. That prevents the planning meeting from affecting the PI timebox or the capacity of other iterations in the PI.

Preparation for the PI Planning Event

Such a significant event requires preparation, coordination, and communication. Product Management, Agile Teams, System Architect/Engineering, the System Team, Business Owners, and other stakeholders must be well prepared.

A successful event requires preparation in three areas:

1. Organizational readiness
2. Facility readiness
3. Content readiness

Organizational Readiness

Before planning, it's essential to ensure that programs have reasonable strategic align-ment among participants, stakeholders, and Business Owners. In other words, they all must agree on exactly what they're building. To address this issue, teams should answer the following preparation questions:

- *Planning scope and context.* Is the scope of the planning process—product, system, or technology domain—understood?

- *Business alignment.* Is there reasonable agreement on priorities among the Business Owners?

- *Agile Teams.* Does each team have dedicated developer and test resources and an identified Scrum Master and Product Owner?

For more on organizational readiness, see chapter 20, 'Implementing Agile Release Trains.'

Facility Readiness

Securing the physical space and technical infrastructure necessary to s̲ number of attendees isn't trivial either, especially if there are remote participants. Considerations include the following:

- *Facility.* The planning venue must be large enough to accommodate all attendees. If there isn't enough space for the teams to plan, nearby breakout rooms may be needed.

- *Technical and communications support.* Support people need to be identified and available during setup, testing, and the event itself.

- *Communication channels.* For distributed planning meetings, primary and secondary audio, video, and presentation channels must be available.

Content Readiness

The PI planning event starts with leadership providing a shared vision and context. Presentation elements include the following:

- *Executive briefing.* A senior executive or line-of-business owner presents the current business context.

- *Product/solution vision briefing.* Product Management presents the vision, highlighting the 'top 10 features' in the program backlog.

- *The architecture vision briefing.* Prepared by the CTO, Enterprise Architect, and/or System Architect/Engineer, this briefing communicates architectural strategy, as reflected by new enablers and nonfunctional requirements (NFRs).

STAYING AHEAD OF PI PREPARATION

Charlene M. Cuenca, SPCT and Lean-Agile Transformation Coach at Icon Technology Consulting, shares her experience about PI preparation: "Staying ahead of PI preparation will enable a consistent flow, with the PI timebox as the heartbeat of program execution. Using a 'just-in-time' (JIT) approach, parallel execution, and PI preparation activities at the portfolio, large solution, program, and team levels allow sufficient lead time for ART leaders and the rest of the enterprise to prepare. Attention needs to be paid to ensure we truly enable JIT decomposition as close as possible to delivery, without doing too much decomposition early in the PI (a big form of waste). This will facilitate the collaborative discovery, discussions, and alignment that PI planning fosters."

Role of the Facilitator

The PI planning event represents a critical point of alignment—it's where the teams decide what they should and can accomplish in the upcoming PI. As such, it can be a politically charged session. Stakeholders can see the work physics of what they are asking for and teams can objectively determine what they can do. Since imagination and market opportunity are largely unlimited, most ARTs are overloaded with expectations and excess work in process (WIP), which must be flushed out of the system. Aligning expectations with reality can be difficult for many stakeholders. As a result, the importance of a well-facilitated event cannot be overstated. Someone has to run an objective process that surfaces and addresses the facts; that responsibility falls to the facilitator.

The facilitator organizes and guides PI planning to ensure that the group meets its planning objectives with good participation and full buy-in from everyone involved. The RTE may be the facilitator; this individual often has experience as a program manager and may have the skills needed to plan and facilitate this type of event. In other cases, the RTE may bring in someone else to handle this responsibility, which allows the RTE to focus on the teams and their needs and enables the other person to manage the timing and progress of the event, free of distraction and without a personal stake in the outcome. The secret of good facilitation is an effective group process that flows—inspiring the flow of the ART's ideas, solutions, and decisions. An agreed-to agenda helps. Over time, SAFe has evolved a standardized agenda that works in most contexts, as shown in Figure 7-2.

Figure 7-2. *Standard PI planning meeting agenda*

Day 1: Create and Review Draft Plans

Day 1 of the event begins with the facilitator reviewing the objectives and agenda, working agreements, planning rules and expectations, and other logistics. The facilitator also presents the upcoming calendar of events, including future PI planning dates, scheduled solution release, milestones, and other events that may affect planning the objectives or teams' capacity.

Business Context

Next, a senior executive or line-of-business owner provides the business context for the planning session. This may include discussions of current business performance and strategy; a strengths, weakness, opportunities, and threats (SWOT) analysis; measures of customer satisfaction; and organizational developments and updates to operating plans.

This discussion *sets the tone* for the PI planning session and can drive the motivation and enthusiasm for the PI and the evolving solution. It's a chance to share success stories, understand the market risks, and rally the troops around challenges and opportunities. The presenter may also provide an overview of strategic themes and upcoming business objectives.

Product/Solution Vision

Product Management then presents the current vision, the objectives for the upcoming PI, and feature priorities. If there are multiple product managers, each may need some time to present the vision and top features for their area of the solution.

Architecture Vision and Development Practices

In this session, the System Architect/Engineer presents the vision for the architecture. This may include descriptions of new architectural epics for common infrastructure, any large-scale refactors under consideration, and system-level NFRs. Also, a technical leader may provide guidance about changes to standard development practices, including new tools and techniques for DevOps and the continuous delivery pipeline as well as built-in quality practices.

Team Planning Breakouts

The next session is the longest and most critical. The teams break out into separate meetings and draft their initial plans to identify the achievable objectives of the PI. During this process, teams will consult with Product Managers, System Architect/ Engineering, the System Team, user experience, and other teams. The goal for the teams is to grasp the scope and priorities necessary for infrastructure development, resolve dependencies, and understand the potential for reuse of common code. *It's an intense and active time.*

Using flipchart paper and story cards (or stickies), teams create and display their plans so that they're visible for all to see. They use one flipchart per iteration, another for team PI objectives, and yet another to capture program risks and impediments. A standard plan might appear as shown in Figure 7-3.

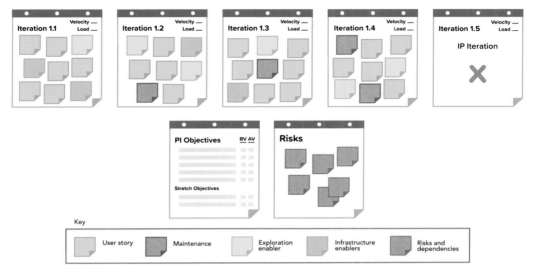

Figure 7-3. Team PI planning deliverables

It's noteworthy that no stories are planned for the IP iteration so as to provide dedicated time for innovation and planning activities. If the ART is releasing on the PI boundary, it may use this time for releasing activities such as final verification, validation, and documentation.

DANGERS OF OVER-PREPARATION

Brian Tucker, SPCT at Ivar Jacobson International, shares an important lesson about preparing stories before PI planning: "I recall one PI planning event where the Product Owner came with all of her stories preloaded into a PowerPoint presentation for the team. The team breakout simply became the Product Owner presenting the stories she created for the team. The team was neither empowered nor engaged during planning since they did not have the choice of how to implement the features. What had changed from the old process? Preparing the stories before PI planning is one of the leading failure modes of PI planning; it rapidly destroys self-organization and limits the choice of what features a team might take."

Starting Fast with Capacity-Based Planning

In the first PI planning session, some teams may not have used Scrum in the past and, therefore, will not have a starting velocity. In this case, teams simply start with eight points per iteration for each full-time technical contributor. They then identify a small story that will take about one day of work and estimate it at one story point. Other stories are then estimated relative to that one-story point. Teams split any story that is larger than eight points into smaller stories. This initial starting process accomplishes two things:

1. It assures that most teams have a reasonable number of right-sized stories in an iteration.

2. It normalizes estimation across teams, which is vital for feature and epic-level estimating and conversion into cost estimates where necessary.

If teams already have known velocities, a quick check will reveal whether they are very close to being normalized. If this is not the case, the facilitator may want to have some teams adjust accordingly so that program velocities make sense.

Hourly Planning Checkpoints

During the team breakouts, the facilitator holds an hourly Scrum of Scrums (SoS) checkpoint to keep the planning on track. In this short stand-up meeting, the RTE and the Scrum Masters from each team meet to review the planning status using a checklist. Figure 7-4 shows an example. A 'meet after' often follows the SoS to deal with any problems that need more discussion.

	A	Team 1	Team 2	Team 3	Team 4	Team 5	Team 6	Team 7	Team 8	Team 9	Team 10	Team 11
	Scrum of Scrums Check-In	B	C	D	E	F	G	H	I	J	K	L
3	**PI Planning Radiator**											
5	**Day 1, Check-In 1: Getting Started**											
6	Do you understand the planning requirements?	y	y	y	y	y	y	y				
7	Do you know who your team is for the whole PI?	y	y	y	y	y	y	n				
8	Is your working space setup?	y	y	y	y	y	y	y				
9	Do you have a Product Owner & Scrum Master?	y	y	y	y	y	y	n				
10	Do you have access to the team members and stakeholders you need?	n	y	y	y	y	y	n				
11	Do you understand (and can you find) the vision that drives your backlog?	y	y	y	y	y	y	y	y			
12	Have you identified the velocity for each Iteration in your PI?	n	n	y	n	n	y	y				
13	Do you understand the architectural context, and who to go to for questions?	y	n	y	y	y	y	y				
14	Do you understand which resources are shared (e.g., UX, Training, and Documentation) and who to go to for questions?	y	y	y	y	y	y	y	y			
15	Do you understand the role of the System Team and DevOps, and who to go to for questions?	y	y	y	y	y	y	n				
16	**Day 1, Check-In 2: Iteration Planning Progress**											

Figure 7-4. Example Scrum of Scrums planning radiator

Draft Plan Review

Based on the agenda, the entire ART gets back together in the main session to review each team's draft plans. At this point, many plans will be incomplete. Even so, the review still occurs as scheduled so everyone can see the planning process and get an initial look at each other's assumptions and dependencies. Each team's presentation is strictly timeboxed (at 5 to 10 minutes) depending on the size of the ART. Business Owners must be present throughout the review to provide early feedback and support the teams. The teams use the agenda, shown in Figure 7-5, to present their plans.

Draft Plan Review Agenda

1. Velocity (capacity) and load

2. Draft PI objectives

3. Program risks and impediments

4. Q&A

Figure 7-5. Sample draft plan review agenda

Typically, there will be a few minutes left for questions and answers, which typically include clarifying misunderstandings, discussing dependencies, and reviewing trade-offs. However, the facilitator must keep the presentations within each team's timebox. The day concludes for most people after all the presentations are done.

Management Review and Problem-Solving Meeting

Some attendees will remain behind to tackle additional, important work. Specifically, the key ART roles[1] will meet to adjust the scope and objectives based on the draft plans. It's likely that there will be more work than the teams can possibly accomplish in the PI timebox.

To address these and the larger challenges identified in the draft review session, some set of managers, Business Owners, Product Managers, System Architects/Engineers, Product Owners, and Scrum Masters must meet. Figure 7-6 shows some common questions asked by the facilitator.

---

1. Key ART roles in this context include RTE, Product Management, System Architect/ Engineer, Business Owners, management and some Scrum Masters, Product Owners, and other subject-matter experts.

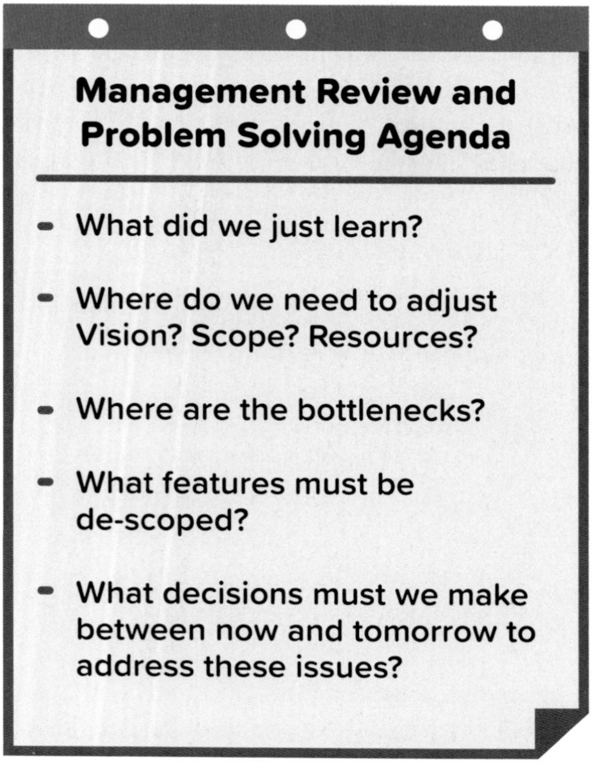

Management Review and Problem Solving Agenda

- What did we just learn?

- Where do we need to adjust Vision? Scope? Resources?

- Where are the bottlenecks?

- What features must be de-scoped?

- What decisions must we make between now and tomorrow to address these issues?

Figure 7-6. Common questions during the management review meeting

The facilitator keeps key stakeholders together as long as necessary to make the decisions needed to increase the likelihood of a successful PI. Resolving these issues may require cuts to scope, rethinking prior commitments, and accepting that some critical milestones will not be met. It may become necessary to reconsider team assignments or to move entire features from one team to another. Any final decisions should be carefully and clearly summarized, as they will inform the next day's planning session.

Day 2: Finalize Plans and Commit

In the opening session of day 2, the facilitator reviews the agenda and the objectives. Figure 7-7 shows a more detailed version of the day 2 agenda.

During day 2, the program must commit to a plan of action that fits the capacity of the teams, while delivering the maximum value in the next PI timebox.

Figure 7-7. Example PI planning day 2 agenda

Planning Adjustments

Based on the previous day's management review and problem-solving meeting, planning adjustments are *discussed* with the ART. The management review group takes responsibility for describing the issues and planning adjustments that were agreed to during the problem-solving meeting at the end of day 1.

Team Breakouts Continue

Based on the new knowledge (and a good night's sleep), teams work to create their final plans.

- Teams finalize their iteration plans and PI objectives.

- Teams make their objectives 'SMART'[2] and establish stretch objectives to provide the guard band (buffer) needed for predictability.

- Business Owners circulate and assign business value to PI objectives from low (1) to high (10).

---

2. Specific, measurable, achievable, realistic, and time-bound (www.scaledagileframework.com/pi-objectives/)

Teams also ensure that the program board (covered later) is updated with all features and cross-team dependencies. In addition, teams consolidate program risks, impediments, and dependencies. As on day 1, the planning SoS convenes hourly to ensure that the teams and plans are ready for the final review.

Team PI Objectives

Toward the end of the planning session, the teams focus on negotiating the final PI objectives with Product Management and Business Owners. Team PI objectives are brief summaries, *expressed in business terms*, of what the teams are prepared to commit to during the PI.

THE ROLE OF PI OBJECTIVES

Eric Willeke, SAFe Fellow, shares his experience with PI objectives as an Enterprise Agile Transformation Coach: "SAFe's use of PI objectives provides a unique tool to create an immediate feedback loop from the teams back to the Business Owners, allowing a quick validation of the teams' grasp of the desired outcomes. In short, we give the teams the following challenge: 'Can you concisely convey, in words the Business Owner understands, the essence of the value implementing this set of features would accomplish?' By asking the teams to summarize the intent and the outcomes they believe the Business Owner wants to achieve, we close the loop of understanding and drive crucial conversations that expose these misunderstandings."

Use Stretch Objectives

Stretch objectives help improve the predictability of delivering business value. The work is planned but is *not* included in the team's commitment. Stretch objectives are used to identify work that can be *variable* within the scope of a PI.

Stretch objectives help avoid loading the teams with more work than they can do. There are two key reasons for categorizing an objective as stretch:

- The team has low confidence in its ability to meet a PI objective.
- The objective has many unknowns. In this case, the team should plan spikes early in the PI to reduce uncertainty.

However, teams agree to do their best to deliver the stretch objectives, and they are included in the capacity for the PI. Since these objectives might not be finished in the PI, stakeholders plan accordingly.

Establish Business Value

The primary evaluation tool of the ART is a predictability *measure* that tracks the percentage of business value achieved for each PI objective in the plan. To execute this, the Business Owners set the business value of each objective toward the end of the PI planning session, as shown in Figure 7-8.

Figure 7-8. Setting business value for team PI objectives

Naturally, not all objectives deliver equal value, and Business Owners are likely to assign higher numbers to externally visible objectives than they would to infrastructure accomplishments and architectural epics. During PI execution, the teams use the Business Owner's rankings to make local trade-off decisions and minor scope adjustments in ways that deliver the maximum value to the business.

Program Board

Typically, the RTE creates a program board in advance of planning and teams update it during planning. The board highlights the feature delivery dates, milestones, and dependencies among teams and with other ARTs, as shown in Figure 7-9.

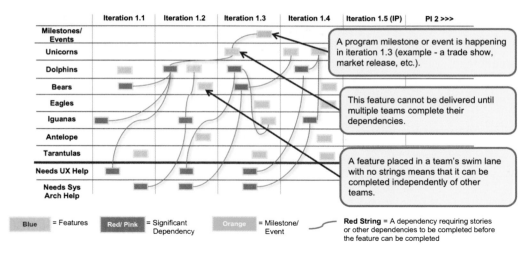

	Iteration 1.1	Iteration 1.2	Iteration 1.3	Iteration 1.4	Iteration 1.5 (IP)	PI 2 >>>
Milestones/ Events						
Unicorns						
Dolphins						
Bears						
Eagles						
Iguanas						
Antelope						
Tarantulas						
Needs UX Help						
Needs Sys Arch Help						

A program milestone or event is happening in iteration 1.3 (example - a trade show, market release, etc.).

This feature cannot be delivered until multiple teams complete their dependencies.

A feature placed in a team's swim lane with no strings means that it can be completed independently of other teams.

Blue = Features   **Red/ Pink** = Significant Dependency   **Orange** = Milestone/ Event   **Red String** = A dependency requiring stories or other dependencies to be completed before the feature can be completed

Figure 7-9. Program board example

THE ORIGIN OF THE PROGRAM BOARD

Drew Jemilo, SAFe Fellow and co-founder of Scaled Agile, Inc., describes how the Program Board came about: "After the first day of PI planning, each team's iteration plans were filled with user stories, and had many red stickies. It was painfully obvious that these 'red' dependencies were killing us, even though we couldn't visualize their true impact.

"When we learned that more than half of the PI objectives were stretch, tempers flared. By chance, I stumbled across a random box with red yarn and other supplies. Then it suddenly hit me, and I ran back with the yarn. We plastered the walls with blank flipchart paper, drew a swim lane for each team, and began mapping our feature dependencies with the yarn. Within an hour, our dependencies resembled a large, chaotic spider web. Craig, the pony-tailed System Architect, said, 'Now you know why we can't get anything done!' Jim, the Product Manager, exclaimed, 'I never knew how many dependencies we had just to get some new features done.' That was the birth of the Program Board (and the architect with the pony tail) on the Big Picture.'"

Final Plan Review

Figure 7-10 shows a sample agenda for the final plan walk-through. This is basically a repeat of the draft plan review session from the day before, but by now the teams will have completed their plans.

Final Plan Review Agenda

1. Changes to velocity (capacity) and load

2. Final PI objectives with business value

3. Program risks and impediments

4. Q&A

Figure 7-10. Final plan review agenda

At the end of each team's time slot, each team states its remaining program risks and impediments; these risks will be addressed later. Next, there is a brief Q&A for the ART and Business Owners. The facilitator asks the Business Owners if the plan is acceptable to them. If it is, the team brings its team PI objectives sheet and remaining program risks sheet to the front of the room. This allows everyone to see the summary of PI objectives unfold in real time. This process continues until all teams have presented their plans.

Addressing Program Risks and Impediments

Even though the plans are now complete, there is still work to do. During the planning, teams were asked to identify the most critical program risks and impediments—the very issues that could affect their ability to meet their agreed-to objectives. Addressing them is vital, as they typically represent things that—left unaddressed—may interfere with the success of the next PI.

ROAMing the Risks

By now, the teams will have addressed the risks that are under their local control. However, the remaining program risks and impediments will need to be addressed in a broader, management context. Every team's program-level risks will be discussed in front of the entire group. Each item is briefly discussed and placed in one of the following ROAM categories:

- *Resolved.* The teams agree that the issue is no longer a concern.
- *Owned.* Someone on the train takes ownership of the item since it cannot be resolved at the meeting.
- *Accepted.* Some risks are just facts or potential problems that must be understood and accepted.
- *Mitigated.* Teams can identify a plan to reduce the impact of an item.

The Commitment

After all the risks have been categorized, it's now time to ask the teams how confident they are about meeting the PI objectives. The teams vote using a 'fist of five,' as shown in Figure 7-11, where one finger equals very low confidence and five fingers represents very high confidence.

Figure 7-11. Fist of five confidence vote

If the average is three or more fingers, management should accept the commitment. However, if the average is less than three, then it's likely that the persons with low confidence have valuable insights into problems with the plan. Scope and resources will need further adjustment, and planning continues until a commitment is reached that day, or even into the evening, or is resumed the next morning.

A Commitment in Two Parts

Leadership must create a culture in which risk-taking *and* commitment are both part of the norm. Given this context, teams can interpret the confidence vote as a commitment. But this commitment has two parts:

1. Teams commit to do everything reasonable to meet the agreed-to objectives.
2. In case the facts change, or new learning occurs that indicates achieving the committed objectives is no longer possible, teams agree to escalate the issue immediately to inform management and initiate corrective action.

In this way, teams learn that they can and should take reasonable risks and also commit to an outcome, knowing that management is fully supportive of this model.

> **THE VALUE OF THE CONFIDENCE VOTE**
>
> Carl Starendal, SPCT at Scaled Agile, Inc., shared his experience about the importance of confidence vote: "During the confidence vote, almost everyone had raised either three, four, or five fingers. However, there was a single person with a one as his confidence (one of the testers), indicating that he did not believe in the plan. I asked him to share his concerns, and he told everyone that the most important feature would not be deployed successfully as the other's team plan did not include performance testing. The tester had information that there would be a drastic increase in the number of users for that specific system mid-PI. The team had been unaware of this and had not planned for it. After a short 20-minute replanning for that team, the ART had a much better plan that everyone believed in."

Planning Retrospective

The next event is a brief retrospective of the PI planning session led by the facilitator. Figure 7-12 shows a simple format to capture the results, along with a few example comments. This session should last no longer than 15–20 minutes. Near the end of that timebox, the facilitator may ask the teams to rank the items in the third column (what we could do better next time) to focus on process improvements for future planning sessions.

Figure 7-12. Method for capturing results during planning retrospective

Moving Forward and Final Instructions to Teams

The last session is typically a discussion about the next steps, along with final instructions to the teams. After PI planning is done, the RTE works with Product Management to summarize the individual team PI objectives into a list of program-level objectives. If the ART is part of a Solution Train, it is rolled up again to the large solution level.

IT'S NEVER TOO LATE TO INSPECT AND ADAPT

It's never too late to inspect and adapt, as Keith de Mendonca, SPC at Ivar Jacobson, learned: "I recently helped a European company prepare for its first PI planning event. A few days before PI planning, a new team popped up apparently out of nowhere and requested some training and an invitation to join the ART planning session. Word had spread down the corridors and in the canteen about the planning event and about the new way of working. This team realized that they would benefit greatly from running as a Scrum team, and by planning their work more closely with other teams on the train. They decided they would prefer to be on this shiny new train, rather than be on the platform watching the train pass every 10 weeks! Now maybe this team should have been included in the scope of this ART from the start. But in any case, they voted with their feet and joined the new train with the organization's blessing. The result? A quantum leap in the level of communication between all teams."

Summary

No event is more powerful in SAFe than PI planning. It's the magic of SAFe. It provides the cadence and rhythm for the ART and brings everyone together to plan toward a common mission, vision, and shared purpose. Gaining that alignment in just two days saves months of delays.

The primary output of PI planning is a committed set of PI objectives that the teams will deliver over the course of the PI. This is supported by a program board, which maps the feature delivery dates, milestones, and dependencies that must be successfully navigated to develop and release value.

8

Iterating

"Few ideas work on the first try. Iteration is key to innovation."
—Sebastian Thrun, chairman and co-founder of Udacity

Overview

In the last chapter, we described Program Increment (PI) planning, which is the seminal event of the Agile Release Train (ART). After PI planning, teams begin developing the solution in iterations.

Iterations are the basic building blocks of Agile development. Each iteration is a standard, fixed-length timebox, during which Agile teams deliver incremental value in the form of working, tested software and systems. The recommended duration of the iteration timebox is two weeks. However, one to four weeks also works, depending on the business context.

Iterations provide a regular, predictable cadence for teams to produce an increment of value, as well as to refine those items previously developed. These short time periods help the team, Product Owners, Product Managers, and other stakeholders test the technical and business hypotheses in a working system. Each iteration anchors at least one system demo, an 'integration point' that assembles various system aspects—functionality, quality, alignment, and fitness for use—across all the teams' contributions.

This chapter describes the typical *iteration cycle*, using the basic Scrum model, and then addresses how to improve flow in Scrum using Kanban techniques. In the next chapter, we cover how the ART explores, executes, and releases value together, as a team of Agile teams.

The Iteration Cycle

Most teams in an ART use Scrum, which has a simple set of roles and a regular set of activities, including iteration planning, execution, review, and the retrospective, as illustrated in Figure 8-1.

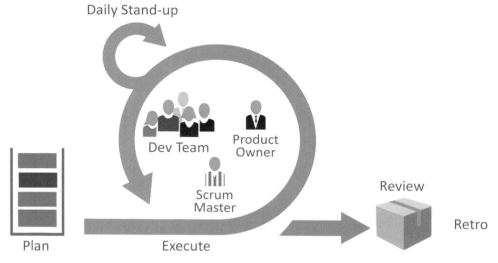

Figure 8-1. Iteration cycle

In each iteration, Agile teams execute a full 'Plan–Do–Check–Adjust' (PDCA) cycle as quickly as possible. The PDCA learning cycle in SAFe is represented in the following iteration events:

- Iteration planning is the 'plan' step.
- Iteration execution is the 'do' step.
- Iteration review is the 'check' step.
- Iteration retrospective is the 'adjust' step.

Iterations are a single development cycle in which each Agile team defines, builds, integrates, and tests the stories from its iteration backlog. Each iteration ends with an inspection of the team's increment to assess progress, as well as an updated backlog for the next iteration. Next, the team prepares and participates in the system demo, which gives an integrated view of the new features for the most recent iteration delivered by all the teams in the ART. Each of these PDCA steps is described in the following sections.

Iteration Planning

Iteration planning is a standard and well-defined Scrum activity. However, in SAFe, it also involves refining the details and adjusting the initial iteration plans created during the PI planning event.

Attendees at the iteration planning event include the Product Owner, Scrum Master, Development Team, and other stakeholders as appropriate. The meeting is timeboxed to a maximum of four hours (for a two-week iteration).

Iteration planning *inputs* include the following:

- Team and program PI objectives
- Stories identified during PI planning
- Existing stories from the team's backlog, defects, enablers, and so on

Iteration planning typically follows a set pattern like the one shown in Figure 8-2.

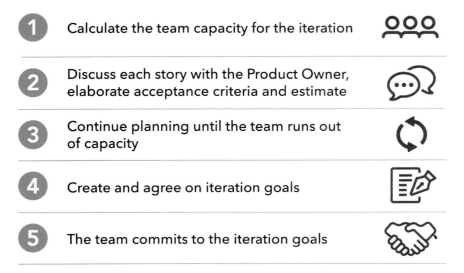

1. Calculate the team capacity for the iteration
2. Discuss each story with the Product Owner, elaborate acceptance criteria and estimate
3. Continue planning until the team runs out of capacity
4. Create and agree on iteration goals
5. The team commits to the iteration goals

Figure 8-2. The iteration planning process

After each team calculates its capacity for the iteration, the Product Owner presents the highest-priority stories. The team discusses implementation options, technical issues, Nonfunctional Requirements (NFRs), and dependencies. Then the team elaborates acceptance criteria, estimates the effort to complete the story, and puts the story in the iteration backlog.

When the team reaches the limit of its velocity for the iteration, it summarizes the stories into a set of iteration goals, adjusted as needed to achieve the broader goal of making progress toward the PI objectives.

The *output* of iteration planning includes the following:

- The iteration backlog, consisting of the stories and acceptance criteria the team committed to in the iteration
- Iteration goals—that is, the business and technical objectives of the iteration
- A commitment to the work needed to achieve the iteration goals

Figure 8-3 shows that the team's commitment has two parts, which helps maintain a healthy balance between commitment and adaptability.

A team meets its commitment:
By doing everything they said they would do
- or -
in the event that it is not feasible, they must immediately raise a red flag

Commitment		Adaptability
Too much holding to a commitment can lead to burnout, inflexibility, and quality problems.		Too little commitment can lead to unpredictability and lack of focus on results.

Figure 8-3. Balancing commitment and adaptability

In exchange for the team's commitment, the business agrees not to change the priorities during the iteration. The team, in turn, commits not just to its own work, but also to helping other teams, the program, and other stakeholders. Thus, if a team is going to change priorities, or miss a deadline that will affect another team or the program, the team must raise that concern immediately.

Iteration Execution

After planning, the team starts implementing new user stories, with each story creating a new baseline of functionality. Teams avoid 'waterfalling' the iteration by ensuring that they complete full define–build–test cycles for each story, as illustrated in Figure 8-4.

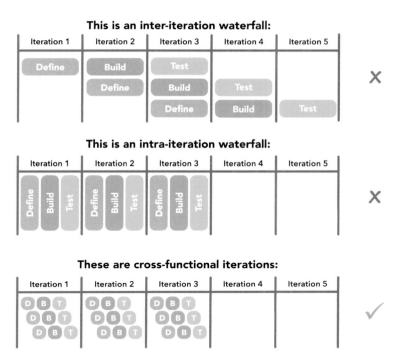

Figure 8-4. Delivering full stories serially avoids the mini-waterfall

Further, implementing stories in thin, vertical slices is the foundation for fine-grained incremental development, integration, and testing, as shown in Figure 8-5.

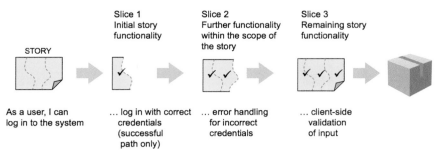

Figure 8-5. Implementing stories in vertical slices

When teams work in vertical slices, it facilitates the shortest possible feedback cycle and allows the teams to integrate and test a small increment of the working system across all architectural layers.

Tracking Iteration Progress

Iteration tracking provides visibility into the status of the stories, defects, and other activities that the team is working on. Most Scrum teams use a Big Visible Information Radiator (BVIR) or 'storyboard' like the one in Figure 8-6.

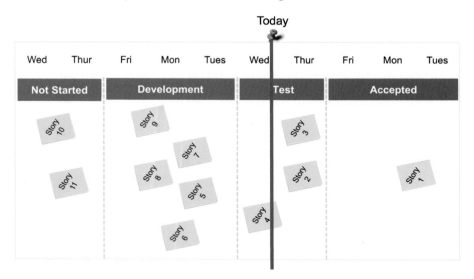

Figure 8-6. A simple storyboard

THE SCRUM MASTER'S ROLE IN TRACKING PROGRESS

During the iteration, the Scrum Master plays a vital role in tracking progress. The Scrum Master has the following responsibilities:

- Facilitating team events
- Fostering backlog refinement throughout the iteration and PI
- Encouraging the team to sound an alarm when the iteration goals or PI objectives may be at risk
- Communicating to and from the Scrum of Scrums and PO Sync
- Fostering the use of Agile software engineering practices
- Ensuring defects are not pushed to the next iteration
- Facilitating preparation for the next PI
- Supporting deployment and release activities

Daily Stand-Up

The team holds a Daily Stand-up (DSU) to coordinate its members' work. The standard format is for each team member to speak and address the following questions:

- Which stories did I work on yesterday to help the team meet the iteration goals?

- What will I do today to advance the iteration goals?

- Which impediments might prevent the team from meeting our iteration goals?

The DSU is *strictly timeboxed* to 15 minutes. The meeting is most effective when it's held in front of a BVIR or Kanban board (covered later in the chapter). The DSU is not a management reporting or problem-solving meeting, but rather a tool to help team members coordinate their work, identify issues, and address dependencies. Often, some attendees remain for a 'meet-after,' where they dedicate time to address any issues raised.

Iteration Review

Each iteration concludes with an iteration review to demo the increment and adapt the backlog as needed. During the review, the team assesses whether it has met the iteration goals and goes over any other metrics it has agreed to analyze, including velocity. The data provides some context for the retrospective that follows. Another objective of the review is to show any working stories that haven't as yet been demonstrated to the Product Owner and other stakeholders for feedback. Teams demo every story, spike, refactor, and new NFR.

The preparation for the review begins during iteration planning, when teams start thinking about how they will demo the stories they've committed to complete. This facilitates planning and alignment and fosters a better understanding of the functionality needed for the increment.

The review starts with a quick evaluation of the iteration goals and then proceeds with a walk-through of all the committed stories. Each is demoed in a working, tested system. Spikes are demoed through a presentation of findings. After all the completed stories are demoed, the team then reflects on any stories that were not completed and why. This discussion usually uncovers impediments or risks, false assumptions, changing priorities, estimating inaccuracies, or over-commitment.

Iteration Retrospective

After the iteration review, the whole team participates in a retrospective to reflect on the work just completed and to develop a plan for improvements in the next iteration. The Scrum Master facilitates this meeting, applying tools and processes for data collection and problem-solving. The team reviews the results of the improvement stories identified in the prior retrospective and points out new stories for improvement in the next iteration. One easy format is to ask three simple questions:

- What went well?
- What didn't go well?
- What can we do better next time?

Building Quality In

Built-in quality is one of the four core values of SAFe. The enterprise's ability to deliver new functionality with the *fastest sustainable lead time,* and to react to rapidly changing business environments, depends on solution quality. But built-in quality is not unique to SAFe: It's a core principle of the Lean-Agile mindset, where it helps avoid the cost of delay (CoD) associated with recall, rework, and defect fixing. As we described earlier, the Agile Manifesto focuses on quality as well: "Continuous attention to technical excellence and good design enhances agility."[1]

The following sections summarize SAFe's recommended practices for achieving built-in quality.

Software Practices

SAFe's software quality practices—many of which are inspired by Extreme Programming (XP) and DevOps—help Agile software teams ensure that their solutions are high in quality and adaptable to change. The collaborative nature of these practices, along with a focus on frequent validation, creates a culture in which engineering and craftsmanship are key business enablers. These software quality practices include the following:

- *Continuous integration (CI).* This practice merges the code from each developer's workspace into a single main branch of code multiple times per day. That lessens the risk of deferred integration issues and the impact on system quality

---

1. http://agilemanifesto.org/principles.html

and program predictability. At the very least, teams perform local integration daily. In addition, to confirm that the work is progressing as intended, full system-level integration should occur at least one or two times per iteration.

- *Test-first.* This set of practices encourages teams to think deeply about intended system behavior before implementing code. In test-driven development (TDD), developers write an automated unit test first, run the test to observe the failure, and then write the minimum code necessary to pass the test. Behavioral-driven development (BDD)[2] expresses story and feature acceptance criteria as automated acceptance tests, which can be run continuously to ensure continued conformance as the system evolves.

- *Refactoring.* Refactoring is "a disciplined technique for restructuring an existing body of code, altering its internal structure without changing its external behavior."[3] A key enabler of emergent design, refactoring is essential to Agile development. To maintain system robustness, teams continuously refactor code in a series of small steps, providing a solid foundation for future development.

- *Pair work.* Some teams engage in *pair programming*, but that approach may be too extreme for some people. More often, pair work couples developers and testers on a story. Other teams prefer more spontaneity, pairing developers for critical code segments, refactoring of legacy code, interface definition, and system-level integration challenges.

- *Collective ownership.* This practice "encourages everyone to contribute to all segments of the system. Any developer can change any line of code to add functionality, fix bugs, improve designs, or refactor."[4] Because big systems have big code bases, and because it's unlikely that the original developer is still on the team or program, this is critical. And even if the original developer is available, waiting for another person to make a change is a hand-off and a certain source of delay.

- *Agile architecture.* This set of principles and practices supports the active evolution of the design and architecture of a system *while implementing new business functionality*. In this approach, the system architecture evolves over time while simultaneously supporting the needs of current users. It avoids Big Design Up Front (BDUF) and the starts and stops of phase-gated development.

---

2. BDD is sometimes known as acceptance test-driven development (ATDD).

3. Martin Fowler, *Refactoring: Improving the Design of Existing Code* (Addison-Wesley Professional, 1999).

4. www.extremeprogramming.org/rules/collective.html

Firmware and Hardware Practices

With firmware and hardware, the quality goal is the same, but the physics and economics—and therefore the practices—are somewhat different. Errors and unproven assumptions in firmware and hardware development can introduce a much higher cost of change and rework over time, as illustrated in Figure 8-7.

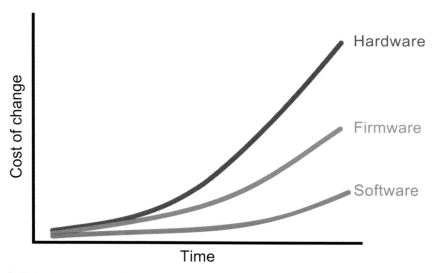

Figure 8-7. Relative cost of change over time for software, firmware, and hardware[5]

The higher cost of change drives developers of complex systems to apply practices that assure quality during solution development:

- *Model-based systems engineering.* MBSE applies modeling and tools to the requirements, design, analysis, verification, and documentation activities in solution development. It provides a cost-effective way to learn about system characteristics before and during development, which helps manage the complexity and cost of large-system documentation.

- *Set-based design.* SBD maintains multiple requirements and design options for a longer period in the development cycle. It uses empirical data to narrow the focus based on emerging knowledge. (SBD is discussed further as part of principle #3, 'Assume variability; preserve options' in chapter 4, 'SAFe Principles.')

---

5. www.innolution.com/blog/agile-in-a-hardware-firmware-environment-draw-the-cost-of-change-curve

- *Frequent system integration.* For many software solutions, CI is an achievable goal. However, systems with physical components—molds, printed circuit boards, mechanisms, fabricated parts, and so on—evolve more slowly and can't be integrated and evaluated daily. Even so, that can't be an excuse for late and problematic integration. That's why builders of complex and embedded systems shoot for *early and frequent* integration of components and subsystems.

- *Design verification.* But even frequent integration is not enough. First, due to the dependencies related to the availability of various system components, it can occur too late in the process. Second, it can't predict and evaluate all potential usage and failure scenarios. To address this issue, builders of high-assurance systems perform design verification to ensure that a design meets the solution intent. This may include specification and analysis of requirements between subsystems, worst-case analysis of tolerances and performance, Failure Mode Effects Analysis (FMEA), modeling and simulation, full verification and validation, and traceability.

Improving Team Flow with Kanban

Kanban is a method for visualizing and managing work. Kanban systems include work in process (WIP) limits, which help to identify bottlenecks and improve the flow of work.

Agile teams, including Scrum teams, can apply Kanban to better understand how their process unfolds, how works flows through their system, and how they can make the development process more effective. The primary aspects of a Kanban system include the following:

- Work moves through the system in a series of defined workflow states, or steps.

- All work is visualized, and the progress of individual items is tracked.

- Teams agree on specific WIP limits for each step and change them to improve flow.

- Teams adopt policies that cover how to manage work (for example, entry/exit criteria for a step, classes of service).

- Work items are tracked from the time they enter the system to the time they leave, providing continuous indicators of flow, WIP, and measures of lead time.

The Team Kanban Board

To start, teams typically create a graphic representation of their current process and define some initial WIP limits. Figure 8-8 shows an example of one team's initial Kanban board.

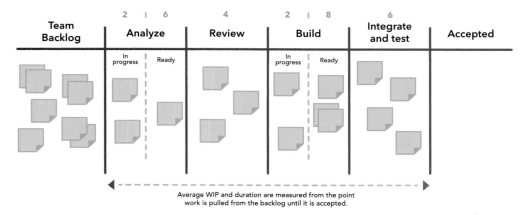

Figure 8-8. Example of a team's initial Kanban board

As shown in Figure 8-8, this team has also included two 'Ready' buffers to manage variability of flow better. One buffer comes before the 'Review' step. (Perhaps it helps smooth the flow of review by external subject-matter experts whose availability may be uneven.) The other buffer comes before the 'Integrate and test' state, which, in this case, requires the use of shared test fixtures and other resources. Since people within the same infrastructure also perform integration and testing, these two steps are combined and treated as a single state.

A team's Kanban board evolves as the team learns how to improve its process. After defining the initial process steps and WIP limits—and executing the process for a while—the team's bottlenecks, resource constraints, and over-specialization will begin to surface. The team can then improve its process accordingly. As they validate assumptions, teams adjust WIP limits. Steps may, in turn, be merged, split, or redefined.

Measuring Flow

To understand and improve their flow and process, Kanban teams use objective measures, including average lead time, WIP, and throughput. One common method is to use a cumulative flow diagram (CFD), as illustrated in Figure 8-9.

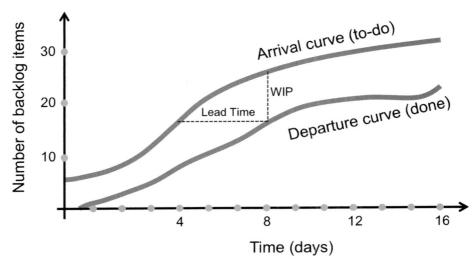

Figure 8-9. The CFD shows how lead time and WIP evolve over time

The CFD provides data for calculating current iteration throughput (average number of stories per day). In addition, it visualizes trends and significant variations, which result from internal impediments the team is unaware of, or external forces that impede the flow.

Managing Work with Class of Service

Figure 8-10 shows three 'classes of service' to help teams optimize their execution of backlog items. Each class has a specific horizontal swim lane on the board and an execution policy for managing that type of work. Here are some examples:

- *Standard.* Normal prioritizing and sequencing practices apply.

- *Fixed date.* Some items are required to meet milestones and dependencies with predetermined dates. These items are pulled into development when necessary to finish the story on time.

- *Expedite.* These high-priority items must be completed as soon as possible. They can be pulled into implementation, even if they violate current WIP constraints. Typically, teams set a policy that there can be only one expedite item in the system at a time. Teams may swarm on that item to make sure it moves through the system quickly.

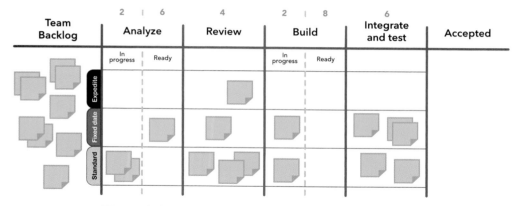

Figure 8-10. Classes of service on the Kanban board

Kanban Teams Are on the Train

Some teams—often the System Team and maintenance teams—choose Kanban as their primary development method. In these contexts, the uneven arrival of the work, fast-changing priorities, and the lower value of planning 'what exactly will be done in the next iteration' reinforce this choice. However, these teams are 'on the train' as well, so certain rules apply.

- *Cadence and synchronization still apply.* Kanban teams participate in ART activities and events. This includes PI planning, the all-important system demo, and Inspect and Adapt (I&A) event.

- *Estimating work.* Kanban teams generally do not invest as much time in estimating as most Scrum teams do. However, they must be able to predict the demand against their capacity for PI planning. They also have to participate in the economic estimation of larger backlog items.

- *Calculating velocity.* To plan and forecast, the teams must understand their velocity. Kanban teams use their CFDs to estimate their real throughput in stories per iteration or simply count and average them. Teams can then calculate their derived velocity by multiplying the throughput by an average story size. This way, both Scrum and Kanban teams participate equally in the larger planning, roadmapping, and economic framework.

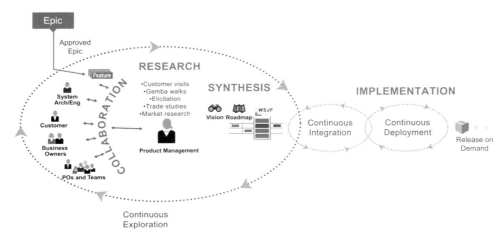

Figure 9-3. Continuous exploration process

The continuous exploration cycle has three major elements:

1. *Collaboration.* Product Management leads a collaboration among customers, Agile teams, architects/engineering, Business Owners, and portfolio stakeholders to provide input.

2. *Research.* Based on this input, Product Management uses a variety of research activities and techniques to help establish the vision, including customer visits, Gemba walks,[1] active requirements elicitation techniques, trade studies, and market research.

3. *Synthesis.* Product Management synthesizes the findings from research into the vision, roadmap, and program backlog, providing a set of prioritized features that are ready for implementation.

Continuous Integration

The second element of the 'pipeline' is continuous integration (CI), the process of taking features from the program backlog and developing, testing, integrating, and finally validating them in a staging environment. When building at the large solution level, CI becomes a three-tiered approach comprising story, system, and solution integration, as shown in Figure 9-4.

---

1. In business, a *Gemba walk* refers to the place where value is created (https://en.wikipedia.org/wiki/Gemba).

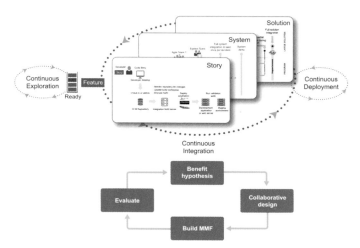

Figure 9-4. Three-tiered continuous integration, supported with the Lean UX cycle

Figure 9-4 also illustrates that each feature implementation follows the 'Lean UX' cycle:

- *Benefit hypothesis.* Each feature has a benefit hypothesis that describes measurable user and business benefits.

- *Collaborative design.* Agile teams apply SAFe Principle #2, 'Apply systems thinking,' to their Lean UX design activities, moving from a siloed, specialist approach to a collaborative, cross-functional design model.

- *Build MMF.* With a hypothesis and design in place, teams can proceed to implement the functionality in a Minimum Marketable Feature (MMF). The MMF should be the minimum functionality that the teams can build to learn whether the benefit hypothesis is valid.

- *Evaluate MMF.* After building the MMF, teams evaluate the feature using a variety of techniques—observation, user surveys, usage analytics, and A/B testing—to determine if it delivers the right outcomes.

In short, the Lean UX cycle provides the knowledge that Agile teams need to adjust and redesign—or even pivot to abandon a feature—based solely on objective data and user feedback, enabling them to iterate toward a successful outcome. With this Lean UX context in mind, we can move on to describing the three-tiered approach to continuous integration.

Story Integration

Since even MMFs are too big and abstract to be coded directly, they must be split into user stories for implementation. Each story is defined, coded, tested, and integrated into the baseline using an automated continuous integration environment. To verify that the new stories work compatibly with all the existing functionality, the system must be continually regression tested as well. To do so, teams apply automated testing and test-first development practices.

System Integration

With the support of the System Team, the work of all teams on the ART must be integrated frequently to assure that the system is evolving as anticipated. Ideally, system-level testing is done daily or as frequently as possible during the iteration. However, whatever the circumstances, such full-system integration must be accomplished at least once per iteration. Otherwise, the late discovery of defects and issues will cause substantial rework and delays. At the all-important system demo, this small batch of work is evaluated objectively and is the only true indicator of solution progress.

Solution Integration

The largest and most complex solutions typically require an additional level of integration, as the work from all the ARTs and suppliers must be integrated together. The solution demo event is where the results are made visible to the customer and other stakeholders. Doing so routinely necessitates ARTs and Solution Trains to invest in solution-level integration, testing, and supporting infrastructure. Even then, the extent of integration and testing may be less than 100 percent, requiring additional early integration points across the PI. Therefore, full or partial integration also occurs over the course of the PI, with a complete solution integration occurring at least once per PI, as illustrated in Figure 9-5.

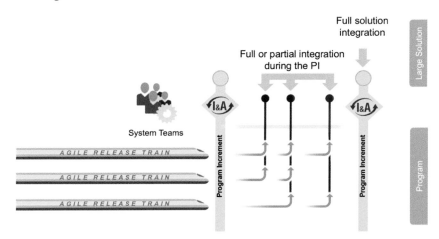

Figure 9-5. Full solution-level integration at least once per PI

The solution integration and demo are the joint responsibility of the ART and solution and system team(s). To lessen the burden, teams can leverage virtualization, environment emulation, mockups, stubs, reduced test suites, and other methods.

Continuous Deployment

Continuous deployment, the third element in the pipeline, is the process that takes features that have passed through continuous exploration and continuous integration and deploys them into the staging and production environments, where they are readied for release. Figure 9-6 identifies six practices to help implement a continuous deployment environment and process.

Figure 9-6. Six recommended practices for continuous deployment

For most traditional IT shops, continuous deployment is a form of agility that takes significant time to build. Incrementally implementing these six practices helps accelerate its realization. The first practice (maintain development environments to match production) shown in Figure 9-6 is especially critical. All too often, teams discover that what seemed to work well in the development environment does not actually work in the production environment. That lack of alignment and collaboration is addressed in the upcoming section on DevOps. The following short story illustrates this point.

A SURPRISING DISCOVERY FROM DOWN UNDER

Em Campbell-Pretty, SAFe Fellow and SPCT at Pretty Agile, Pty. Ltd., notes from her experience in adopting SAFe at Telstra in Australia, "The team quickly made a surprising discovery: Only 50 percent of the source code in their development and test environments matched what was running in production."

Release on Demand

Release on demand is the fourth and last element of the 'pipeline.' It moves deployed features, gradually or immediately, to customers and enables evaluation of the benefits hypothesis. Several strategies for releasing may be applied, depending on the context and situation:

- *Release on the PI cadence.* The simplest case is when an enterprise can release at the end of the PI, allowing PI planning, releasing, and Inspect and Adapt (I&A) events to have predictable calendar dates.

- *Release less frequently.* Releasing on the PI cadence may not always be possible or desirable due to the current service level, license agreements, and the overhead and disruption of deployment. In these cases, the planning and releasing activities are decoupled.

- *Release more frequently.* For many enterprises, the goal is to release as often as possible—hourly, daily, weekly, and so on. Achieving frequent releases requires DevOps capabilities, an efficient continuous delivery pipeline, and an architecture that supports incremental delivery practices.

- *Release on demand.* Large and complex solutions often contain different types of components and subsystems, each of which may leverage a different release model. In this case, the guidance is to release whatever you want and whenever it makes sense, within an appropriate governance and business model.

Releasing is not always automatic, nor is it an 'all-or-nothing' proposition, as Figure 9-7 illustrates.

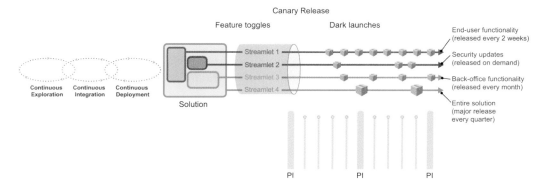

Figure 9-7. Releasing is not a monolithic, all-or-nothing process

Rather than releasing the entire solution as a single event, *elements* of the system can be released as they become available, or as the business demands. Figure 9-7 shows an example with four 'value streamlets,' each of which uses a separate release model. Releasing can be more flexible by applying modern software engineering techniques such as feature toggles, dark launches, and canary releases.

> ### A STORY FROM FACEBOOK ABOUT DARK LAUNCHES
>
> "The secret for going from zero to seventy million users overnight is to avoid doing it all in one fell swoop. We chose to simulate the impact of many real users hitting many machines by means of a 'dark launch' period in which Facebook pages would make connections to the chat servers, query for presence information, and simulate message sends without a single UI element drawn on the page. With the 'dark launch' bugs fixed, we hope that you enjoy Facebook chat now that the UI lights have been turned on."[2]

Finally, after a feature is released, the enterprise can evaluate the benefit hypothesis. For example, were the intended outcomes achieved? The feature is considered done once the benefit hypothesis is evaluated in a production environment. At that time, teams may discover they must either remove the feature toggles to avoid technical debt, or add new backlog items to extend the functionality (persevere), or pivot (remove the feature) to find a different solution. Together, continuous exploration, continuous integration, continuous deployment, and release on demand provide an integrated Lean and Agile strategy for rapidly accelerating the delivery of value to the customer.

Release Management

Releasing on demand is often supported by a release management function, which helps guide the value stream toward its business goals. This function facilitates the process of planning, managing, and governing upcoming releases. Sometimes release management can be handled by the teams and the trains themselves as part of their DevOps capability but, often—especially for systems with significant regulatory and compliance criteria—it requires a more dedicated, specialty function. In either case, the release management function facilitates the activities needed to help stakeholders receive and deploy the new solution, ensuring that the most critical governance and quality elements are resolved before deployment.

---

2. http://www.25hoursaday.com/weblog/2008/06/19/DarkLaunchesGradualRampsAnd IsolationTestingTheScalabilityOfNewFeaturesOnYourWebSite.aspx

Enabling Continuous Delivery with DevOps

DevOps[3] is the cornerstone of continuous delivery and enables the enterprise to economically develop and release small batches of functionality to the business or end user, providing faster feedback and time-to-market. Moreover, SAFe enterprises implement DevOps to break down silos and empower trains to continuously deliver new features. Over time, the separation between development and operations is greatly reduced, enabling delivery of solution elements to the end user, without hand-offs or excessive external production or operations support.

From planning through delivery, the primary goal of DevOps is to improve collaboration between development and IT operations by developing and automating a continuous delivery pipeline. SAFe's 'CALMR' approach to DevOps covers five main aspects, as illustrated in Figure 9-8.

Figure 9-8. SAFe's CALMR approach to DevOps

Each aspect of DevOps is briefly described next.

---

3. DevOps is the combination of two words: development and operations.

- *Culture of shared responsibility.* In SAFe, DevOps leverages the culture created by adopting the Lean-Agile values, principles, and practices of the entire framework. Just about every principle of SAFe, from Principle #1, 'Take an economic view,' to Principle #9, 'Decentralize decision-making,' applies to DevOps. This approach supports shifting some operations responsibilities upstream, while following development work downstream into deployment, and operating and monitoring the solution in production.

- *Automation of the continuous delivery pipeline.* DevOps recognizes that manual processes are the enemy of fast value delivery, high productivity, and safety. But automation is not just about saving time: It also enables the creation of repeatable environments and processes, which are self-documenting and, therefore, easier to understand, improve, secure, and audit. The entire continuous delivery pipeline is automated to achieve a fast, Lean flow.

- *Lean flow accelerates value delivery.* SAFe teams strive to achieve a state of continuous flow, enabling new features to move quickly from concept to cash. The three primary keys to implementing flow make up SAFe Principle #6: (1) Visualize and limit work in process (WIP); (2) reduce the batch sizes of work items; and (3) manage queue lengths. All three aspects of Lean flow are integral to relentless improvement and systems thinking.

- *Measurement of everything.* In a DevOps environment, problem resolution is often less complex and time-consuming, because changes are made more frequently and in smaller batches. Telemetry—that is, automated collection of real-time data regarding the performance of solutions—helps teams quickly assess the impact of frequent application changes. Resolution happens faster because teams don't need to wait for a different group to troubleshoot and fix the problem. It's also important to implement application telemetry to automatically collect data on the business and technical performance of the solution.

- *Recovery enables low-risk releases.* To support the continuous delivery pipeline and the concept of release on demand, the system must be designed for low-risk component or service-based deployability, releasability, and fast recovery from operational failure. Also, the following techniques support fast recovery: stop-the-line mentality, automatically build the environment, and have the capability to fix problems forward or roll back, and plan for and rehearse failures. Planning for and rehearsing failures might seem a bridge too far for many, but that's exactly what Netflix does to improve the recovery and reliability of its systems, as described in the following story.

To achieve these recovery capabilities, the organization will typically need to undertake certain enterprise-level initiatives to enhance its architecture, infrastructure, and other nonfunctional considerations to support deployment readiness, release, and production.

Enabling Continuous Delivery with Architectural Runway

The SAFe concept of the architectural runway provides the means by which Agile architecture is implemented. An architectural runway exists when the system has sufficient existing technological infrastructure to support the implementation of the highest-priority features in a near-term PI, *without* excessive redesign and delay. This runway provides the necessary technical basis for quickly implementing new features to continuously deliver new value. Indeed, it is a key enabler of development flow.

As Figure 9-9 illustrates, the architectural runway is constantly consumed by new functionality. In turn, ARTs must continually invest in extending the runway by implementing enablers to support new functionality. Some of these enablers fix existing problems with the solution—for example, the need to enhance performance—while others might implement foundational technical capabilities and services that will be used by future system behaviors.

---

4. https://github.com/Netflix/SimianArmy/wiki/Chaos-Monkey

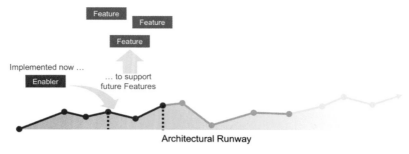

Figure 9-9. Building and consuming the architectural runway

For this reason, teams need some intentional architecture—a set of planned architectural initiatives that enhance the solution design, performance, and usability, and that provide guidance for cross-team design and implementation synchronization. Together, intentional architecture and emergent design enable ARTs to create and maintain large-scale solutions.

Managing Continuous Delivery with the Program Kanban

Each ART delivers valuable features every PI, which requires maintaining a small backlog of new features that are visible to everyone, have been socialized, and are ready to implement. ARTs use a program Kanban system to analyze features and get them ready for implementation, as shown in Figure 9-10.

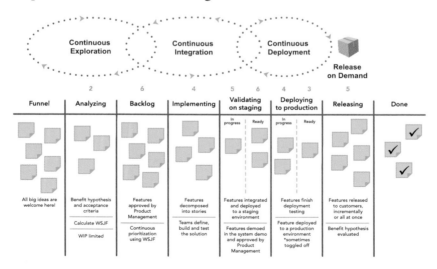

Figure 9-10. Example program Kanban system

The program Kanban facilitates the flow of features through the continuous delivery pipeline. Features begin with continuous exploration and may originate locally from the ART or flow down from an upstream Kanban (e.g., solution or portfolio Kanban). The local content authority (Product Management and System Architects) manages this Kanban.

Some ART initiatives are simply too big to be completed in a single PI. These program epics are identified and managed in a separate program epic Kanban system. The primary purpose of this Kanban system is to analyze and approve program epics, splitting them into features that will be further explored and implemented using the program Kanban. Depending on how frequently program epics occur in the local context of the ART, this Kanban system may not be required.

Supporting Continuous Delivery with Program Events

In chapter 8, 'Iterating,' the iterating loop of program execution (see Figure 9-11) was described. In the remainder of this chapter, we'll describe the program events that support continuous delivery. After all, managing work through the continuous delivery pipeline is not trivial. Indeed, a sequence of program events is needed to create a closed-loop system to 'keep the train on the tracks,' as illustrated in Figure 9-11. Each program event is described briefly in the next sections.

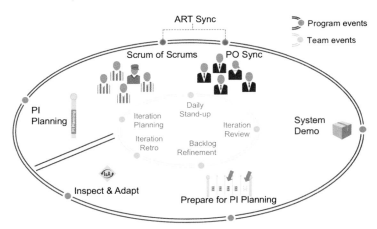

Figure 9-11. Program execution events support continuous delivery

PI Planning

The first program event, PI planning, was described in chapter 7, 'Planning a Program Increment.' The outputs of planning—that is, the PI objectives and program board—guide what will be delivered and highlight the dependencies with other Agile teams and trains.

Scrum of Scrums and PO Sync

To assess and manage progress and dependencies, ARTs coordinate through various synchronization (sync) meetings. These typically include the following:

- *Scrum of Scrums (SoS)*. The Release Train Engineer (RTE) typically facilitates the 'SoS' that meets to coordinate ART dependencies and to provide visibility into progress and impediments. Scrum Masters and others update their progress toward milestones and PI objectives and manage interteam dependencies. The SoS is held weekly or more frequently, as needed.

- *Product Owner (PO) sync*. The purpose of the PO sync is to gain visibility into how well the ART is progressing toward achieving PI objectives, to discuss problems or opportunities with feature development, and to assess any scope adjustments. Also, this meeting can be used for program backlog refinement. The PO sync meeting is held weekly or more frequently, as needed.

Sometimes, it makes sense to combine the SoS and PO sync meetings. This event is called an 'ART sync' meeting, as illustrated in Figure 9-12.

ART Sync

Scrum of Scrums

- ▸ Visibility into progress and impediments
- ▸ Facilitated by RTE
- ▸ Participants: Scrum Masters, other select team members, SMEs if necessary
- ▸ Weekly or more frequently, 30 – 60 minutes
- ▸ Timeboxed and followed by a 'Meet After'

PO Sync

- ▸ Visibility into progress, scope, and priority adjustments
- ▸ Facilitated by RTE or PM
- ▸ Participants: PMs, POs, other stakeholders, and SMEs as necessary
- ▸ Weekly or more frequently, 30 – 60 minutes
- ▸ Timeboxed and followed by a 'Meet After'

Figure 9-12. ART Sync

System Demo

The primary measure of ART progress is the objective evidence provided by a working system. Every two weeks, the full system—the integrated work of all teams on the train for that iteration—is demoed to the train's stakeholders. (This demo event is in addition to each team's iteration demo.) Stakeholders provide the feedback the train needs to stay on course and take corrective action.

At the end of each PI, a final system demo is held as part of the I&A event. This demo is a significant and somewhat more structured affair, as it demos all the features (from all teams on the train) that have been developed over the course of the PI. In large value streams, in addition to the system demo, the results of all the development efforts, from all the ARTs in the Solution Train (including suppliers), are demoed to the customers and other key stakeholders. For more information, see chapter 13, 'Solution Train Execution.'

Prepare for PI Planning

While 'prepare for PI planning' is shown as an event in Figure 9-11, in reality, preparing for the upcoming PI is a continuous process, with three primary focus areas:

- Organizational readiness
- Facility readiness
- Content readiness

The first two aspects of this preparation were described in chapter 7, 'Planning a Program Increment.' The last, and perhaps the most important, aspect of preparation is content readiness. Appearing at a PI planning event without a well-elaborated program backlog adds unacceptable risk to the upcoming PI. Making the backlog refinement process visible and achieving backlog readiness for the upcoming PI is the primary purpose of the program Kanban system.

Inspect and Adapt

The I&A event is held at the end of each PI and provides time to demonstrate the solution, get feedback, and then reflect, problem solve, and identify improvement actions. The improvement items can then be immediately incorporated into PI planning. This is such an important event that it is the entire subject of chapter 10, 'Inspect and Adapt.'

Innovation and Planning Iteration

Innovation and Planning (IP) iterations conclude each PI, providing a dedicated opportunity for teams to work on activities that are difficult to fit into a continuous, incremental value delivery pattern. The following activities may be included in these iterations:

- Time for innovation and exploration beyond the iterations dedicated to delivery
- Work on technical infrastructure, tooling, and other systemic impediments to delivery
- Education to support continuous learning and improvement
- A dedicated time for the PI planning events and backlog refinement
- The I&A event, including the final PI system demo
- Final integration of the solution, including final verification and validation, final user acceptance testing, and other readiness activities if releasing on the PI boundary

IP iterations fulfill another critical role by providing an estimating buffer for meeting PI objectives and enhancing release predictability. However, routinely using that buffer for completing work left over from prior iterations is a failure pattern.

Summary

To release value continuously, each ART builds a continuous delivery pipeline encompassing continuous exploration, continuous integration, continuous deployment, and the ability to release on demand. A sequence of program events and activities creates a closed-loop system to 'keep the train on the tracks.' Each feature implementation follows the Lean UX cycle, producing an initial minimum marketable feature, followed by enhancements that deliver appropriate and additional economic value. ARTs use a program Kanban system to analyze features and get them ready for implementation. Each ART's DevOps capability provides the technical and philosophical infrastructure needed to enable the enterprise to economically develop and release small batches of functionality, providing faster feedback and faster time-to-market.

10

Inspect and Adapt

"At regular intervals, the team reflects on how to become more effective, then tunes and adjusts its behavior accordingly."

—Agile Manifesto

Overview

In chapter 9, 'Executing the Program Increment,' we described how Agile Release Trains (ARTs) build and maintain the continuous delivery pipeline to explore, execute, and release value, including the program events and activities that support delivery. Although the Inspect and Adapt (I&A) event was briefly described there, this event is such an integral part of SAFe and Lean-Agile success that we've devoted this entire chapter to it.

As previously described, the I&A is a significant SAFe event, held at the end of each Program Increment (PI). During this event, the current state of the full solution is demonstrated and evaluated. The result is an objective assessment of the current state and a set of improvement items that the teams add to their backlog for the next PI. In this way, every ART improves every PI.

The I&A event has three parts:

1. *PI system demo*: a demo of all features completed by the ART during the previous PI.

2. *Quantitative measurement*: a review of the quantitative metrics that the teams have agreed to collect and discuss.

3. *Retrospective and problem-solving workshop*: a short retrospective for the PI, along with a structured problem-solving workshop that systematically addresses the broader impediments that are limiting velocity.

Wherever possible, all the people involved in building the system attend this workshop. These include the Agile teams, the Release Train Engineer (RTE), the System Architect/Engineer, Product Management, Business Owners, and other stakeholders. Additionally, and where applicable, Solution Train stakeholders may attend this workshop.

PI System Demo

The PI system demo is the first part of the I&A event, though this system demo is somewhat different from the biweekly versions that preceded it. Specifically, this demo shows *all the features* that have been developed by the ART during the course of the PI. Also, the audience is typically broader, including additional customer representatives and internal stakeholders. As such, this demo tends to be more formal and is set up to demonstrate and evaluate the full solution. It typically requires additional preparation and technical 'scaffolding' to reflect all the elements of the solution.

But like any other system demo, the PI system demo should be timeboxed to an hour or so, presented at a level of abstraction high enough to keep the critical stakeholders engaged and providing feedback.

Quantitative Measurement

In the second part of the I&A event, teams review the quantitative metrics they have agreed to collect and then discuss the data and trends. The RTEs and Scrum Masters are often responsible for gathering the data, analyzing it to showcase interesting findings, and presenting the measurements.

During the PI system demo, or just prior to it, the Business Owners, Agile teams, and other stakeholders collaboratively rate the actual business value achieved for each team's PI objectives and record it on the *Team PI Performance Report*, as shown in Figure 10-1. This report compares the actual business value achieved to the planned business value assigned during PI planning.

Since stretch objectives are *not* part of the commitment, they don't count in the planned value but do count in the achievement score, which is also shown in Figure 10-1. In other words, it is possible to achieve more than 100 percent of committed objectives.

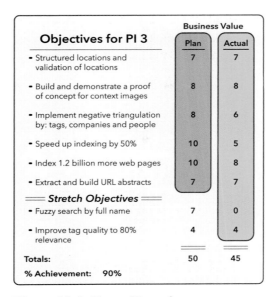

Figure 10-1. Team PI performance report

The *Team PI Performance Report* is summarized for all teams on the train to calculate the *Program Predictability Measure*, as illustrated in Figure 10-2.

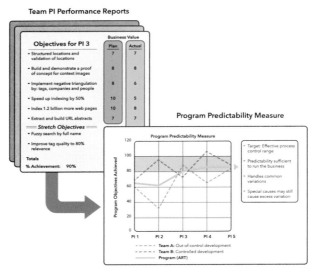

Figure 10-2. Program predictability measure

Reliable trains should generally operate in the 80 percent to 100 percent range (highlighted by the green band in Figure 10-2), which allows the business and its internal and external stakeholders to plan effectively.

Retrospective and Problem-Solving Workshop

Retrospective

In the next phase of the I&A event, the teams run a brief retrospective with the goal of identifying the broader program impediments they would like to address. This session is typically timeboxed to 30 minutes or less. There's no right way to do this, and several Agile retrospective formats can be used.[1] The objective of the selected format is to identify a small number of significant problems that the teams can potentially address.

Based on attendance at the retrospective and the types of problems identified, the groups decide which items to tackle. Attendees have a choice of resolving team-level problems or, more typically, selecting a program-level challenge and joining others who want to work on the same issue. This self-selection helps provide cross-functional and differing views. Essential ART stakeholders—including Business Owners, customers, and management—join the teams in this retrospective. They're often the only ones who can remove impediments that exist outside the team's control.

Problem-Solving Workshop

When addressing significant problems, a structured root-cause analysis and problem-solving workshop format can be useful. Root-cause analysis is a set of problem-solving tools that identifies the origins of an issue, versus just addressing the symptoms. The steps are shown in Figure 10-3 and described in the paragraphs that follow.

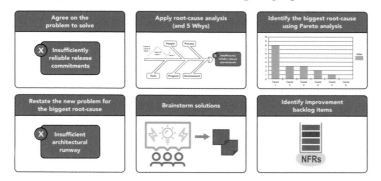

Figure 10-3. Six steps in the problem-solving workshop

---

1. Esther Derby and Diana Larsen, *Agile Retrospectives: Making Good Teams Great* (Pragmatic Bookshelf, 2009).

Agree on the Problem(s) to Solve

At this point, the teams will have selected the problem they want to work on. But have they agreed on what the problem really is? Could it be that they have differing perspectives? American inventor Charles Kettering is credited with saying, "A problem well stated is a problem half solved." To resolve those questions, the teams should spend a few minutes restating the problem—the what, where, when, and impact—as succinctly as they can. Figure 10-4 illustrates an example.

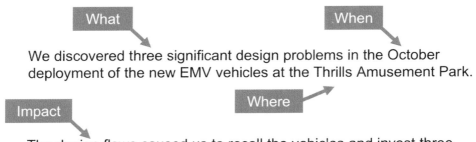

Concept contributed by Beth Miller

Figure 10-4. Example problem statement[2]

Perform Root-Cause Analysis

Next, the working group performs root-cause analyses, using proven problem-solving tools such as fishbone diagrams and the 'five whys.'[3]

Also, known as an Ishikawa diagram, the fishbone is a visual tool used to explore the causes of events or the sources of variation in a process. As shown in Figure 10-5, the team describes the problem at the right end of the 'backbone.' Causes are identified and then grouped into major categories as 'bones' off the 'main bone'—for example, people, process, tools, program, and environment. Team members then brainstorm factors they think contributed to the problem to be solved. Once a factor is named, its root cause is identified with the 'five whys' technique. After some number of 'whys' are addressed, the root cause will start to appear.

---

2. Concept contributed to SAFe by Beth Miller.
3. Originally described by Sakichi Toyoda and Taichi Ohno of Toyota, where it was integral to the Toyota Production System, the foundation of Lean thinking.

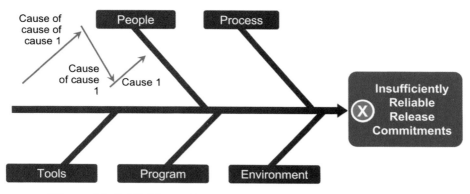

Figure 10-5. Fishbone diagram with major sources identified

Identify the Biggest Root Cause

Complex problems often have many root causes. Therefore, Pareto analysis is applied to narrow down the number of actions that produce the most significant overall effect. It applies the principle that 20 percent of the root causes may contribute to 80 percent of the problem. Once all the possible cause-of-causes have been identified, team members then dot vote[4] on the items they think are the most relevant to the end problem. To summarize the findings and assure their consensus, the team creates a Pareto chart, like that shown in Figure 10-6.

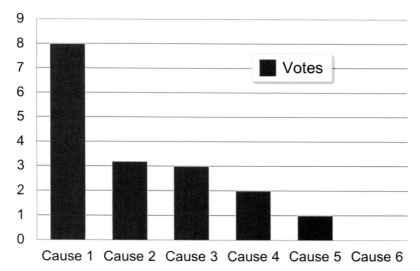

Figure 10-6. Pareto chart of probable causes

---

4. Dot-voting is a facilitation technique used to describe voting with stickers or a marker pen.

Restate the New Problem

The next step is to pick the primary cause from the Pareto analysis and restate it clearly as the new problem. This should take only a few minutes, as the teams should now be closing in on an understanding.

Brainstorm Solutions

At this point, the root cause should be clear enough that it suggests potential solutions. The working group then identifies as many potential corrective actions as they can think of, applying these rules of brainstorming:

- Generate as many ideas as possible.
- Suspend judgment of the ideas; do not allow criticism or debate during the ideation period.
- Let the imagination soar; combine and mutate ideas.

Create Improvement Backlog Items

Next, the team identifies (votes on) up to three potential solutions, which become the improvement stories that are fed into the PI planning session. During that event, the RTE and Scrum Masters help assure that the stories are incorporated into the iteration plans. Like any other backlog item, they will require people, resources, and visibility to complete.

This step concludes the retrospective. When these kinds of I&A events are held regularly, problem-solving becomes routine, and continuous improvement becomes a habit, firmly ingrained in the culture of the Lean enterprise.

Inspect and Adapt at the Large Solution Level

The previous section described a rigorous approach to problem-solving in the context of the ART. Many ARTs, however, are part of a larger Solution Train. In that case, some large solution stakeholders may attend the program-level I&A to provide feedback. In addition, as Figure 10-7 illustrates, a large solution-level I&A event is typically required, which follows the same format as the program-level I&A. Attendees include the customers and primary stakeholders at the large solution level, as well as representatives from the various ARTs and suppliers.

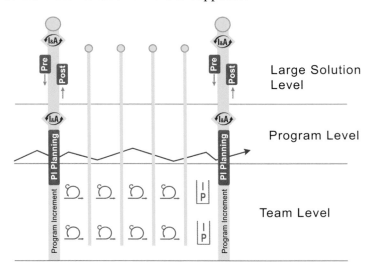

Figure 10-7. I&A events may occur at both the program and large solution levels

Summary

The I&A is a regular event held at the end of each PI. It provides time to demonstrate the solution, get feedback, and then reflect, problem-solve, and identify improvement actions. It is integral to SAFe's focus on relentless improvement. When there are several ARTs in a large solution, a similar Solution Train I&A event is typically required. It usually follows the same format as the program-level I&A but is attended by only a subset of the Solution Train stakeholders.

Part IV
Large Solution SAFe

"No solution can ever be found by running in three separate directions."

—Deepak Chopra

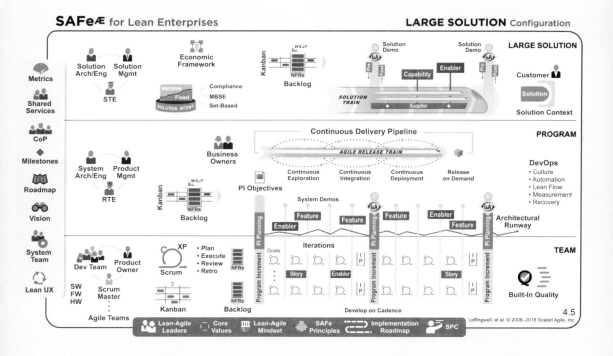

Introduction of the Large Solution SAFe Configuration

The Large Solution SAFe configuration is intended for developing the largest and most complex solutions that typically require multiple Agile Release Trains (ARTs) and the contribution of suppliers, but do not require portfolio-level considerations. This situation is commonly encountered in industries like aerospace and defense, automotive, and government, where the large solution—not portfolio governance—is the primary concern.

In this part, we provide an overview of the large solution configuration in chapter 11, then describe how to define large and complex solutions in chapter 12, and finally explore how to build these solutions via Solution Train execution in chapter 13.

Large Solution SAFe Overview

"Everything must be made as simple as possible. But not simpler."
—Albert Einstein

Overview

Building on Essential SAFe, the Large Solution SAFe configuration includes additional practices, roles, and events to support building and deploying these highly complex systems in a Lean and Agile manner, thereby replacing many of the constructs and challenges of traditional, phased-gated development.

But Einstein's quote reminds us that we should strive to make things as simple as possible, but not simpler than what is needed. Similarly, when building these large and complex systems, theoretically the simplest thing that could *possibly* work would be a single team. But we know that even teams with more than 11 people are problematic. And a single 'team' of hundreds, or even thousands, of people just isn't feasible. Instead, we need teams-of-teams (Agile Release Trains [ARTs]) and teams-of-teams-of-teams (Solution Trains). Coordinating these activities requires additional roles, events, and artifacts, which is the purpose of the large solution level.

SAFe supports enterprises building the world's largest, most important, and most complex solutions. Examples include medical devices, domestic and international banking and trading systems, aerospace and defense systems, aircraft and automotive manufacturing, shipping and other transportation systems, and more. Our modern world depends on these systems for convenience, utility, and safety—and in some cases, for our very survival. Building these solutions may require hundreds, thousands, or even tens of thousands of mechanical, electrical, and software engineers, not to mention physicists, scientists, medical professionals, and other experts, along with the integral contributions of an extensive network of external suppliers. Moreover, these systems are often so mission-critical that a failure of a single component can have serious, and even life-threatening, consequences.

The Solution Train

The *Solution Train* is the primary organizational construct of Large Solution SAFe. It is used to coordinate multiple ARTs, as well as the contributions of suppliers, as illustrated in Figure 11-1.

Figure 11-1. The Solution Train

The Solution Train enables multiple ARTs and suppliers to operate like a single entity, but with the advantages inherent in organizing using Agile teams and ARTs as a means to scale the enterprise's work. The Solution Train has a stronger focus on capturing requirements in solution intent, which provides robust mechanisms to ensure compliance with regulations and standards. In addition, the Solution Train provides ARTs with a shared business and technology mission via the solution vision, backlog, roadmap, and aligned Program Increments (PIs).

Similar to an ART, a Solution Train executes in PIs, providing shared cadence and synchronization for all its ARTs and suppliers. Each ART and supplier within a Solution Train contributes to the development of the solution, as shown in Figure 11-2.

Figure 11-2. ARTs power the Solution Train

Solution Train Roles

Similar to an ART, the Solution Train has its own trio of critical functions and roles needed to coordinate and advance the solution, as Figure 11-3 shows.

Figure 11-3. Solution Train Engineer, Solution Architect/Engineer, and Solution Management trio

- The *Solution Train Engineer (STE)* is a servant leader and coach who supports and facilitates the work of all ARTs and suppliers.

- *Solution Management* represents the customer's overall needs across trains as well as communicates the strategic themes of the portfolio vision.

- The *Solution Architect/Engineer* collaboratively defines the technology and architecture that connects the solution across trains.

Customers work closely with Solution and Product Management and other key stakeholders to shape the solution intent, the vision, and the economic framework in which development occurs. They help define and prioritize the solution's development and participate in solution planning, demos, and process improvement.

Solution Intent

When building systems that have an unacceptably high cost of failure, there is a need for a more rigorous definition and validation of system behavior. Therefore, solution behavior and decisions are managed in *solution intent*—the single source of truth and the repository for specifications as they move from variable to fixed intent. In addition to the solution vision and roadmap, the development of solution intent in an *adaptive manner* is supported by three additional practices, as shown in Figure 11-4.

Figure 11-4. Solution intent

- *Compliance* includes how solution intent facilitates built-in quality and meeting regulatory and industry standards using Lean-Agile development.

- *Model-Based Systems Engineering (MBSE)* describes how emergent requirements and design can be developed, documented, and maintained in more flexible and accessible models.

- *Set-Based Design (SBD)* encompasses practices that support preservation of options and the move from variable to fixed requirements over time, while deferring decisions to the last responsible moment.

ADAPTIVE NATURE OF SOLUTION INTENT

Harry Koehnemann, SAFe Fellow and SPCT at Scaled Agile, Inc., shares an important insight about solution intent: "While we use SAFe's solution intent to manage requirements and design, that does not mean we use it in a traditional way. Instead of creating and recording requirements and design decisions once, Lean-Agile development continually evolves them. Since the content will evolve, System Architects/Engineers must concern themselves with what content is worth keeping and maintaining. The solution intent does not replace face-to-face conversation. Instead, it provides the minimally sufficient information necessary to align everyone on the systems' current and future states, as well as support compliance. While we encourage Agile teams to visually collaborate on designs and sketch or model their solutions, the decision to persist that information is driven by economic trade-offs of aiding communication and supporting compliance needs versus the effort to maintain over the life of the system." As such, when building such large and critical systems, defining and documenting the solution intent is a science unto itself. This is the topic of chapter 12, 'Defining Large and Complex Solutions.'

Capabilities and the Solution Backlog

Solution intent captures and elaborates 'capabilities' that are used by the Solution Train to identify and define higher-level solution behaviors. Capabilities typically span multiple ARTs and often require the contributions of suppliers, as shown in Figure 11-5.

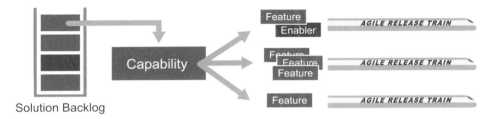

Solution Backlog

Figure 11-5. Capabilities describe higher-level solution behavior

Capabilities have attributes and practices similar to features:

- They're written using a phrase, benefit hypothesis, and include acceptance criteria; they are structured to fit within a single PI.

- Associated *enabler* capabilities describe and bring visibility to all the technical work required to support effective development and delivery of business capabilities.

- They're developed, analyzed, and approved using the solution Kanban.

- Capabilities approved for implementation are maintained in the solution backlog and are prioritized using the Weighted Shortest Job First (WSJF) model.

- Solution Managers approve capabilities that have been implemented by using acceptance criteria to determine whether the functionality is fit for purpose.

Implemented by ARTs, capabilities must be first split into features. Features are subsequently split into user stories that are implemented by Agile teams within an iteration timebox. Figure 11-6 illustrates an example of splitting a capability into features.

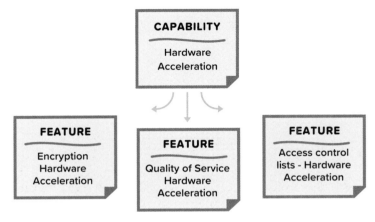

Figure 11-6. Example of a capability split into features

Solution Epics

Solution epics are initiatives large enough in scope and cost to warrant analysis and a Lean business case. Unlike capabilities, which can be split to fit inside a single PI, solution epics usually take several PIs to develop. They may also arise as a result of splitting portfolio epics, or they may occur locally as the Solution Train plans larger initiatives.

More details about epics (for example, the Lean business case and epic value statement) are covered in the discussion of portfolio epics in chapter 14, 'Lean Portfolio Management.'

Economic Framework

Building large solutions is a material economic undertaking for the system builders, suppliers, and, in many cases, the general public. In support of this, the Large Solution SAFe configuration introduces an economic framework that is designed to permit fast, effective decision-making, within the bounds of the broader economic requirements.

While described here in one place for convenience of understanding, many aspects of the economic framework are directly embedded in various SAFe practices, including the following:

- Lean budgets
- Epic funding and governance
- Decentralized economic decision-making
- Job sequencing based on the Cost of Delay (CoD)

Figure 11-7 illustrates where many of the decision rules and decision-making authority may occur within the framework. These four practices are briefly described in the following sections.

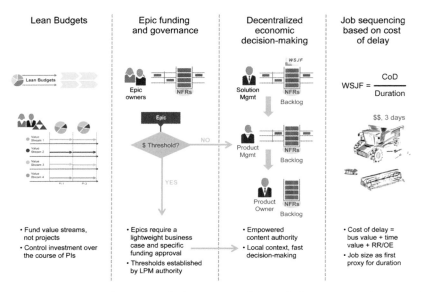

Figure 11-7. Economic framework decision rules and decision-making authority

Lean Budgets

SAFe helps the Lean-Agile enterprise move from project-based, cost-center accounting to a more streamlined, leaner budget process, in which funding is allocated to long-lived value streams. This process is described in chapter 15, 'Strategy and Investment Funding.'

Epic Funding and Governance

Allocating funds to the value streams (and, as a result, to the ARTs) is all well and good. But what happens when there are substantial financial decisions to make, such as portfolio, solution, or program epics? Empowered funding comes with the responsibility to communicate any investments that are not routine. This is the role of the Kanban systems at the portfolio, large solution, and program levels.

Decentralized Economic Decision-Making

With these budget elements in place, the enterprise empowers people to make content decisions at each level of the framework—for example, Solution Management for Solution Trains, Product Management for ARTs, and Product Owners for teams. Of course, these decision-makers don't act alone: They collaborate with the broader stakeholder community to determine the best course of action.

Job Sequencing Based on Cost of Delay

Every significant program has a backlog of new jobs—features and capabilities—waiting to be implemented. In a flow-based system, optimizing the sequence of jobs based on CoD produces better economic outcomes than prioritizing work by theoretical return on investment (ROI) or 'first-come, first-served' methods. Job sequencing is enabled by the program and solution Kanban systems and their associated backlog holding areas. When capacity exists, jobs are 'pulled' for implementation based on the WSJF algorithm.

Applying Large Solution Elements to Other Configurations

Enterprises that build smaller and largely independent systems may not need the large solution configuration. However, some ARTs build systems that are mission- or life-critical. In such a case, many SAFe elements that are pictured at this level may applied to the Essential SAFe or Portfolio SAFe configurations. For example, solution intent and compliance might be used by a single ART building a medical device of modest scale, as illustrated in Figure 11-8.

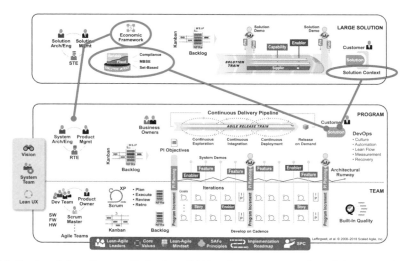

Figure 11-8. Applying Large Solution SAFe elements to other SAFe configurations

Summary

The Large Solution SAFe configuration supports enterprises that build some of the world's largest, most important, and most complex solutions. Such solutions typically require multiple ARTs, as well as the contributions of suppliers. This configuration includes additional practices, roles, and events to support building and deploying these highly complex systems in a Lean and Agile manner.

The Solution Train is the primary organizational element of the large solution level. It enables multiple ARTs and suppliers to operate like a single entity, but with the advantages inherent in organizing using Agile teams and ARTs to scale up the enterprise's efforts. Given the complexity and criticality of large solutions, the Solution Train has a stronger focus on solution intent, which provides robust mechanisms to capture requirements and designs and to help ensure compliance with regulations and standards. Given the scope and investment in large solutions, the solution train also focuses on the larger economic framework, which provides the financial boundaries for effective solution development and deployment.

Defining Large and Complex Solutions

"At its heart, engineering is about using science to find creative, practical solutions. It is a noble profession."[1]
—Queen Elizabeth II

Overview

Building large-scale and complex systems is one of the most difficult and challenging endeavors today. In addition, as we described in the last chapter, many such large systems have an unacceptably high cost of failure. This has created a barrier to Agile adoption, as the need for a more rigorous definition and validation of solution behavior may appear to conflict with the Agile Manifesto's value of "working software over comprehensive documentation."[2] Clearly, the people who build these systems need both.

The engineering of these complex and highly reliable solutions also requires and creates large amounts of technical information, resulting in far more 'comprehensive documentation.' Much of this information reflects the intended behavior of the solution.

Other relevant information records some of the key decisions and findings about the system. This may include information from trade studies, results of experiments, the reasons for design choices, and more. In many cases, this information and traceability between artifacts must become part of the official record, whether out of necessity or to satisfy regulations.

---

1. https://www.brainyquote.com
2. http://agilemanifesto.org

To manage the complexity and intensity of this information, the following concepts are described further in this chapter:

- *Solution.* The products, systems, or services.

- *Solution intent.* The knowledge repository that stores the previously mentioned information.

- *Solution context.* The broader ecosystem in which the solution operates.

The Solution

A *solution* is the set of final products, systems, or services that is delivered to the external customer or that enables the work of an operational value stream[3] within the organization. Solution development is the subject of each Agile Release Train (ART) and value stream. The Large Solution SAFe configuration supports developing solutions that require multiple ARTs, and typically multiple suppliers, to build them. At this level, solution development involves several core practices and elements of SAFe, as Figure 12-1 illustrates.

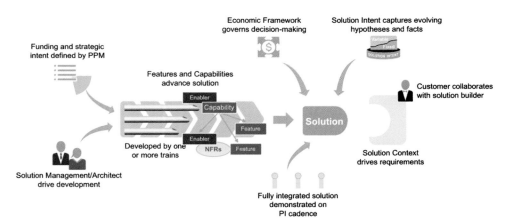

Figure 12-1. Overview of large solution development

As previously described, large solutions are delivered by multiple ARTs and suppliers operating together as a *Solution Train.* ARTs build the solution simultaneously in fully integrated increments, measuring progress during the *solution demo*, which occurs at least once during every Program Increment (PI) and provides an objective evaluation of

---

3. The steps used to provide goods or services to a customer, be they internal or external (Martin, Karen, and Mike Osterling. *Value Stream Mapping* [McGraw-Hill, 2014]).

the working solution. The solution intent is used to capture the evolving benefit hypotheses for the intended system behavior. It also facilitates exploring and defining fixed and variable requirements and designs that are derived, in part, from the *solution context*. The solution intent and context are described in the following sections.

The *customer* interacts with the development teams to clarify intent, validate assumptions, and review progress. *Solution Management* and *Architects/Engineering* help drive development, make scope and priority decisions, and manage the flow of features, capabilities, and *nonfunctional requirements (NFRs)* in the solution Kanban. Governance is provided, in part, by the *economic framework*, which was described in chapter 11, 'The Large Solution SAFe Overview.'

Solution Intent

Solution intent is a knowledge repository used to define, store, manage, and communicate 'what is being built' and 'how it will be built,' as shown in Figure 12-2. It serves many purposes:

- Provides a single source of truth for solution behavior
- Records requirements, design, and architecture decisions
- Facilitates exploration and analysis activities
- Aligns customers, teams, and suppliers to a common understanding
- Supports compliance and contractual obligations

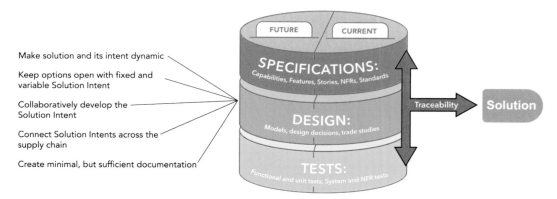

Figure 12-2. Anatomy of solution intent

As Figure 12-2 illustrates, builders of large and complex systems must constantly know two things about the solution.

- *Current state*: describes what the current system does at any point in time
- *Future state*: defines the intended changes for the future state of the system

Knowledge of both the current and future states can be captured in any form suitable to the teams but includes three primary elements:

- *Specifications*: capabilities, features, stories, NFRs, and standards
- *Designs*: models, prototypes, drawings, and trade studies
- *Tests*: functional and unit tests and system and NFR tests

Fixed and Variable Solution Intent

As mentioned earlier, teams use solution intent for a variety of purposes. None of these, however, mandates creating fully defined up-front 'point-solution' specifications. 'Such early decisions restrict exploration of better economic alternatives and often lead to waste and rework.'[4] SAFe principle #3, 'Assume variability; preserve options,' tells us that defining requirements and designs too tightly up-front leads to less successful outcomes. Fixed and variable solution intents support a more adaptive approach, as described here:

- *Fixed intent.* This represents required and/or known solution behaviors. Those behaviors might be non-negotiable, or they may have emerged during the course of development.
- *Variable intent.* These solution behaviors allow the teams to explore the economic trade-offs of requirements and design alternatives that could meet the needs of the customer (for example, 'the launch pad elevator can carry a load of between 200 kg and 800 kg').

Developing Solution Intent

SAFe's Lean-Agile approach to developing system knowledge differs from the traditional waterfall approach. Figure 12-3 illustrates the artifacts and processes used to develop solution intent using an *emergent* method.

---

4. Allen C. Ward and Durward Sobek, *Lean Product and Process Development* (Lean Enterprise Institute, 2014).

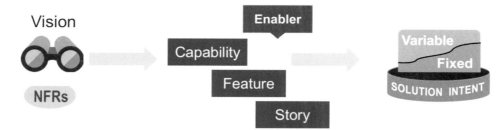

Figure 12-3. Developing solution intent

Solution intent begins with a vision. It describes at a high level the purpose and key capabilities of the intended solution, as well as the critical NFRs. This information, along with the emerging roadmap and critical milestones, guides teams in creating backlogs and planning their work. At the same time, the roadmap and solution intent are filled with assumptions. SAFe's guidance for continuous delivery tests assumptions through minimum viable products (MVPs) that provide validated learning through frequent, quantifiable experiments. Although the validated learning in the solution intent is predominately technical, the *Lean Startup* principles of 'leap–test–measure–pivot' still apply.

Collaborating on Solution Intent

ARTs help define the solution intent and build the capabilities and subsystems that support it. This requires collaboration between the customer, Architects/Engineers, and Solution and Product Management.

Typically, the Solution Architect/Engineering team drive the highest-level, system-wide decisions. This could include system decomposition, interfaces, and allocations of requirements to various subsystems and capabilities. In turn, required solution behaviors are allocated to the ARTs, where they influence the program backlogs.

Solution Engineering also establishes how the solution intent is structured and may define where information is managed to support analysis and compliance needs.

Moving from Variable to Fixed Solution Intent

Building and deploying a solution requires moving from *variable* to *fixed* intent. This process entails exploring options and keeping them open for as long as possible—within the constraints of the economic framework. As more information becomes known, the teams implement new features, and more requirements become fixed, as Figure 12-4 illustrates.

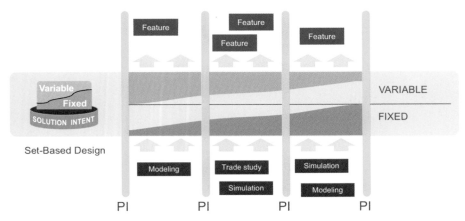

Figure 12-4. Moving from variable to fixed solution intent

System-of-Systems Solution Intent

A system's solution intent doesn't always stand alone. Many solutions are systems that participate in a higher-level system of systems. In those cases, other systems, as well as suppliers, provide teams with unique knowledge and solution elements that accelerate development. Suppliers, for example, will often have separate and independent requirements, designs, and other specifications for their subsystem or capability. From their perspective, that's their solution intent. The top-level solution intent must, therefore, include the relevant supplier knowledge and information to communicate decisions, facilitate exploration, align teams, and support compliance. Figure 12-5 shows this chain of requirements, which moves design decisions up and down the solution intent hierarchy.

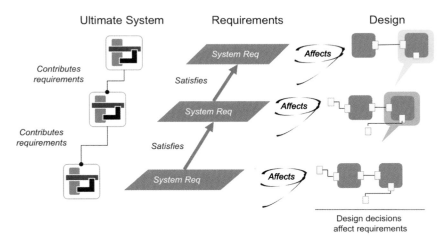

Figure 12-5. Solution intent hierarchy

Minimum Responsible Documentation

Solution intent is a means to an end—that is, a means to guide builders of systems to communicate decisions and demonstrate compliance. But more is not necessarily better—design and architecture documentation should be as *lightweight* as possible. Best practices include the following:

- *Favor models over documents.* An environment of continuous change challenges a document-centric approach to organizing and managing solution intent. Model-based systems engineering provides an easier way to maintain and manage this information.

- *Keep options open.* Defer decisions to local teams, and make those decisions at the last responsible moment. Set-based design practices help the teams avoid committing to design and requirements too early.

- *Communicate at a high level.* Describe system behavior with solution intent, at the highest possible level. Don't over-specify. Provide a range of acceptable behaviors.

- *Keep it simple.* Record only what is needed. Solution intent is a tool to help build a product and meet compliance and contractual obligations. Less can be more.

Solution Intent Documentation in High-Assurance Environments

Complex and/or regulated environments may require substantially more investment in solution intent documentation. Compliance may mandate the creation of standards-based documentation or other technical specifications. Some regulations even require recording the results of exploration and design decisions. Others mandate traceability to support analysis, feasibility, and demonstration of the solution's compliance with approved requirements.

In these cases, some elements of solution intent will be more formally documented. However, this documentation can be 'compiled' during solution development, rather than defined in an up-front mandate. Traceability connects the artifacts of solution intent to each other and to the components of the systems that realize the full system behavior.

Solution Context

An understanding of the solution context is integral to the solution's ability to produce the desired result. The solution context helps identify critical aspects of the target solution environment and its impact on usage, installation, operations, support, and even marketing, packaging, and selling. Here are a few examples of solution context:

- System of systems (e.g., an avionics system as part of the aircraft, or a word processor as part of an office productivity suite)

- Production infrastructure (e.g., a cloud environment where the solution is deployed)

- A single solution used in different usage models (e.g., a passenger airplane that can fly both domestic and international routes economically)

Understanding and aligning solution intent with solution context requires frequent interaction with the customer, as shown in Figure 12-6. Customers understand the vision and have the required decision-making authority. The degree of interaction and collaboration depends on the level of connection between the solution and its environment.

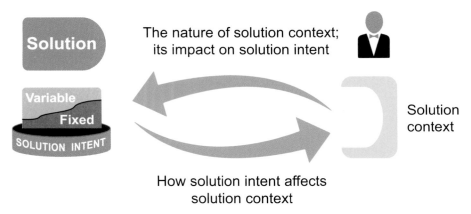

Figure 12-6. Solution intent and solution context inform each other

To ensure this alignment, the customer should participate in the pre- and post-PI planning meetings and solution demos as frequently as possible. This regular cadence of collaboration and integration allows for building solution increments based on correct assumptions and provides for validation of the result within the customer's environment.

Solution Context for a System of Systems

The solution supplier-to-customer relationship in large system-of-systems contexts is a unique and cascading entity, as Figure 12-7 shows.

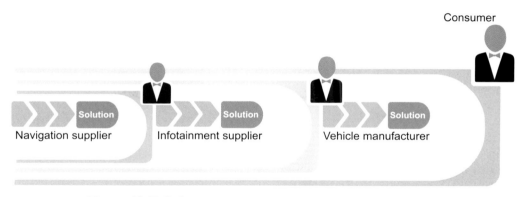

Figure 12-7. Solution contexts wrap in a system of systems

Each organization in the supply chain delivers its solution to the customer's context, which specifies how the solution is packaged, deployed, and integrated. That customer, in turn, provides a solution in context to its own customer, and so on.

Solution Context for IT Deployment Environments

Even when the software being developed is for an internal customer, the solutions for the production environment still require context. Deployment must consider specific interfaces, deployed operating systems, firewalls, APIs to other applications, and hosted or cloud infrastructure, as Figure 12-8 illustrates.

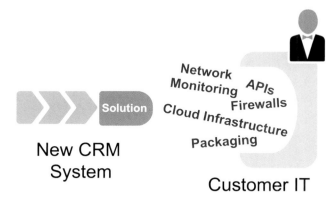

Figure 12-8. Solution contexts for internal IT deployment

Understanding the solution context is particularly relevant to help make deployment as routine as possible, which is the primary goal of DevOps and the continuous delivery pipeline.

Solution Context Includes Portfolio-Level Concerns

One final consideration is relevant to the solution context: Generally, the products and services of a business must work together to accomplish the enterprise's broader business objectives. These solutions do not stand alone, but rather are part of a larger solution portfolio, which makes them a portfolio-level concern. As such, emerging initiatives (typically in the form of portfolio epics) also drive solution intent and affect the solution's development and deployment.

For internally hosted systems, compatibility with other solutions is often required, further extending the solution context. For example, larger operational value streams often use solutions from multiple development value streams, as Figure 12-9 illustrates.

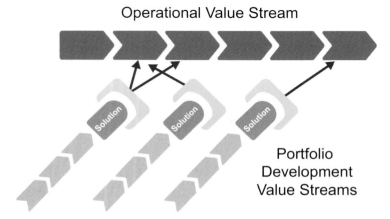

Figure 12-9. Solutions work together to support the full operational value stream

Providing a seamless, end-to-end solution to the operational value stream requires each of these solutions to collaborate and become integrated with the other solutions.

Summary

The engineering of complex and highly reliable solutions necessarily requires large amounts of technical documentation, which initially may appear to be in conflict with Agile values. SAFe provides a Lean-Agile approach to solution definition that fosters lightweight design and architecture documentation, which favors models over documents. Such an approach captures the intended system behavior in the solution intent—a knowledge repository that communicates 'what is being built' and 'how it will be built.' The solution intent also describes the solution context—the ecosystem in which the solution operates. The solution intent facilitates exploring and defining fixed and variable requirements and designs.

Compliance concerns may mandate the creation of standards-based documentation or other technical specifications, which may require more investment in solution intent documentation. These efforts may include recording the results of exploration and design decisions in support of analysis and feasibility, and demonstrating of traceability to requirements.

13

Solution Train Execution

"Principle of Alignment: There is more value created with overall alignment than with local excellence."

—Don Reinertsen

Overview

In part III of this book, we discussed planning and executing a Program Increment (PI), as well as the Inspect and Adapt (I&A) event for a single Agile Release Train (ART). But as discussed in chapter 12, 'Defining Large and Complex Solutions,' when it comes to building really big systems, a single ART cannot do the job alone. With this context in mind, we described a Solution Train that is used to define and build large and complex solutions that require the coordination of multiple ARTs as well as the contributions of suppliers.

In this chapter, we describe *Solution Train execution* and cover the Solution Train topics that are illustrated in Figure 13-1.

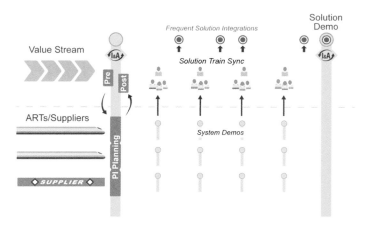

Figure 13-1. Overview of Solution Train events

Pre-PI Planning

The first element on the left of Figure 13-1 is Solution Train pre-PI planning. The purpose of this event is to establish the broader solution context and goals for the ART PI planning meetings that follow. Inputs to preplanning include the solution vision and roadmap, context from the most recent solution demo, any updates to the solution intent, and the highest-priority capabilities from the solution backlog. Attendees at this event typically include customers, the Solution Train Engineer (STE), Solution Management, Solution Architect/Engineering, the solution-level system team and release management, and representatives from the ARTs and suppliers.

The pre-PI planning meeting is used to build the context that allows the ARTs and suppliers to effectively create their plans during their individual PI planning sessions. There is no prescribed format for such a meeting, and it may occur as a single event or multiple sessions over time. For simplicity's sake, let's assume pre-PI planning takes place as a single event and follows the agenda shown in Figure 13-2. Each item of the sample agenda is described next.

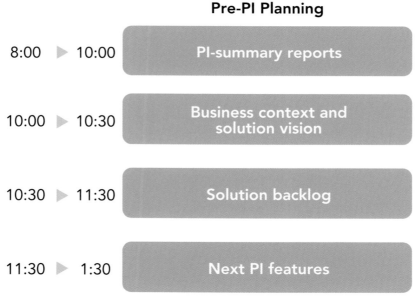

Figure 13-2. Example pre-PI planning meeting agenda

- *PI-summary reports.* Each ART and supplier briefly report on the accomplishments of the previous PI. This discussion does not replace the need for the solution demo, but rather summarizes what has been achieved to date.

- *Business context and solution vision.* A senior executive presents a briefing about the current state of the solution within the larger context of the full portfolio. Solution Management presents the current solution vision and highlights changes from the previous PI. Solution managers may also present a roadmap for the upcoming three PIs, as well as milestones that occur during that period, to ensure that they are known and addressed.

- *Solution backlog.* Solution Management reviews the top capabilities for the upcoming PI. Solution Architect/Engineering discusses upcoming enabler capabilities and epics.

- *Next PI features.* Each ART's Product Management presents the features backlog the ART has prepared for the upcoming PI and discusses any known dependencies with other trains and the potential impact on the solution.

ART PI Planning

The next step is where the individual ARTs perform their PI planning (the entire topic of chapter 7, 'Planning a Program Increment'), as illustrated in Figure 13-3.

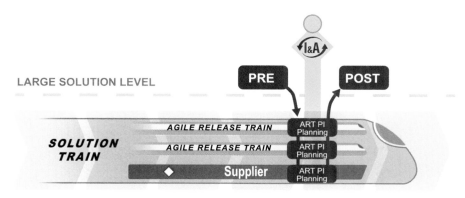

Figure 13-3. ART PI planning follows Solution Train pre-PI planning

Following this sequence, ART Product Managers will have reviewed their initial plans at the pre-PI planning meeting and made whatever adjustments are necessary. Product Management, along with the Release Train Engineer (RTE) and System Architect, will have a better understanding of the Solution Train context and will be more prepared to fulfill their mission.

Solution Train stakeholders should attend as many of the ART PI planning sessions as possible. In many cases, ART planning sessions occur at the same time, and Solution Train stakeholders participate by circulating among the various sessions. Suppliers and customers should also be represented during ART PI planning.

Post-PI Planning

The post-PI planning meeting, which occurs after the ARTs have held their respective PI planning sessions, aims to synchronize the ARTs and create the overall solution plan and roadmap. Participants include Solution Train and key ART stakeholders. Figure 13-4 shows an example agenda, followed by a description of each agenda item.

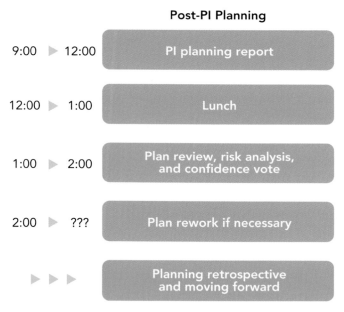

Post-PI Planning

9:00 ▷ 12:00	PI planning report
12:00 ▷ 1:00	Lunch
1:00 ▷ 2:00	Plan review, risk analysis, and confidence vote
2:00 ▷ ???	Plan rework if necessary
▷ ▷ ▷	Planning retrospective and moving forward

Figure 13-4. Example post-PI planning meeting agenda

- *PI planning report.* Each ART's Product Management presents the plans devised at the individual PI planning meetings, explaining the ART PI objectives and when each is expected to be available. The STE works with RTEs to build the solution planning board and discuss dependencies with other ARTs and suppliers.

- *Plan review, risk analysis, and confidence vote.* All participants in the post-PI planning session review the complete plan. One by one, risks are addressed and 'ROAMed.' (See chapter 7, 'Planning a Program Increment,' for more information on ROAMing risks.) Once all risks have been addressed, the group votes on its confidence in meeting the solution PI objectives.

- *Plan rework if necessary.* If necessary, the group revises its plans for as long as necessary to reach commitment. This could cascade into follow-up meetings in the ARTs, as teams will need to be involved in any change to the plans.

- *Planning retrospective and moving forward.* Finally, the STE facilitates a brief retrospective of the pre- and post-PI planning sessions. Following this, next steps are discussed, including capturing objectives, entering data into Agile project management tooling, and finalizing the schedule of key upcoming Solution Train activities and events.

Solution Planning Outputs

A successful event delivers three primary artifacts.

1. *A set of solution PI objectives.* Solution Management, Solution Architect/ Engineering, and customers set business value and objectives. This may include stretch objectives and goals built into the plan, but not committed to by the Solution Train.

2. *A solution planning board.* This artifact highlights the objectives, anticipated delivery dates for capabilities, dependencies between ARTs, and any other relevant milestones; it is created by summarizing the data from the ART's program boards.

3. *An agreed set of solution PI objectives.* The confidence vote demonstrates the group's support and agreement for meeting these objectives.

Thereafter, the solution roadmap is updated based on the objectives for the planned PI.

MULTIPLE ARTS PLANNING TOGETHER

Inbar Oren, SAFe Fellow and methodologist, shares his experience with Solution Train planning: "It's a complex thing when you have a Solution Train trying to coordinate the work of multiple ARTs and shared services. In one Solution Train, we held all four ART PI planning sessions together at the same location. This allowed the STE and the RTE to walk between the rooms, identify and resolve dependencies, and coach their ARTs. Each ART had swim lanes for the other trains on their program board, and as dependencies were raised, they were resolved and visualized. Shared services had their own program board to map the work to the different trains. During the ART's management review and problem-solving meeting, we identified cross-cutting concerns, which were raised to a Solution Train management review and problem-solving meeting and the decisions were available for day two of PI planning."

Frequent Solution Integration

Solution integration across ARTs and suppliers is critical to success, as illustrated in Figure 13-5.

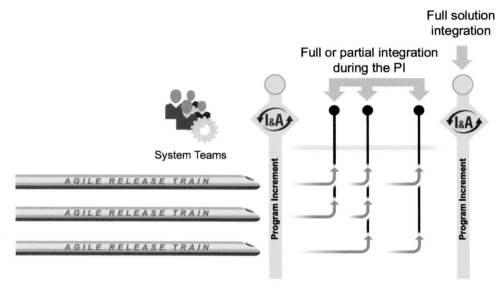

Figure 13-5. Frequent solution integration is the real measure of progress

System integration for ARTs occurs at least once at the end of each iteration, driven by the system demo. But that frequency clearly isn't sufficient for Solution Trains, where it's significantly more difficult to integrate across multiple ARTs and suppliers. Such solutions typically involve building multidisciplinary, large, and complex systems, where an integrated solution demo happens at least once at the PI boundary, *and more frequently wherever possible*. That mitigates the risk of a larger solution being developing for months and never being fully integrated.

Solution Train Sync

The STE typically facilitates a once-per-iteration (or more frequently, as conditions require) meeting to continuously coordinate work across multiple ARTs and to provide visibility into progress and impediments. The STE, Solution Management, RTEs, System/Solution Architect/Engineer, and others (where appropriate) meet to update their progress toward milestones, program PI objectives, and dependencies among the ARTs. The meeting is often timeboxed to less than 60 minutes and is followed by a "meet-after" to solve problems identified. This team is also responsible for keeping other large solution stakeholders informed as required.

Solution Demo

The Solution Train demos a fully integrated solution, showing the accomplishments of the previous PI. It provides a regular opportunity for senior managers and high-profile stakeholders to review the progress and evaluate the fully integrated solution.

The solution demo is usually coordinated by Solution Architect/Engineering, and Solution Train stakeholders (who include Solution Management and the STE) typically attend the event. The insights gleaned from the demo inform these stakeholders of the current objective assessment of solution progress, performance, and potential fitness for customer use. While the timing of the solution demo will vary based on Solution Train and solution context, it provides a critical context for the next pre- and post-PI planning meetings.

> **THE SOLUTION DEMO ROADSHOW**
>
> Inbar Oren, SAFe Fellow and methodologist, shares his experience with solution demo: "When building large cyber-physical systems, it's sometimes hard to demo the solution under development. At a customer site, we had solutions at various labs that were too heavy or complex to move around. We arranged a 'roadshow' demo, where people were going between the different labs, and team members were waiting to demo and show them the solution that they had worked on during the PI. During half a day, we visited many labs and got to see all the work that was done. Business Owners could review the results and assign business value, and the teams got the pride of demoing their work to multiple people at all levels of the organization."

Solution Train Inspect and Adapt

At the end of the PI, a Solution Train I&A event is held to assess the current state of the solution and identify improvement backlog items via a structured, problem-solving workshop. This workshop follows the same format as the ART I&A event (see chapter 10, 'Inspect and Adapt'); however, due to the number of people involved, participants in the

Solution Train I&A event cannot include everyone, so stakeholders are selected who are best suited to address that context. This group typically includes the primary stakeholders of the large solution level (e.g., STE, Solution Management, Solution Architecture/Engineering, and Business Owners), as well as representatives from the various ARTs and suppliers. As with the ART I&A event, improvement items are identified and added to the solution backlog.

Summary

When it comes to building really big systems, a single ART typically cannot do the job by itself; instead, it requires a Solution Train to complete the system. In turn, a Solution Train requires additional roles (STE, Solution Management, and Solution Architect/Engineering) and a set of additional events to coordinate multiple ARTs, as well as the contribution of suppliers. The Solution Train events include pre- and post-PI planning, the solution demo, and an I&A event. Because the solution demo requires frequent system integration that can be difficult to coordinate, it's often necessary to do *partial integrations* across ARTs and suppliers during PI execution before concluding the PI with a full system integration during the solution demo.

Part V
Portfolio SAFe

"Being able to enter new categories and exit old ones is fundamental to freeing your company's future from the pull of the past—but it is not easy."

— Geoffrey Moore

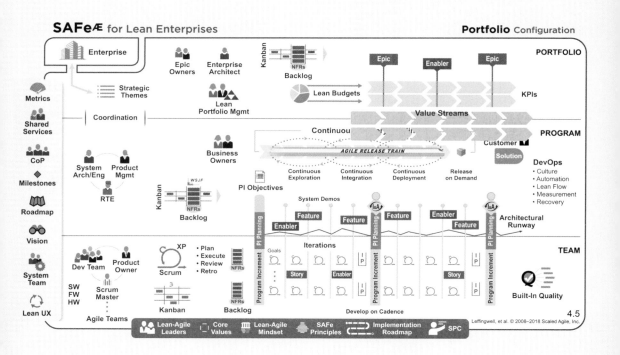

- **Chapter 14 – Lean Portfolio Management**
- **Chapter 15 – Strategy and Investment Funding**
- **Chapter 16 – Agile Portfolio Operations**
- **Chapter 17 – Lean Governance**

Introduction to the Portfolio SAFe Configuration

The Portfolio SAFe configuration helps align portfolio execution to the enterprise strategy by organizing Agile development around the flow of value through one or more value streams. It provides business agility through the principles and practices for Lean Portfolio Management (LPM).

In this part, we'll provide an overview of LPM in chapter 14 and then describe its three primary portfolio collaborations in the following chapters:

- Strategy and investment funding (chapter 15)
- Agile portfolio operations (chapter 16)
- Lean governance (chapter 17)

Together these three collaborations provide a leaner, and more agile, governance model that helps each portfolio in the enterprise achieve its larger business objectives.

14

Lean Portfolio Management

> *"Most strategy dialogues end up with executives talking at cross-purposes because . . . nobody knows exactly what is meant by vision and strategy, and no two people ever quite agree on which topics belong where.*
>
> *That is why, when you ask members of an executive team to describe and explain the corporate strategy, you frequently get wildly different answers. We just don't have a good business discipline for converging on issues this abstract."*
>
> —Geoffrey Moore, *Escape Velocity*

Introduction

As Moore's quote reminds us, the apparently simple act of defining and communicating an aligned strategy for the enterprise is not so simple. And yet nothing could be more critical to applying Principle #1, 'Take an economic view,' to improve the overall business outcomes of the enterprise.

To address this issue, SAFe describes a *Lean Portfolio Management (LPM)* function that has the highest level of decision-making and financial accountability for the products and solutions in a SAFe portfolio. The people who fulfill these responsibilities have various titles and roles, and they may be distributed throughout the organization hierarchy. But the LPM responsibilities are critical, and they must be fulfilled by the business managers and executives who understand the enterprise's financial, technical, and business contexts, and who are ultimately responsible for business outcomes.

As shown in Figure 14-1, SAFe describes three primary portfolio collaborations: *strategy and investment funding*, *Agile portfolio operations*, and *Lean governance*.

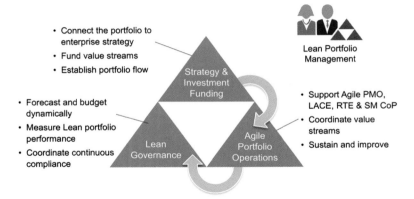

Figure 14-1. Three Lean Portfolio Management collaborations

Each is described briefly in the sections that follow.

Strategy and Investment Funding

Of these three primary collaborations, strategy and investment funding is perhaps the most important. Only by allocating the right investments to building the right things can an enterprise achieve its ultimate business objectives. This requires the focused and continued attention of LPM, which is the topic of chapter 15, 'Strategy and Investment Funding.'

This collaboration engages enterprise executives, Business Owners, technologists, and Enterprise Architects—who discuss, debate, and ultimately *agree and communicate* portfolio strategy. As Figure 14-2 illustrates, they do so by fulfilling the responsibilities of *connecting the portfolio strategy to the enterprise strategy*, *funding value streams*, and *establishing portfolio flow*.

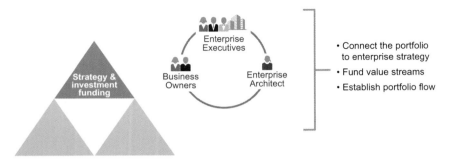

Figure 14-2. The strategy and investment funding collaboration and responsibilities

Each of these responsibilities is described next.

Connect the Portfolio Strategy to the Enterprise Strategy

It's critical that the portfolio strategy supports the enterprise's broader business objectives. However, an effective enterprise strategy also relies on the existing assets and distinctive competencies of its solutions portfolios. It's a bidirectional process; you can't have one without the other.

One key output of this strategy collaboration is the *strategic themes* that provide the differentiation needed to achieve the desired future state. To ensure that the entire portfolio is aligned to the overall business strategy, these themes must be developed and communicated broadly within the portfolio.

> ### CLARITY CAN BE UPSETTING
>
> Isaac Montgomery, SPCT and Principal Consultant at Scaled Agile, Inc., shares an interesting dilemma that a client had with strategic themes: "Safely decentralizing decision-making requires that leaders at all levels create contextual awareness and strategic alignment. This is accomplished at the portfolio through strategic themes. Recently, while leading a Lean Portfolio Management workshop for a major data communications company, we got bogged down crafting their strategic themes. Certain executives wanted to have themes that were specific, in order to inform trade-off decisions. Others wanted to keep them more general, to allow flexibility. The CEO told me, "If we make them too specific, I'm afraid that people will be upset if their work is not viewed as a strategic priority." I explained to him, "The purpose of strategic themes is to create clarity and alignment as to strategic direction. You've told me that your strategic direction must change. If that doesn't upset anyone, it's either not clear or they're not aligned."

Fund Value Streams

The role of a SAFe portfolio is to identify, fund, and nurture a set of development value streams that deliver end-user value directly or support internal business processes. Lean budgets provide value stream funding aligned with the business strategy and current strategic themes. This eliminates the need for traditional project-based funding and cost accounting. Moving away from these legacy approaches reduces friction, delays, and overhead. This is a significant change, and one that often requires some significant analysis and understanding of the enterprise's value streams.

Establish Portfolio Flow

To implement the business objectives, the flow of work originating from the portfolio must be balanced with the extensive work that arises as each Agile Release Train (ART) and Solution Train responds directly to customer needs. Portfolio business and enabler epics are used to capture, analyze, and approve new business and technology initiatives that require collaboration of multiple value streams or that cause the formation of entirely new ones.

The portfolio Kanban system is designed for this purpose. It is used to visualize and limit work in process (WIP), reduce batch sizes of work, and control the length of longer-term development queues. Epic Owners, Enterprise Architects, and—where applicable—Solution Portfolio Management support this particular Kanban system.

As we will see in chapter 15, 'Strategy and Investment Funding,' successful implementation relies on knowing the total capacity for each ART in the portfolio, as well as understanding how much is available for new development work versus ongoing maintenance and support activities. When the necessary balancing act is understood, the enterprise can then evaluate and originate portfolio-level initiatives in a logical, objective, and practical manner.

Agile Portfolio Operations

Since assuring operating alignment and execution consistency across the portfolio is a constant and urgent concern for managers and executives, chapter 16 is devoted to 'Agile Portfolio Operations.' Historically, much of this work was centralized, along with planning, program management, and solution definition. This approach was adopted in part to help assure that solution development was aligned with portfolio strategy and in part to help foster consistent approaches to critical elements such as information security, common platforms, and financial and progress reporting.

Often, a centralized Program Management Office (PMO) carried out these responsibilities. In contrast, the SAFe Lean-Agile mindset fosters the decentralization of strategy execution to empowered ARTs and Solution Trains. Even then, though, systems thinking must be applied to ensure that ARTs and Solution Trains are aligned and operate within the larger enterprise context. Typically, some form of Agile portfolio operations is required to accomplish these goals in larger enterprises. Figure 14-3 illustrates the collaboration and responsibilities of this function.

Figure 14-3. Agile portfolio operations collaboration and responsibilities

The primary responsibilities of this collaboration include supporting an Agile PMO (APMO), a Lean-Agile Center of Excellence (LACE), and Release Train Engineer (RTE) and Scrum Master Communities of Practice (CoPs). Further, it facilitates the coordination of value streams and helps the enterprise improve its overall portfolio performance with sustain and improvement activities.

Support an APMO, LACE, and RTE and Scrum Master CoPs

Many enterprises have discovered that centralized decision-making and traditional mindsets can undermine the move to Lean-Agile practices. In response, some enterprises have abandoned the PMO approach, distributing all the responsibilities to ARTs and Solution Trains. However, many organizations appear to be better served by redesigning the traditional PMO to become an APMO that provides a consistent context for delivering new value in a Lean and Agile manner.

The LPM also has a leadership role in helping the organization relentlessly improve and achieve its business goals. This is often accomplished through a small, but persistent Lean-Agile Center of Excellence (LACE).

The APMO may also sponsor and support CoPs for RTEs (and Solution Train Engineers) as well as Scrum Masters. These role-based CoPs provide a forum for sharing effective Agile program execution practices and other institutional knowledge.

Coordinate Value Streams

Although many value streams operate independently, cooperation among a set of solutions can provide some portfolio-level capabilities and benefits that competitors can't match. Indeed, in some cases, this is the ultimate goal: to offer a set of differentiated solutions in which new integrated capabilities may emerge to respond to expanding end-user patterns.

Sustain and Improve

LPM—as supported by the APMO—also has a leadership role in helping the organization relentlessly improve and thereby achieve its evolving business goals. This is the entire topic of chapter 22, 'Sustain and Improve.'

Lean Governance

The final collaboration, Lean governance, is illustrated in Figure 14-4 and further described in chapter 17, 'Lean Governance.' This important collaboration influences spending, future expense forecasts and milestones, and governance of the development effort. The stakeholders of this collaboration include the relevant enterprise executives, the Enterprise Architects and Solution Portfolio Management, and the APMO. Together with the ART and Solution Train, Business Owners and other stakeholders share the responsibilities described in the following sections.

Figure 14-4. Lean governance collaboration and responsibilities

Forecast and Budget Dynamically

SAFe describes a Lean approach to budgeting—a lighter-weight, more fluid, and more Agile process that replaces the fixed, long-range budget cycles, financial commitments, and fixed-scope expectations of a legacy planning process. It includes Agile approaches to estimating, forecasting, and longer-term roadmapping.

Measure Lean Portfolio Performance

Each portfolio must also establish the minimum metrics needed to assure that strategy is being implemented, that spending aligns with the agreed-upon boundaries, and that results are constantly improving.

Coordinate Continuous Compliance

No solution is an island unto itself. Rather, each operates in the context of its larger environment, typically containing audit and compliance requirements. These may include internal or external financial auditing requirements and industry legal or regulatory requirements. These obligations impose significant constraints on solution development and operations.

Traditional approaches to compliance tend to defer these activities to the end of development, subjecting the enterprise to the risk of late discovery and subsequent rework, and even compromising regulatory or legal exposure. A more continuous approach coordinating continuous compliance with relevant standards is required.

Summary

The apparently simple outcome of 'agreeing on strategy' is not such a simple thing in the enterprise. Opinions abound; important stakeholders don't always agree. But clearly misalignment on strategy has an unacceptably high cost, as only by allocating the right investments to building the right things can an enterprise achieve its ultimate business objectives. To address this challenge, SAFe defines a set of three Lean Portfolio Management collaborations—strategy and investment funding, Agile portfolio operations, and Lean governance—intended to help bring leadership together at the right times for the right strategic reasons. Each of these collaborations has a set of stakeholders and a set of responsibilities. When the right people work together in the right context and fulfill these responsibilities appropriately, the enterprise is well along its way to achieving the best possible business outcomes.

Strategy and Investment Funding

"Do our innovation investments focus on leveraging our crown jewels, or are we spreading ourselves too thin and failing to achieve genuine competitive separation?"

—Geoffrey Moore

Introduction

In the first chapter of part V, we introduced the Portfolio SAFe configuration from the perspective of Lean Portfolio Management (LPM) and the three collaborations around *strategy and investment funding*, *Agile portfolio operations*, and *Lean governance*.

We also highlighted that *strategy and investment funding* is arguably the most important of these collaborations. When this collaboration operates with strategic alignment and effective communication, then the enterprise can be confident that each solution portfolio is addressing the right opportunities and challenges, with the right solutions.

We also noted that defining and communication strategy concisely is no small feat, and a task that seems to challenge many enterprises. Opinions abound. Voices are loud. Really important people do not always share the same vision.

To this end, SAFe describes the strategy and investment funding collaboration intended to address these challenges. As shown in Figure 15-1, this collaboration involves (1) some of the highest-level executives in the portfolio or enterprise, (2) the Business Owners of the Agile Release Trains (ARTs) that build the solutions that deploy the strategy, and (3) typically the CTO/vice president/technology directors and Enterprise Architects who are responsible for the technical underpinnings—both within, and across, solution sets.

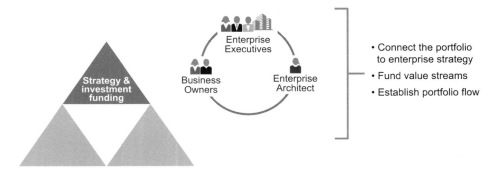

Figure 15-1. Strategy and investment funding collaboration responsibilities

This collaboration has three primary responsibilities, which are described next.

Connect the Portfolio Strategy to the Enterprise Strategy

As illustrated in the Big Picture and in Figure 15-2, portfolios have a two-way connection to the enterprise.

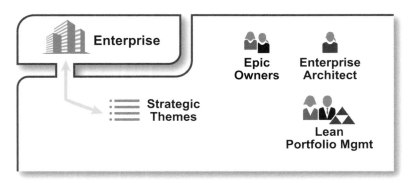

Figure 15-2. Portfolio strategy is bidirectional

The first direction helps the enterprise communicate the evolving strategy in the form of strategic themes. These themes align the portfolio to the larger enterprise business objectives. But the reverse direction is important, too: It informs the enterprise of the portfolio context, which in turn influences the decisions on strategic themes. This context includes the current state of the portfolio's solution set and assessments of strengths, weaknesses, opportunities, and threats across the portfolio.

Larger Enterprises Have Multiple SAFe Portfolios

Each SAFe portfolio contains a set of value streams and provides funding and governance for the products, services, and solutions needed to fulfill some aspect of the enterprise strategy. However, one solution portfolio may not be able to reflect the entire business. In the larger enterprise (typically those organizations with more than 500 to 1,000 technical practitioners), multiple portfolios will likely be required— one for each line of business, each with its own budgets and mission, as shown in Figure 15-3.

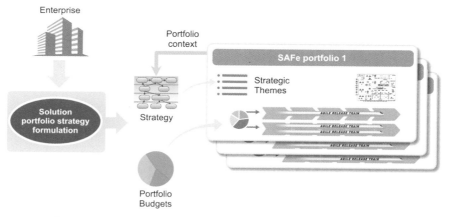

Figure 15-3. Enterprise view of multiple SAFe portfolios

Defining Strategic Themes

"The way to get strategy executed is not by telling people what to do. It's by sharing the strategy in a way that everyone can understand and buy into it, and see how their jobs relate to it. Then by putting the people processes in place to enable and encourage strategy execution."[1]

---

1. Strategy Execution: Leadership to Align Your People to the Strategy. https://millian.nl/ artikelen/strategy-execution-leadership-to-align-your-people-to-the-strategy

To this end, strategic themes help simplify and amplify the communication of the portfolio's strategy to the value streams and ARTs. Further, strategic themes provide the enterprise with the differentiators (to set its products, services, and solutions apart from those of its competitors) needed to move from the current state to a more desirable future state. These themes help drive innovation and competitive differentiation, which are achievable only through effective portfolio solutions. Some examples of strategic themes follow:

- Appeal to a younger demographic (online video streaming service)

- Implement product and operational support for trading foreign exchange instruments (securities company)

- Establish a single sign-on from portfolio applications to internal enterprise apps (independent software vendor)

- Standardize on three software platforms (large IT shop)

Defining the portfolio budget and strategic themes is part of a strategy formulation process that requires *extensive collaboration* among LPM, enterprise executives, enterprise architects, and portfolio stakeholders, as illustrated in Figure 15-4.

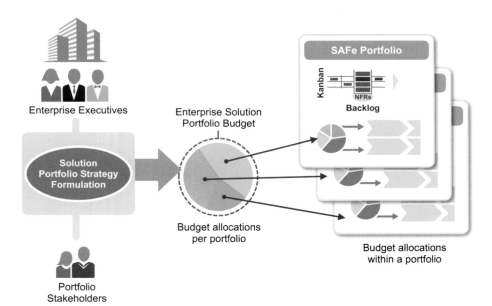

Figure 15-4. Strategic themes collaboration

THE IMPORTANCE OF SHAPING AND COMMUNICATING THE STRATEGY

Robert Kaplan and David Norton of the Harvard Business School conducted research that found a staggering 95% of employees in a company are either unaware of, or do not understand, the enterprise's strategy.[2] They noted, "Too often, strategy is formulated in a vacuum, and then centrally broadcast as a 'done deal.' The communication is either too vague or too detailed for anyone to understand what it really means. The more people are involved in helping to shape the strategy, and/or shape the execution plan, the more they feel part of the process and are likely to support it."

Indeed, formulating the strategy and communicating it to the entire portfolio influences everyone involved in solution delivery. In the next section, we explore the significant influence of strategic themes.

Influence of Strategic Themes

Most generally, strategic themes define *what needs to be new and different* from the *current state*. As such, these themes heavily influence many aspects of SAFe:

- *Value stream budgets.* Strategic themes heavily influence value stream budgets, which provide the money, resources, and people necessary to accomplish the portfolio vision.

- *Portfolio backlog and Epic Kanban decision filters.* Strategic themes provide decision-making filters in the portfolio Kanban system, influencing the content of the portfolio backlog.

- *ART and Solution Train vision and roadmap.* Strategic themes influence the ART and Solution Train vision and roadmap.

- *Economic framework.* Strategic themes may have a significant impact on the economic framework, affecting any of its parameters, including cycle time, product cost and value, development expense, and risk.

Fund Value Streams

The next responsibility of strategy and investment funding is to allocate budgets to value streams. Doing so requires first identifying and understanding value streams and then organizing ARTs to realize those value streams. Furthermore, organizing around value streams enables value stream mapping to be used to identify and address delays and non-value-added activities to accomplish delivering value in the *shortest sustainable lead time*.

---

2. Strategy Execution: Leadership to Align Your People to the Strategy. https://millian.nl/artikelen/strategy-execution-leadership-to-align-your-people-to-the-strategy

The Problem of Traditional Project Cost Accounting

Applying value stream thinking provides an excellent opportunity to rethink one of the most important problems with conventional portfolio funding practices: Traditional project-based funding and cost accounting tends to drive overhead, and even worse, creates 'temporary work for temporary people.' This outcome is in direct conflict with stable, long-lived Agile teams and the need for persistent knowledge acquisition. Also, project cost accounting requires significant administrative overhead, defense of cost overruns for unforeseen technical challenges, constant personnel reassignments, and more, as shown in Figure 15-5, which illustrates a traditional cost- and project-based funding model.

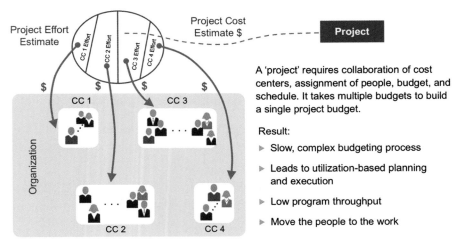

Figure 15-5. Traditional project-based cost budgeting and cost accounting model

Each cost center must contribute people to the project, which causes the following problems:

- The process for forming teams is slow and complicated because it requires many individual cost center budgets to fund the project. People are assigned on a temporary basis. When the project is complete, people return to their functional silos. If these people don't go back as planned, other projects that rely upon them will suffer.

- Cost center managers are driven to make sure everyone is fully allocated to one or more projects, resulting in 100% planned utilization (or even higher!) and causing significant bottlenecks.

- The project model prevents people from working together for longer than the duration of a single project. This reduces learning, velocity, team performance, and employee engagement.

- It drives teams to follow traditional project management practices and develop plans by identifying all tasks up front, when the least amount of knowledge exists.

Project-Based Constraints Impede Agility and Economic Outcomes

Once a project is initiated, the problems with this model continue. The needs of the business and the project change rapidly. However, because the budgets and personnel are fixed for the project term, the projects can't adapt to the changing priorities, as Figure 15-6 illustrates.

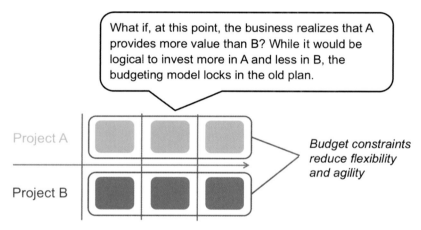

Figure 15-6. Project funding inhibits the ability to react to change

The result is an organization that is unable to adjust to changing business needs (it lacks agility) because doing so incurs the overhead of urgently changing budgets and personnel assignments. The Cost of Delay (CoD)—the cost of not doing the thing you should be doing—increases.

Delays Happen. Things Get Uglier

But we are not done. Product development cannot innovate without takings risks.[3] Because innovation inevitably involves a high degree of technical uncertainty, it's

3. Don Reinertsen. *Principles of Product Development Flow: Second Generation Lean Product Development* (Celeritas Publishing, 2009).

challenging to estimate the work. Of course, everyone knows that most things take longer than planned. Moreover, even when things go well, stakeholders may want more of a specific feature—which requires approval from a change control board, which adds further delay. Again, project-based funding hinders progress, culture change, and transparency, as Figure 15-7 illustrates.

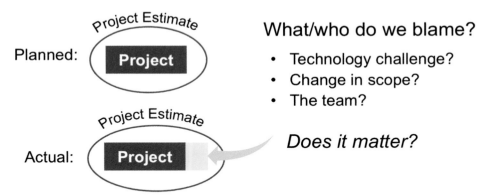

Figure 15-7. When overruns happen, project accounting analysis and rebudgeting occurs

When a schedule overrun occurs for any reason, it's necessary to analyze the variances, replan the schedule, and adjust budgets. Resources are scrambled. Personnel are reassigned. As a result, other projects are negatively impacted. Now, the 'blame game' sets in, pitting project managers against each other and financial analysts against the teams. Casualties include transparency, productivity, and morale.

Solution: Fund Value Streams, Not Projects

There is a better way: Move the day-to-day spending and resource decisions to the people closest to the solution domain by funding the value streams. Figure 15-8 illustrates this approach.

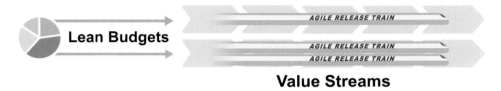

Value Streams

Figure 15-8. Operating budgets are defined for each value stream

Then, when the inevitable happens and features take longer than anticipated, the ART is empowered to make the decision locally, as illustrated in Figure 15-9. The budget for the PI is fixed, which avoids any cost overruns.

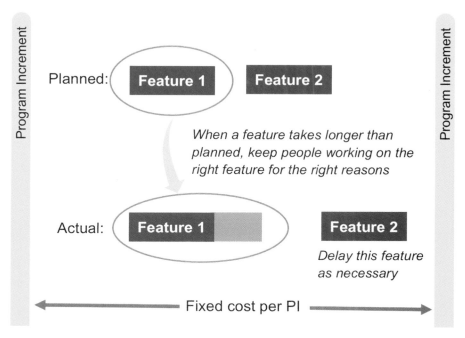

Figure 15-9. Value stream funding empowers ARTs to make local decisions

The funding of value streams delivers many benefits over traditional project funding:

- *Local empowerment.* Value stream stakeholders are empowered to allocate the budget to the personnel and resources that make sense based on the current backlog and roadmap.

- *Higher throughput and improved morale.* People work together for an extended time, increasing engagement, knowledge, competency, and productivity.

- *Full control of total spend.* The expenses across a Program Increment (PI) are fixed. If a feature takes longer than planned, the budget is not impacted; personnel adjustments are a local concern.

- *Flexibility and agility.* Most importantly, trains can flex to the work, swarming on critical features as necessary and generally doing whatever makes the most sense based on the changing flow of work.

Establish Portfolio Flow

Establishing the portfolio flow is the third and final responsibility of strategy and investment funding. This is accomplished in part through the use of portfolio *epics*, artifacts that are used to define and manage the largest initiatives within a portfolio. Typically, these epics affect more than one value stream and ART. There are two types of epics:

- *Business epics* directly deliver customer and end-user value.

- *Enabler epics* are used to evolve the architectural runway to support upcoming business epics.

Typical drivers of new epics include

- Portfolio strategic themes

- Unanticipated changes in the marketplace

- Business acquisitions, mergers, and response to competitors

- Improvements of the efficiency or cost of a solution or its operation

- Problems with existing solutions that affect business or technical performance

Epics are initially written as a simple phrase and then documented with an epic hypothesis statement, as shown in Figure 15-10. Each is also supported by a Lean business case, which highlights the elaboration of the analysis in support of the epic.

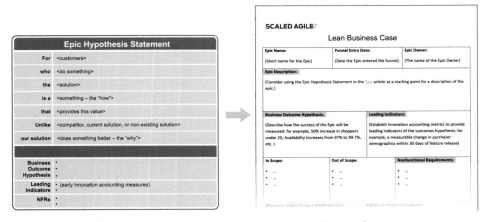

Figure 15-10. Epic hypothesis statement and Lean business case

Fostering Innovation with the Lean Startup Cycle

Epics also give the enterprise a way to leverage the *Lean startup cycle*.[4] Inspired in part by the emergence of Agile methods, the Lean startup approach recognizes that 'Big Design Up-Front' (BDUF), along with big financial commitment up front, is a poor way to foster innovation. Simply put, it assumes and overcommits the enterprise before any validated learning exists.

As an alternative to BDUF, the Lean startup movement embraces the highly iterative 'hypothesize–build–measure–learn' cycle, which fits quite naturally into SAFe, as reflected in Figure 15-11.

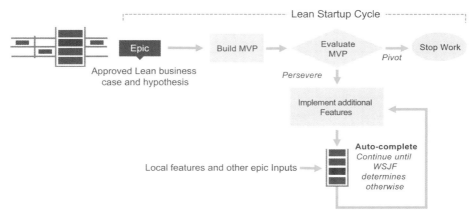

Figure 15-11. Lean startup cycle in the SAFe portfolio

As Figure 15-11 implies, approved epics deserve additional investment—but not a fully committed investment up front. After all, the work up to that point has been analytical and exploratory. As such, we need to apply the 'hypothesize–build–measure–learn cycle,' which includes the following steps:

- *Hypothesize.* Each epic has a Lean business case, which includes the hypothesis that describes the assumptions and potential measures that can be used to assess whether an epic will deliver value commensurate with the investment.

- *Build an MVP.* Based on the hypothesis of the epic, the next step is to implement a minimum viable product (MVP)—that is, the minimum effort necessary to sufficiently validate or invalidate the hypothesis. In SAFe, this translates to the minimum feature set required to deliver some holistic, but minimal, solution.

---

4. Eric Ries. *The Startup Way: How Modern Companies Use Entrepreneurial Management to Transform Culture and Drive Long-Term Growth* (Random House, 2017).

- *Evaluate the MVP.* Once the feature set is implemented, teams evaluate the MVP against the hypothesis. Teams apply 'innovation accounting,' and design the systems to provide fast feedback on the leading indicators of future success.

- *Pivot or persevere.* With the objective evidence in hand, teams and stakeholders can decide what to do next: either pivot (i.e., stop doing that work and start doing something else) or persevere (i.e., define features to further develop and refine the innovation).

- *Implement additional features.* Choosing to persevere means work continues until the new epic-inspired features that hit the backlog can't compete with other features as determined via the Weighted Shortest Job First (WSJF) prioritization model.

The Portfolio Kanban System

Finally, to assist with enterprise value flow, the portfolio Kanban system is used to capture, analyze, approve, and track portfolio business epics and enablers. Figure 15-12 shows an example system.

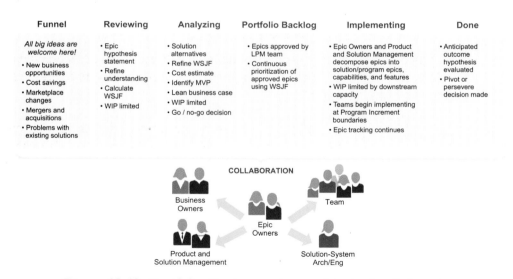

Figure 15-12. Portfolio Kanban system and typical collaborators

This portfolio Kanban system describes the steps an epic passes through on its way to implementation (or rejection), as well as the collaboration that is required for each step.

- *Funnel.* The funnel is used to capture all new big ideas. Epics that meet some decision criteria are then moved to the next state, 'reviewing.'

- *Reviewing.* Epics that reach this state are elaborated in the epic hypothesis statement format. Epics are prioritized using the WSJF algorithm, and those that rise to the top are pulled into the next state, 'analyzing,' as soon as space is available in this state.

- *Analyzing.* Epics that make it to this step merit more rigorous analysis and require further investment. Alternatives are explored for solution design and implementation. A Lean business case is developed, and options for internal development and outsourcing are considered. An MVP is defined (described in the next section). Epics that meet the 'go' criteria are moved to the 'portfolio backlog' state.

- *Portfolio backlog.* This step is used to maintain epics that have been approved by LPM. They're reviewed and prioritized on a periodic basis. When sufficient capacity from one or more ARTs is available, the highest-priority item advances to 'implementing.'

- *Implementing.* As capacity becomes available, epics are pulled into the ART (or Solution Train) Kanban. There they split into features, and acceptance criteria are established. While responsibility for implementation moves to development teams, Epic Owners remain available as necessary.

- *Done.* Once its anticipated business outcome has been achieved, the epic is considered done. If the hypothesis is refuted, the portfolio pivots to another approach or drops the initiative.

The portfolio Kanban states detailed in this list are just examples. As learning occurs, the design of the Kanban evolves. This evolution may include adjusting WIP limits, splitting or combining states, or adding classes of service to optimize the flow and priority of epics.

The Role of Epic Owners

Epics don't move through the Kanban system by themselves. Epic Owners are responsible for driving individual portfolio business epics from identification through the analysis process and into implementation. Typically, Product Managers, Enterprise Architects, program managers, or business analysts fulfill this role.

Epic Owners may work with Product and Solution Management to assist them with splitting the epic into value stream epics, program epics, or features. They may also help prioritize these items in the appropriate backlogs. Figure 15-13 highlights the key participants in the collaboration.

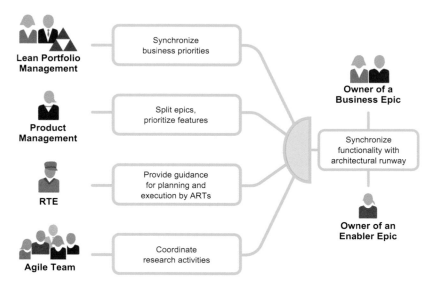

Figure 15-13. Collaborative nature of the Epic Owner role

The Role of the Enterprise Architect

Enterprise Architects work with business stakeholders and Solution and System Architects to guide holistic technology implementation across value streams. Their key responsibilities include the following:

- Act as the Epic Owner for portfolio enabler epics and participate in business epic analysis where applicable

- Participate in the strategy for building and maintaining the enterprise architectural runway

- Understand and communicate strategic themes and other key business drivers for architecture to System Architects and nontechnical stakeholders

- Influence common modeling, design, and coding practices

- Facilitate the reuse of components and patterns

Summary

Strategy and investment funding is perhaps the most important element of Lean Portfolio Management and the Portfolio SAFe configuration. It has three main functions: connecting the portfolio strategy to the enterprise strategy, providing value stream funding, and establishing a continuous flow of new value initiatives across the entire portfolio. When this collaboration operates with strategic alignment and effective communication, then the enterprise can be confident that each solution portfolio is addressing the right opportunities and challenges with the right solutions.

16

Agile Portfolio Operations

"The thing is, continuity of strategic direction and continuous improvement in how you do things are absolutely consistent with each other. In fact, they're mutually reinforcing."

—Michael Porter, Harvard Business School professor[1]

Introduction

In part V, we have introduced the Portfolio SAFe configuration within the context of the Lean Portfolio Management (LPM) function, and described the three critical collaborations of strategy and investment funding, Agile portfolio operations, and Lean governance. In chapter 15, 'Strategy and Investment Funding,' we described the first of these three collaborations and its responsibilities of connecting the portfolio strategy to the enterprise strategy, funding value streams, and establishing a flow of value across the entire portfolio.

In this chapter, we'll continue our journey through the portfolio by describing the second collaboration, Agile portfolio operations, which has three key responsibilities (as shown in Figure 16-1). Each of these responsibilities is described next.

---

1. Michael Porter is an American academic known for his theories on economics, business strategy, and social causes.

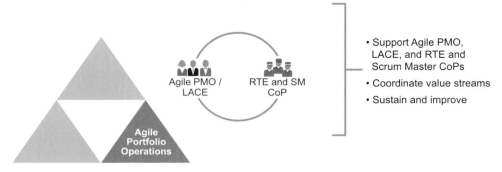

Figure 16-1. The LPM collaboration and responsibilities for Agile portfolio operations

Support an Agile PMO, LACE, and RTE and Scrum Master Communities of Practice

The Agile PMO

The centralization of certain functions such as planning and program management represents a traditional mindset—one that can undermine the move to SAFe. To address this threat, some enterprises have abandoned the Program Management Office (PMO) approach altogether, distributing all the responsibilities to Agile Release Trains (ARTs) and Solution Trains. However, this can be a bridge too far for other organizations, particularly larger enterprises. Instead, these organizations may be better served by an Agile PMO (APMO), one that provides a consistent portfolio context for delivering value in a leaner and more agile manner.

Indeed, we now see many enterprises in which the APMO leads the change to the new way of working. In this case, the APMO becomes part of a 'sufficiently powerful coalition for change' (see chapter 18, 'The Guiding Coalition'). In this expanded role, the APMO often

- Sponsors and communicates the change vision
- Participates in the rollout (some members may even deliver training)
- Leads the move to objective milestones
- Helps implement Lean budgets

- Fosters more Agile contracts and leaner supplier and customer partnerships
- Provides consistent support for effective program execution

These aims can be accomplished, in part, by sharing common and consistent enterprise patterns and practices for optimal value delivery. Indeed, standardizing such work is one of Lean's most effective tools. "By documenting the current best practice, standardized work forms the baseline for Kaizen or continuous improvement. Improving standardized work is a never-ending process."[2]

The Lean-Agile Center of Excellence

But even the APMO cannot do the job alone. Fortunately, most organizations have no shortage of potential change agents. We know them when we see them, as they are strong advocates for organizational improvement. The smart enterprise can harvest their energy as active catalysts for change. These change agents are typically ready and willing to lead the implementation of SAFe.

The challenge, of course, is that most of the people have full-time responsibilities in their current roles. While a significant portion of their time can perhaps be devoted to supporting the change, a smaller, but dedicated group of people is typically required to drive the transformation. Although these groups go by different names—the Agile center of excellence, Agile working group, Lean-Agile transformation team, learning and improvement center—they are all staffed with people whose primary task is to implement the change.

We use the generic term 'Lean Agile Center of Excellence' (LACE) to describe this group, and consider it an integral part of Agile portfolio operations. The LACE may be a function of the organization's emerging APMO, or it may exist as a stand-alone team, but in any case, its responsibilities typically include the following:

- Communicating the business need, urgency, and vision for change
- Developing the implementation plan and managing the transformation backlog
- Establishing the metrics and communicating progress
- Conducting or sourcing coaching and training for executives, managers, leaders, and teams
- Identifying value streams and helping define and launch ARTs

---

2. https://www.lean.org/Workshops/WorkshopDescription.cfm?WorkshopId=20

- Extending Lean-Agile practices to other areas of the company, including Lean budgets, Lean Portfolio Management, Agile contracts, and Agile human resources

- Helping to establish relentless improvement

This is a pretty significant list of responsibilities—but it's important to note that many of them are shared with numerous SAFe Program Consultants (SPCs), who may or may not be regular members of the LACE.

In any case, the LACE serves as a focal point of activity, a continuous source of energy that can help power the enterprise through the necessary changes. Additionally, because the evolution to a Lean-Agile enterprise is an ongoing journey rather than a destination, the LACE often evolves into a longer-term center for continuous improvement.

The LACE is a credible, cross-functional team, with respected members who can proactively address significant organizational impediments. It operates as an Agile team, with a Product Owner, Scrum Master, and Dev Team roles. It applies common iteration and Program Increment (PI) cadences, which allows the LACE to plan and inspect and adapt in harmony with the newly formed ARTs, while also serving as an example of Agile team behavior.

LACE Team Size and Distribution

Depending on the scope of the transformation, a question naturally arises as to how many dedicated individuals are necessary, as assigning talented resources to the LACE will have both organizational and financial impacts. The LACE should be proportionate to the size and distribution of the development organization. For smaller enterprises, a single, centralized LACE can balance speed with economies of scale. In larger enterprises—typically those with more than 500 to 1,000 practitioners—it's useful to consider a decentralized model or the hub-and-spoke model illustrated in Figure 16-2:

- *Centralized.* One LACE supports a single SAFe portfolio.

- *Decentralized.* There are multiple portfolios, and each portfolio has its own LACE.

- *Hub-and-spoke.* Certain aspects of the LACE are centralized, such as certain core practices, which are then adapted by spokes, funding for central hub personnel, and common tooling. Learning is exchanged between the hubs and central spokes. and vice versa.

Centralized	Decentralized	Hub-and-Spoke
• Single portfolio, single SAFe instance of SAFe (hundreds of practitioners).	• Independent business units, each with their own, largely autonomous SAFe portfolios.	• Large enterprises – a small LACE typically serves as the 'hub' for decentralized spokes. Spokes coordinate local operations.
• Value streams and ARTs operate under a common budget.	• Funding for LACE personnel, tooling, coaching, etc., comes from the business unit's budget.	• Core practices developed centrally, shared and adapted locally. Local practices are communicated to the hub.
• Funding for LACE personnel, tooling, and coaching all under the same budget.	• Cross-business unit collaboration is effective to provide knowledge sharing.	• Funding for hub personnel, as well as common tooling, may be centralized. The costs for consulting and coaching are funded locally.

Figure 16-2. LACE organizational models

For perspective, we've observed that a LACE of four to six dedicated people can support a few hundred practitioners, while teams of about twice that size can support proportionally larger groups. Beyond that, the LACE size is beyond an 'Agile team size' and gets unwieldy. In this case, a fully decentralized or hub-and-spoke model is typically more effective.

RTE and Scrum Master Communities of Practice

It's a principle of systems thinking that optimizing for one thing—almost by definition—sub-optimizes another thing. In this case, the move to product- and flow-based organizational models comes at a cost. One such cost is that specialty functional and skill areas that may have been combined under one organizational structure in the past now become distributed. Once operations are distributed, it can be hard to share lessons learned and grow distinctive competencies together.

Communities of practice (CoPs) help address this new challenge. CoPs are organized groups of people who have a common interest in a specific technical or business domain. They collaborate regularly to share information, improve their skills, and actively work on advancing the general knowledge of the domain. As Figure 16-3 illustrates, CoPs organized by job function can focus on the skills, competencies, and knowledge sharing required for that particular role.

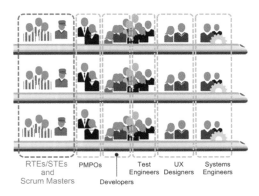

Figure 16-3. CoPs organized by function

For example, each of the following roles plays a critical role in facilitating the flow of value within and across the portfolio: Release Train Engineers (RTEs), Solution Train Engineers (STEs), and Scrum Masters. Each role is optimized to perform as servant leader for the train or team.

The CoPs discussed here can focus on the larger picture by assuming the following responsibilities:

- Share common team and ART practices and emerging standards
- Evolve methods for cross-ART coordination
- Establish meaningful Lean-Agile metrics and reporting
- Assist with PI planning and readiness for Solution Trains
- Provide coaching and extend Agile practices outside of solution development
- Address portfolio impediments that affect multiple value streams

In addition, these CoPs can extend system thinking to address larger systemic issues and simultaneously correct some of the imbalances that may be created with the introduction of an entirely new product, value stream, and ART.

Coordinate Value Streams

The second responsibility of Agile portfolio operations is to coordinate value streams. Although in theory value streams could be independent, cooperation among a set of solutions can provide portfolio-level capabilities and benefits that competitors can't match.

Indeed, in some cases, this is the ultimate goal: to offer a set of differentiated solutions in which new integrated capabilities can emerge to respond to expanding end-user needs. Portfolio coordination provides many additional benefits, including the following:

- Assure that value streams don't build overlapping solutions that can confuse the market

- Coordinate component and technology strategies to support efficient reuse, thereby minimizing total investment

- Coordinate and facilitate availability of scarce skill sets and shared services (such as security or compliance expertise)

Ultimately, this means that the value streams often need some level of portfolio coordination. Achieving this requires some additional roles and strategies, as illustrated in Figure 16-4:

- *Solution Portfolio Management.* This individual (or small team) has the overall responsibility for guiding a portfolio to a set of integrated solutions.

- *Enterprise Architect.* The Enterprise Architect provides technical guidance for the long-term evolution of the technologies and platforms and the larger Nonfunctional Requirements (NFRs) for the portfolio solution set.

- *Agile Program Management Office.* The APMO—along with the RTEs and STEs—is typically responsible for supporting decentralized, but efficient, program execution.

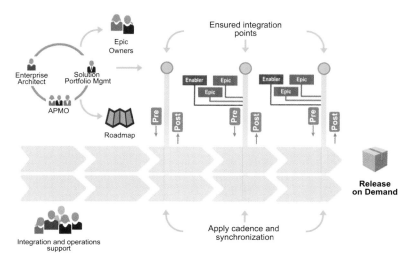

Figure 16-4. Cross-value stream coordination

In addition to the roles, aspects of cross-value stream coordination include those discussed in the following subsections.

Portfolio Cadence and Synchronization

Figure 16-4 depicts how the principles of cadence and synchronization apply just as well to the portfolio as they do to ARTs and Solution Trains. The merits are the same: making events and activities routine, thereby lowering the transaction costs associated with change and synchronizing the solution development of multiple value streams.

A shared cadence enables the portfolio-level solution to progress through routine planning and integration points via portfolio epics. Each integration point provides an opportunity for objective evaluation of the combined solution and is the only true measure of portfolio progress.

Starting New Portfolio Level Work

Figure 16-4 also illustrates another key concept: The portfolio cadence determines the rate and timing of starting new portfolio-level work. During each PI, the value streams and ARTs are focused on achieving their committed objectives. Clearly, if new work enters the system in the interim, it causes interruptions, task switching, realignment, and movement of people and other resources to the newly revised objectives. The portfolio PI cadence provides a steady rhythm for introducing new portfolio work.

Portfolio Roadmap

Like the other roadmaps, a portfolio roadmap highlights how new content, primarily in the form of epics, contributes to the plan of intent. This higher-level roadmap also provides an opportunity to integrate aspects of lower-level roadmaps, and their associated milestones, into a more comprehensive view. This helps communicate the larger picture to enterprise stakeholders.

Deployment and Release

Due to the nature of the value streams and dependencies, deploying integrated value may also depend on effective DevOps capabilities. In some cases, ARTs and Solution Trains provide all the DevOps capability that's needed. In others, additional considerations must be addressed. In some cases, dedicated (or shared services) System Teams may be needed to help integrate multiple solutions into a portfolio-level release.

Sustain and Improve

Lean Portfolio Management—and by proxy, the APMO—also has a leadership role in helping the organization relentlessly improve and achieve its business goals. This is the entire topic of chapter 22, 'Sustain and Improve.'

Summary

The LPM Agile portfolio operations collaboration has three key responsibilities: supporting an Agile PMO, LACE, and RTE and Scrum Master CoPs; aligning and coordinating activities across value streams; and sustaining and helping the organization relentlessly improve to achieve its business goals. Fulfilling these responsibilities often requires changing the existing PMO to become an Agile PMO—one that provides a consistent portfolio context for delivering value, in a leaner and more agile manner. In addition, most value streams need some portfolio-level coordination, which often requires additional roles, such as Solution Portfolio Management, Enterprise Architects, and the APMO. Such coordination typically involves portfolio cadence and synchronization, practices for starting new portfolio-level work, maintenance of the portfolio roadmap, and integration of multiple solutions into a portfolio-level release. Finally, LPM—and by proxy, the APMO—has a significant leadership role in helping the organization relentlessly improve and achieve its business goals.

17

Lean Governance

"A bad system will beat a good person every time."
—W. Edwards Deming

Introduction

The last three chapters provided an overview of Lean Portfolio Management (LPM) and described the collaborations of *strategy and investment funding* and *Agile portfolio operations*. In this final chapter of part V, we'll describe the third and final collaboration, *Lean governance*.

Lean-Agile development practices are so different from traditional methods that many of the legacy practices for governance—planning and forecasting, reporting, investment spending, and assuring regulatory compliance—are no longer effective. Worse, continuing to apply traditional governance to the new ways of working 'creates a bad system' that will often hinder the adoption of the new Lean-Agile methods, to the detriment of the organization as a whole.

As Figure 17-1 illustrates, the final LPM collaboration, Lean governance, describes a new approach intended to address this problem.

Like the other aspects of the LPM, these practices are a result of a collaboration among stakeholders, including the relevant enterprise executives, Solution Portfolio Management, Enterprise Architects, and the Agile Program Management Office (APMO). Together this group shares governance responsibilities including dynamic forecasting and budgeting, Lean measures of portfolio performance, and continuously coordinating compliance activities. Each of these responsibilities is described in the next sections.

Figure 17-1. Lean Governance collaboration and responsibilities

Forecast and Budget Dynamically

Agile has an intense focus on near-term value delivery—but that doesn't mean planning and forecasting have no value. The enterprise, its partners, and its customers *all* need a near-term roadmap. For example, marketing needs to understand when new products and features will be released, sales needs to forecast revenue and plan activities, and development needs to establish budgets. Clearly, the ability to do effective forecasting is a key economic driver and an essential ability of a Lean enterprise.

Estimating

Forecasting requires estimating the work. Such estimates must be fast, efficient, and reasonably accurate and support 'what if' analysis of various incremental implementation scenarios. To this end, epics are split into potential features during the portfolio Kanban analysis stage. Product Managers and System Architects—working with Product Owners and teams wherever appropriate—can use historical data to fairly quickly estimate the size of these features in story points. The story point estimates are then rolled up into the epic estimate, as illustrated in Figure 17-2.

Whenever the economics justify further investment in estimating, teams can split larger features into smaller backlog items to get a more granular estimate.

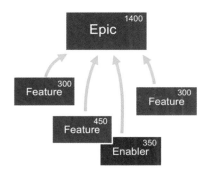

Figure 17-2. Estimating epics

Forecasting

Given knowledge of the epic estimates and Agile Release Train (ART) velocities, and by applying capacity allocation, epic delivery can be forecasted over a near-term timeline, as illustrated in Figure 17-3. SAFe provides mechanisms for estimating and planning that have been proved to be more reliable than traditional methods.

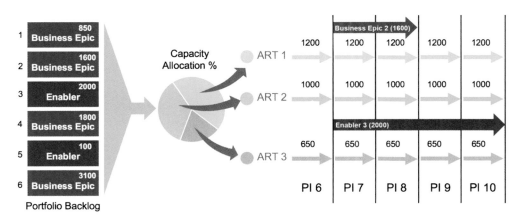

Figure 17-3. Portfolio forecasting

Budget Dynamically

Finally, although value streams are long-lived and mostly self-organizing and self-managing, they are not *self-initiating* or *self-funding*. That responsibility lies with LPM, which must regularly adjust the value stream budgets to adapt to changing business priorities, as shown in Figure 17-4.

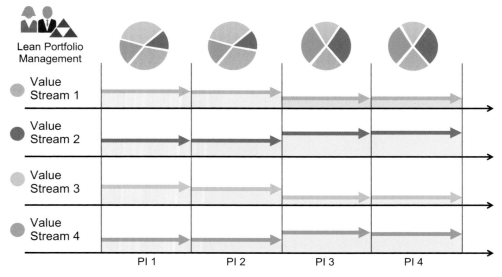

Figure 17-4. Value stream budgets are adjusted dynamically

At a minimum, these budgets can be adjusted twice annually. If adjustments occur less frequently than that, then spending is fixed for too long, limiting real business agility. If adjustments occur more frequently, then the enterprise may seem to be very Agile, but people become uncomfortable in their assignments. After all, no one can plan for a completely uncertain future.

Measure Portfolio Performance

Lean governance's second responsibility is measuring tangible and intangible aspects of performance: Did the solution ship? Is productivity improving? These and other intangible aspects offer an uncomfortable challenge to leaders. That is, when you measure a thing, that measure of the thing tends to improve, but there is a legitimate concern as to whether the underlying objectives are truly improving, or whether the focus becomes the measure, not the real outcome.

For this reason, many people have a skeptical view of some of these measurements. For example, how do we know that outcomes, rather than the symptoms, are really improving? Fortunately, Agile development is inherently more measurable than traditional, document-driven methods. Moreover, measurement is absolutely integral to DevOps and continuous delivery. To this end, SAFe offers a wide variety of potential measurements, each of which can be used for a specific purpose.

Figure 17-5 provides an example set of 'Lean portfolio metrics' that have proved effective in many implementations. More information on portfolio metrics can be found on the SAFe website.[1]

Benefit	Expected Result	Metric Used
Employee engagement	Improved employee satisfaction; lower turnover	Employee survey; HR statistics
Customer satisfaction	Improved net promoter score	Net promoter score survey
Productivity	Reduced average feature cycle time	Feature cycle time
Agility	Continuous improvement in team and program measures	Team, program, large solution, and portfolio self-assessments; release predictability measure
Time-to-market	More frequent releases	Number or releases per year
Quality	Reduced defect counts and support call volume	Defect data and support call volume
Partner health	Improved ecosystem relationships	Partner and vendor surveys

Figure 17-5. A set of Lean portfolio metrics

Applying Innovation Accounting

Many desirable portfolio measures of intent are *lagging* economic indicators. Success factors, such as return on investment (ROI) and new markets penetrated, can take a long time to achieve. Thus, the organization needs fast feedback from *leading indicators*, many of which are not financial metrics. Lean organizations apply innovation accounting to address this challenge.[2]

---

1. www.scaledagileframework.com/metrics
2. Eric Ries. *The Lean Startup: How Today's Entrepreneurs Use Continuous Innovation to Create Radically Successful Businesses* (Crown Business, 2011).

At the portfolio level, applying innovation accounting requires a thoughtful look at which leading indicators for an epic are likely to produce the desired long-term results. This is directly encouraged by the epic hypothesis statement and Lean business case.

Capitalization of Agile Software Development

Of course, monitoring development expense is a primary aspect of Lean governance. This includes measuring both capital expenses (CapEx)—that is, tangible, capital assets that are purchased to support the effort—and operating expenses (OpEx)—that is, salaries and other current expenses necessary to develop the system. There is an in-between case as well: Certain labor expenses required to build intangible assets like software and intellectual property may be capitalized. For example, many U.S. companies are subject to U.S. Financial Accounting Standards Board (FASB) regulations, which require that a company should begin capitalizing software development costs when a project or product meets certain criteria:[5]

- The product has achieved technical feasibility.
- Management has provided written approval to fund the development effort.

---

3. https://www.scaledagileframework.com/guidance-applied-innovation-accounting-in%20-SAFe

4. http://lexicon.ft.com/Term?term=innovation-accounting&mhq5j=e5

5. Disclaimer: The authors have no formal training or accreditation in accounting. The treatment of software costs and potential for capitalization treatment varies by country, by industry (for example, while many companies in the United States are subject to one set of rules, suppliers to the U.S. federal government have an entirely different set of rules), and even by individual company policy. Some companies choose not to capitalize software development costs at all.

- Management has committed the resources to development.

- Management is confident that the product will be successfully delivered.

Before software can be capitalized, finance departments typically require documented evidence that these specific activities have been completed. Once these criteria are met, further development costs may be subject to capitalization. Although these capitalization rules apply to companies operating in the United States, similar accounting rules exist for other countries.

Agile Development Capitalization Strategies

In any case, the process for capitalizing Agile software development can be challenging for companies moving to Agile development. Historically, capitalization has been applied in the context of traditional waterfall development, which has a well-defined 'up-front phase' during which requirements are created, the design is produced, and feasibility is established. The requirements and design milestones often serve as phase gates for starting capitalization, as Figure 17-6 illustrates.

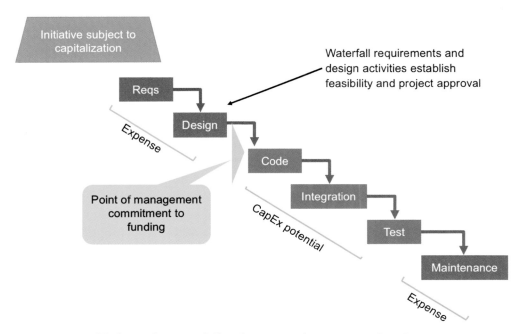

Figure 17-6. Early waterfall milestones often trigger CapEx treatment

In Agile, however, requirements and design emerge continuously, so there is no formal gate to serve as a prelude to capitalization. However, the majority of the work of most ARTs usually focuses on building and extending software assets that are past the point of feasibility analysis. They do this by developing new features for the solution. Since features 'increase the functionality of existing software,' the stories associated with those features constitute much of the work of the ART personnel. Therefore, feature development costs may be subject to potential capitalization. As a consequence, both types of work may be present within any Program Increment (PI) and, by extension, in any relevant accounting period.

In addition, maintenance, infrastructure work, and other routine tasks may occur during the period. As Product Management identifies features, teams associate new stories with those features and perform the essential work of realizing the behavior of the features by implementing stories in the new code base. Most user stories contribute directly to new functionality of the feature, so the effort for those stories may be subject to CapEx treatment. Other stories, such as enabler stories for infrastructure, exploration, defects, refactors, and any other work, may not be.

By associating stories with features when applicable in the ALM tooling,[6] the work related to feature development can be identified for potential capital expense treatment. More information on capitalizing and expensing software can be found on the Scaled Agile website.[7]

Governance via Agile Contracts

Throughout this book, we've described the application of SAFe as a means for enterprises to build systems that help them meet their business objectives. Rarely, though, are truly large systems developed exclusively 'in-house.' More likely, enterprises will work with a variety of suppliers to achieve their mission objectives. These suppliers may be external (e.g., the U.S. government purchasing IT systems from contractors) or internal (e.g., a large company using components or systems provided by other divisions). In either case, buyer and suppliers have a governance duty to manage the investment wisely and to help assure the desired results are achieved. Formally, this is achieved via a written contract between buyer and supplier. Traditionally, enterprises have used a variety of approaches to contracts, ranging from 'firm fixed price' to 'time and materials,' with almost every variation in between, as Figure 17-7 illustrates.

---

6. Application Life-Cycle Management.

7. http://www.scaledagileframework.com/capex-and-opex

Figure 17-7. A range of traditional contract types

A Collaborative Approach to Agile Contracts

Since neither endpoint in Figure 17-7 provides much assurance, perhaps the range in the middle is the sweet spot? Perhaps so, but even then, the biases of traditional contracts will likely creep into these agreements and expectations. What's needed is a different approach—one that 'trusts and verifies' that the suppliers are building the right thing in the right way. For example, such an Agile contract would include the ability to optimize the economic value for both parties, exploit variability and adapt the response to new knowledge, and motivate all parties to build the best solution possible within agreed-to economic boundaries.

We call one such approach a *SAFe managed-investment contract*. To oversimplify things a bit, there are two different phases of engagement: pre-commitment and execution. The pre-commitment phase, illustrated in Figure 17-8, gives the buyer and supplier time to do their due diligence. In this case, the customer and supplier work together to agree on terms for the basis of the contract.

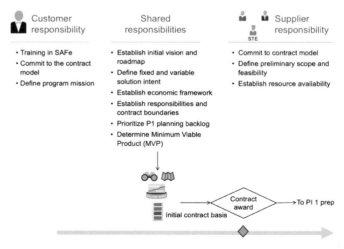

Figure 17-8. SAFe managed-investment contract: pre-commitment phase

During pre-commitment, the *customer* has specific responsibilities, including understanding the basic constructs and responsibilities of this form of Agile contract, as well as defining and communicating the program mission to the supplier. The *supplier* has responsibilities as well, including analysis of potential feasibility, assurance that the supplier's core competence aligns with the buyer's needs, and a rough cost estimate. The *shared responsibilities* in the middle, however, start the customer and supplier down a path to a more measured investment. Based on the agreements, the customer will agree to fund the supplier for the initial PIs.

Depending on context, the customer may engage with multiple potential suppliers. If significant technical feasibility is involved, this can often be done under a separate contract, which compensates the supplier(s) for the efforts to get to the commitment phase. At this point, the execution phase is entered for the first PI. A description of the contract activities that occur within this timebox follows:

- *PI preparation.* The supplier and customer invest time and effort in preparing the first PI planning session.

- *PI planning.* Customer and supplier stakeholders plan the first PI in iteration-level detail.

- *PI execution.* Depending on the context, customers participate at various levels in iteration execution. At a minimum, direct customer engagement is usually required for each system and solution demo.

- *PI evaluation.* Each PI marks a critical milestone for both the customer and the supplier, when the solution demo is held and is evaluated during the Inspect and Adapt (I&A) event.

The I&A event is also used to assess progress and to plan improvements for the upcoming PI. Based on whether sufficient value has been achieved, the customer may decide to keep funding steady, increase it, or begin winding down. This process is repeated until the solution has delivered the value the customer requires. The SAFe contract model *trusts and verifies* that both parties are on the path to the best economic outcomes—to the long-term benefit of both. More information on Agile contracts can be found on the Scaled Agile website.[8]

---

8. http://www.scaledagileframework.com/agile-contracts

Coordinate Continuous Compliance

Enterprises use SAFe to build some of the world's largest and most important systems, many of which have unacceptable social or economic costs of failure. To protect the public's safety, these systems are often subject to government, regulatory, or customer oversight and rigorous compliance requirements. To satisfy compliance requirements, organizations must provide objective evidence that their system meets its intended purpose and has no unintended consequences.

Historically, organizations have relied on comprehensive quality management systems (QMS) based on phase-gated development models to reduce risk and ensure compliance. In addition, compliance activities have typically been deferred until the end of the project, providing little insight into compliance progress. And as Deming notes, "Inspection is too late. The quality, good or bad, is already in the product."

A Lean Quality Management System

Lean-thinking enterprises are moving rapidly from traditional QMS systems to Lean QMS systems to improve compliance and achieve better business outcomes. In turn, those who want to reap the benefits of Lean-Agile development (faster time-to-market and higher quality, to name a few) will typically have to evolve toward a Lean QMS.

The five principles for implementing a Lean QMS are as follows:

1. Build the solution and compliance incrementally.
2. Organize for value and compliance.
3. Build in quality and compliance.
4. Continuously verify and validate.
5. Release validated solutions on demand.

Summary

Lean-Agile development practices are so different from traditional methods that many of the legacy practices for governance are no longer effective. Moreover, continuing to apply traditional governance to the new ways of working will often impede the transformation, to the detriment of the organization as a whole. This is the driving force behind Lean governance, which is the third and final LPM collaboration. It describes a new approach intended to address governance, including dynamic forecasting and budgeting, Lean measures of portfolio performance, and continuous coordination of compliance activities using a Lean QMS. In turn, Lean governance provides the oversight needed to assure that investments track to strategic intent and that the portfolio is always mindful and compliant with applicable standards and regulations.

Part VI
Implementing SAFe

"Many leaders pride themselves on setting the high-level direction and staying out of the details. It's true that a compelling vision is critical. But it's not enough. Big picture, hands-off leadership isn't likely to work in a change situation, because the hardest part of change—the paralyzing part—is in the details.

Any successful change requires a translation of ambiguous goals into concrete behaviors. In short, to make a switch, you need to script the critical moves."

—Chip and Dan Heath

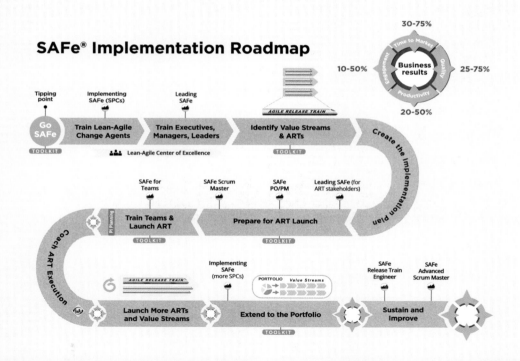

Introduction to the SAFe Implementation Roadmap

Throughout this book, we've described the values, principles, and practices of the SAFe. Our goal was to show how a SAFe enterprise operates and achieves the business benefits that only Lean-Agile development at scale can provide. But what we haven't done yet is describe *how* an enterprise implements SAFe. That's where the real journey begins: Part VI—which comprises the final five chapters of this book—is dedicated to that purpose.

To begin, we note that to achieve the desired organizational change, leadership must "script the critical moves."[1] Fortunately, hundreds of the world's largest enterprises have already gone down this path (see the case studies on the SAFe website),[2] and successful adoption patterns have emerged. While every transformation journey is unique, and there is rarely a perfectly sequential step-by-step implementation, we know that businesses getting the best results typically follow a path similar to that shown in the *SAFe Implementation Roadmap*. The roadmap consists of 12 steps, which are described in the following five chapters:

Chapter 18, 'The Guiding Coalition'

1. Reach the tipping point
2. Train Lean-Agile change agents
3. Train executives, managers, and leaders
4. Create a Lean-Agile Center of Excellence

Chapter 19, 'Designing the Implementation'

5. Identify value streams and ARTs
6. Create the implementation plan

---

1. Chip Heath and Dan Heath, *Switch: How to Change Things When Change Is Hard* (Crown Business, 2010).

2. www.scaledagileframework.com/case-studies

Chapter 20, 'Implementing Agile Release Trains'

7. Prepare for ART launch
8. Train teams and launch the ART
9. Coach ART execution

Chapter 21, 'Launching More ARTs and Value Streams; Extending to the Portfolio'

10. Launch more ARTs and value streams
11. Extend to the portfolio

Chapter 22, 'Sustaining and Improving'

12. Sustain and improve

18

The Guiding Coalition

"A strong guiding coalition is always needed. One with the right composition, level of trust, and shared objective."
—John P. Kotter

Introduction

Once the rationale for a significant change to a new way of working becomes obvious, the difficult work begins. In *Leading Change*, Kotter discusses eight stages of guiding organizational transformation and what it takes to make that transformation stick. As Kotter notes: "In a rapidly moving world, individuals and weak committees rarely have all the information needed to make good non-routine decisions. Nor do they seem to have the credibility or the time required to convince others to make the personal sacrifices called for in implementing changes. Only teams with the right composition and sufficient trust among members can be highly effective under these circumstances."[1]

Once the need for change is established, forming the *guiding coalition* is a critical step. To be effective, this coalition must include people from across the organization. Selecting the right people for this coalition is essential and requires that the following criteria be met:

- Leaders who can set the vision, remove impediments, and make blocking the change difficult
- Practitioners, managers, and change agents who can implement specific process changes
- People with sufficient organizational credibility to be taken seriously
- The expertise and confidence needed to make fast, smart decisions

---

1. John P. Kotter, *Leading Change* (Harvard Business Review Press, 1996).

As our experience shows—and the SAFe Implementation Roadmap implies—there are four essential steps to achieve an effective 'guiding coalition' for change:

Step 1. Reach the tipping point.

Step 2. Train Lean-Agile change agents.

Step 3. Train executives, managers, and other leaders.

Step 4. Create a Lean-Agile Center of Excellence (LACE).

This chapter describes these four steps of the journey.

Step 1. Reach the Tipping Point

Changing the way of working—the habits and culture of a large organization—is hard. People naturally resist change. Accepting change means accepting the possibility that the organization is currently not doing things the best way, or worse, challenging people's long-held beliefs or values. Therefore, there must be a reason for such a change—a reason so compelling that the status quo becomes simply unacceptable.

In other words, the enterprise must reach its *tipping point*[2]—the crossroads at which the organization's imperative is to achieve the change rather than resist. We've observed two primary reasons that cause an organization to tip to SAFe.

- *A burning platform.* Sometimes the need to change is obvious. The company is failing to compete, and the existing way of doing business is inadequate to achieve a new solution within a survivable time frame. This is the easier case for change. While there will always be those who resist, the wave of energy that drives the needed change through the organization is overwhelming. Survival of the enterprise depends on it.

- *Proactive leadership.* In the absence of a burning platform, leadership must drive change proactively by 'taking a stand' for a better future state. This is often the less obvious reason to drive change, as people may not see or feel the urgency. In this case, senior leadership must continuously communicate the reasons for change, making it clear that maintaining the status quo is unacceptable.

---

2. Malcom Gladwell, *The Tipping Point: How Little Things Can Make a Big Difference* (Little, Brown and Company, 2006).

Establish the Vision for Change

There must be a compelling vision to go along with the reason for change. Kotter notes that establishing a 'vision for change' is a primary responsibility of leadership.[3] The vision provides three vital benefits:

- *Purpose.* It clarifies the objective and direction for the change and sets the mission for all to follow. It focuses everyone on the 'why,' not the 'how,' of the change.

- *Motivation.* The vision helps motivate people by giving them a compelling reason to make the change and start moving in the new direction. A compelling vision makes it clear that there is no job security in the status quo.

- *Alignment.* The vision aligns and empowers everyone to take the actions necessary to achieve the change, without the constant need for management supervision.

Communicate the Benefits

Whether the reason for change is a burning platform or proactive leadership, the goal is the same: Realize the business benefits that the change is intended to deliver. SAFe's principle #1 reminds us to always 'Take an economic view.' In this context, the leaders should communicate the goal of the change in terms that everyone can understand. Dozens of case studies[4] can help people understand the journey and its benefits, which are summarized in four major areas, as Figure 18-1 illustrates.

Figure 18-1. SAFe business benefits

---

3. John P. Kotter, *Leading Change* (Harvard Business Review Press, 1996).

4. http://www.scaledagileframework.com/case-studies/

Leaders should communicate these intended outcomes as part of the vision for the change. Also, leaders should describe any other specific, tangible objectives they hope to accomplish. This will provide the fuel necessary to *escape the inertia of the status quo.*

Step 2. Train Lean-Agile Change Agents

The next step in the roadmap is to develop change agents with the knowledge and skills needed to successfully implement SAFe. Most enterprises source these change agents from both *inside* and *outside* the organization. Such agents may be business and technology leaders, program and project managers, process leaders, and many others.

One path to success is to take the 'Implementing SAFe with SPC Certification' class. This course prepares change agents to lead the transformation.

In addition, scaling Agile across the enterprise requires training all the people who do the work. To make it practical and cost-effective, SPCs are licensed to teach other SAFe courses. This affordable strategy supplies the trainers needed to initiate and implement the change.

Step 3. Train Executives, Managers, and Leaders

Leading SAFe is a two-day course designed to teach leaders and managers the SAFe Lean-Agile mindset, principles, and practices, as well as the most effective leadership values in managing the new generation of knowledge workers. This course helps the organization reach the tipping point for change and seeds the enterprise with knowledgeable, active leaders prepared to guide it.

Some of these key stakeholders will provide ongoing executive sponsorship. Others will be directly involved in implementing SAFe, managing others who do, and participating directly in Agile Release Train (ART) execution. All of these stakeholders need the knowledge and skills to lead, rather than follow, the implementation.

Step 4. Create a Lean-Agile Center of Excellence

In chapter 16, 'Agile Portfolio Operations,' we noted how a Lean-Agile Center of Excellence (LACE) can be a powerful and persistent force in both achieving the transformation and fostering relentless improvement. Indeed, experience has shown that the LACE is a significant differentiator between companies practicing Lean-Agile development in name only and those truly committed to adopting Lean-Agile practices and thereby achieving the best business outcomes.

The LACE operates as an Agile team and typically applies the same iteration and Program Increment (PI) cadences as the ARTs. The Product Owner works with stakeholders to prioritize the team's transformation backlog. The Scrum Master facilitates the process and helps remove roadblocks along the path. Members of various functional organizations are selected to serve as integral members of the cross-functional team. A 'C-level' leader typically acts as the organization's Product Manager for the team.

Like any Agile team, the LACE needs to align itself with a common mission. An example mission statement is included in Figure 18-2.

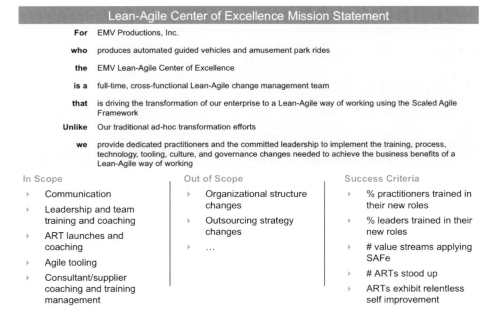

Figure 18-2. Sample LACE mission statement

As we noted in chapter 16, the LACE may be part of an emerging Agile Product Management Office, or it may exist as a separate group. In either case, it serves as a focal point of knowledge and transformational activities that can power the enterprise through the changes. In addition, the LACE often evolves into a permanent center for Lean-Agile learnings, communication, and relentless improvement.

Summary

After 'reaching the tipping point'—that is, the point at which the need for changing to a Lean-Agile way of working is clear and compelling—forming a 'guiding coalition' is the next critical move. An effective coalition must include the right people from across the organization, especially leaders who can set the vision, remove impediments, and make blocking the change difficult. The people in this coalition need sufficient organizational credibility to be taken seriously and must have the expertise and confidence to make fast, smart decisions. The coalition also requires practitioners, managers, and change agents who can implement local and specific process changes.

Our experience shows that there are three essential steps to achieve an effective guiding coalition for change: (1) training Lean-Agile change agents; (2) training executives, managers. and other leaders; and (3) creating a Lean-Agile Center of Excellence.

Designing the Implementation

"Break down barriers between departments."
—W. Edwards Deming

Introduction

In the previous chapter, we described how the first four steps of the SAFe Implementation Roadmap help form 'the guiding coalition'—a powerful team of knowledgeable and enthusiastic people who can drive the implementation. In this chapter, we will describe how to 'design the implementation' with the next two steps:

Step 5. Identify value streams and Agile Release Trains (ARTs).

Step 6. Create the implementation plan.

Step 5. Identify Value Streams and Agile Release Trains

Value streams are the primary means for understanding, organizing, and delivering value in SAFe. Identifying enterprise value streams, and forming ARTs to create and deliver value, is the next critical step. After all, ARTs contain the people and other resources that build the solutions to realize this value.

As a refresher, each value stream is a long-lived series of steps used to create value—from concept to the delivery of a tangible result (value) for the customer, as illustrated in Figure 19-1.

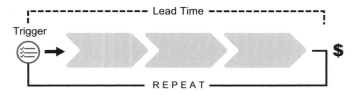

Figure 19-1. The anatomy of a value stream

Some important event triggers the flow of value—perhaps an *internal* request for a new feature, or maybe an *external* request for a consumer loan. The middle of the value stream represents the steps needed to develop, produce, and deliver a product or service to the market. It ends when all the steps in the middle have been executed and the customer receives value.

Types of Value Streams

As shown in Figure 19-2, enterprises typically have two types of value streams.

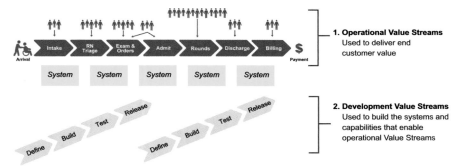

Figure 19-2. Example operational and development value streams

1. *Operational value streams.* These are the people and steps that provide goods or services to a customer or the end user. Examples might include manufacturing a medical instrument, or ordering and receiving a part from a supplier.

2. *Development value streams.* These are the people and steps used to develop the new products, systems, solutions, and services the enterprise sells or that support internal operational value streams.

Development value streams are what constitute a SAFe portfolio and are the primary concern of the Framework. However, typically (especially in IT) the enterprise's

2. *A single development value stream can fit within an ART.* Often, a small value stream (50–125 people) can be realized by a single ART. Many development groups are already organized into units of about that size, so it's a common case.

3. *Multiple ARTs are required for large development value streams.* When a lot of people are involved, the development value stream must be split into multiple ARTs to form a *Solution Train*, as described in the next section.

Forming a Solution Train with Multiple ARTs

The last pattern in Figure 19-8 is fairly common in large enterprises and requires additional analysis. Whenever possible, ARTs should focus on a single, primary system, or a set of closely related products or services in that value stream. However, in the case where many people are needed to deliver a single system, the best approach is for the teams developing features and components that have a high degree of interdependence to work together. This leads us to the next decision about organizing ARTs around 'feature areas' or 'subsystems.'

- *Feature-area ARTs are optimized for flow and speed.* But pay attention to subsystem governance; otherwise, the system architecture will eventually decay. As a countermeasure, a System Architect (one or more individuals, or even a small team) is dedicated to maintaining platform integrity and subsystem governance.

- *Subsystem ARTs (components, platforms, and so on) are optimized for architectural robustness and reuse of components.* However, organizing ARTs around subsystems may create too many dependencies between ARTs, resulting in slow value flow.

There's another common pattern where ARTs realize just a segment of a larger value stream. That might not seem to be a fully end-to-end approach, but in reality, the 'beginning' and the 'end' of a value stream are relative notions. The types of systems and operational value streams being served may be very different in these segments, creating a logical dividing line.

There's no one right solution to split value streams into ARTs, and large systems typically require both types of ARTs. An example is when multiple ARTs provide services or solutions based on a common platform. In this case, a platform ART may support one or more feature ARTs, as Figure 19-9 illustrates.

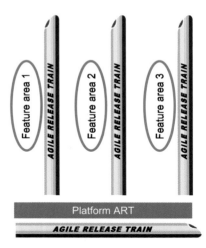

Figure 19-9. Feature area ARTs with a platform ART

Of course, combinations of these models often appear in the larger value streams, as our final example in Figure 19-10 illustrates.

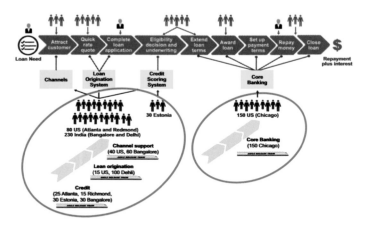

Figure 19-10. ARTs in the bank loan example

Finally, other ART design and considerations may be driven by geography, spoken language, and cost centers—all of which may influence the ART design. These structures are generally far less desirable.

> ### TREAT THE ART DESIGN AS A HYPOTHESIS
> It's important to carefully consider the different options for splitting value streams into ARTs and to choose the option that best balances the fast flow of value with the right amount of architectural integrity. Treat each design option as a hypothesis and implement the best-known alternative based on your assumptions. If the chosen option works well, persevere and continue with that design; otherwise, pivot and try a different way.

Once a development value stream is selected, some additional analysis is required to further define the development value stream's boundaries, people, deliverables, potential ARTs, and other parameters. To assist, we offer Figure 19-11, a 'development value stream canvas' that stakeholders can use to capture their emerging understanding.[2]

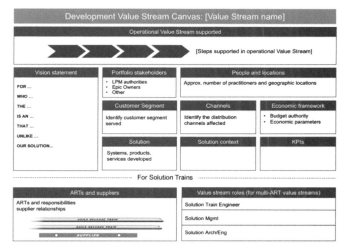

Figure 19-11. A development value stream canvas

And as highlighted in the bottom section of Figure 19-11, some additional analysis is needed to define prospective Solution Trains and governance for multi-ART value streams.

Step 6. Create the Implementation Plan

The next step is to plan for implementing SAFe in each value stream. In a smaller portfolio, there may be only one value stream of interest, in which case the target is obvious. The larger enterprise, however, requires additional analysis, and leadership often needs to pick the first value stream to be addressed.

---

2. Thanks to SPCT Mark Richards for contributing the value stream canvas concept.

Select the First Agile Release Train

It's typical for the organization to focus initially on one value stream (and correspondingly, the first ART). This can create an initial success and gain institutional knowledge to apply to other value streams. To start, many companies look for a first 'opportunistic' ART, which can be found at the intersection of the four factors highlighted in Figure 19-12.

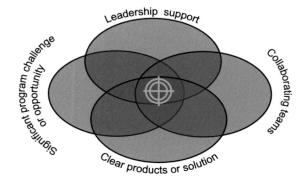

Figure 19-12. Finding an opportunistic ART to start the transformation

The 'target' for the first ART is often one that best meets the following criteria:

- Leadership support
- Clear products or solutions
- Collaborating teams
- Significant challenge or opportunity

Once this ART is selected, the enterprise is nearly ready to move forward.

Create a Preliminary Plan for Additional ARTs and Value Streams

Before we move on to launching that first ART, it's likely that a broader implementation plan may already be forming. Although it's still early in the process, strategies for rolling out additional ARTs and for launching additional value streams may be starting to take shape. In short, change is beginning to happen, and the signs are everywhere:

- The new vision is being communicated around the company.
- Principal stakeholders are aligning.
- Something big is in the air, and people are catching on. There is a growing sense of excitement for the change.

As we described in Chapter 18, 'The Guiding Coalition,' the Lean-Agile Center of Excellence (LACE) and various SPCs and leaders typically guide the transformation using Agile and SAFe as their operating models. In keeping with SAFe practices, the LACE holds internal Program Increment (PI) planning events and invites other stakeholders, such as Business Owners, to help further define the implementation strategy. One natural output would be a PI roadmap for the implementation, which provides a plan and a PI cadence for implementation, as illustrated in Figure 19-13.

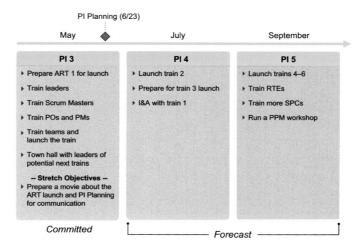

Figure 19-13. An example PI roadmap

Before they commit to the roadmap, stakeholders should reflect on the existing culture and the 'how' of the larger implementation strategy. The change is not optional for members of the enterprise, but how it is received depends on many factors. Often, mandated change can be uninspiring to those on the receiving end of the decision.

INVITATION-BASED ROLLOUT STRATEGY

Yuval Yeret, CTO and SPCT, at Agile Sparks describes an alternative rollout approach that invites people to change. The default approach for implementing organizational change is typically the 'mandate' or 'push' approach. This may appear to be the fast and easy way, in which a central group of change agents decide when people will 'board' the Agile Release Train, as well as how the train should operate. The problem with this approach is that people don't like to 'be changed.' Instead, an invitation-based approach may serve the enterprise better. Read more about this strategy and how to implement it at the SAFe website.[3]

---

3. http://www.scaledagileframework.com/invitation-based-safe-implementation/

Again, don't be overly concerned about getting the rollout strategy, perfect, right at the start. Any plan is only the current hypothesis; it will improve incrementally as the implementation evolves. Once the value streams are identified, the enterprise can move on to 'preparing for the ART launch,' which is the subject of the next chapter.

Summary

After creating a powerful guiding coalition, the next step is to design the implementation. This includes identifying the initial enterprise value streams, forming ARTs to develop and deliver that value, and creating a first draft of the broader implementation plan.

For some organizations, identifying value streams is an easy task. Many are simply the products, services, or solutions that the company develops and sells. For others, the process is more complicated, and some analysis is required to figure out what the deliverable value is and how it flows though the organization. Creating the implementation plan begins with selecting the first ART in the selected value stream—the one that best meets the criteria of leadership support, clear products or solutions, collaborating teams, and a significant challenge or opportunity. The LACE and various SPCs and leaders typically guide the implementation by applying Agile and SAFe practices as their operating model.

Implementing Agile Release Trains

"Train everyone and launch trains."
   —SAFe advice

Introduction

In the previous two chapters of this part of the book, we described steps 1–6 of the implementation roadmap. In this chapter, we'll cover the next three steps, including the most important part of the transformation: implementing Agile Release Trains (ARTs). The steps described here focus on the following aspects of SAFe:

Step 7. Prepare for the ART launch.

Step 8. Train teams and launch the ART.

Step 9. Coach ART execution.

In addition, we'll describe an accelerated, one-week ART 'Quickstart' approach to the ART launch, which—after some preparation—is the fastest way to get an ART structured, started, and delivering value.

Step 7. Prepare for the ART Launch

By now, the enterprise or business unit will have identified the value streams and established an initial implementation plan. It will have a rough strategy for the first ART to launch in the target value stream. This is a pivotal moment, as the focus now shifts to implementation.

From a change-management perspective, the first ART will have a profound effect on the transformation's success. After all, it's introducing a material change in the enterprise's way of working. It should generate the first 'short-term win' that helps build momentum for the rest of the rollout.

SAFe Program Consultants (SPCs) often lead the implementation of each ART and are supported by ART stakeholders and members of the Lean-Agile Center of Excellence (LACE). The main steps in preparing the launch include the following:

- Defining the ART
- Setting the program cadence and launch date
- Training the ART leaders and stakeholders
- Organizing the Agile teams
- Training Product Managers and Product Owners
- Training the Scrum Masters
- Assessing and evolving launch readiness
- Preparing the program backlog

Each of these activities is described in the sections that follow.

Defining the ART

In chapter 19, 'Designing the Implementation,' we described the process for defining the first value stream and the ART. At that stage of planning, the ART is expressed with just enough detail to determine that it's a potential ART. However, the details and boundaries of the ART are left to those who better understand the local context, expressed in an 'Agile Release Train canvas,' as shown in Figure 20-1.[1]

A key benefit of the ART canvas is that it helps teams identify the principal ART roles. Systems thinking teaches us that the people, management, and processes of the organization that builds the system are also a system, and by extension, the ART itself is a *system*. The responsibilities of system definition, building, validation, and deployment have to be realized for the *system* to function properly.

---

1. Thanks to SPCT Mark Richards for the ART canvas inspiration.

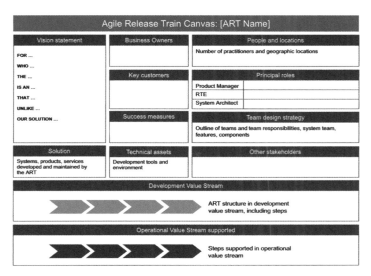

Figure 20-1. Agile Release Train canvas

WHO ARE THE BUSINESS OWNERS?

Business Owners are a small group of stakeholders who have the primary business and technical responsibility for governance, compliance, and return on investment for the ART's solution. To identify Business Owners, ask the following questions:

- Who is ultimately responsible for business outcomes?
- Who can speak to the technical competence and security of the solution now and in the near future?
- Who should participate in planning, help eliminate impediments, and speak on behalf of development, the business, and the customer?
- Who can approve and defend a set of Program Increment (PI) plans, knowing full well that they will never satisfy everyone?
- Who can help coordinate the efforts of the ART with other organizations within the enterprise?

The answers to these questions will help identify the Business Owners, who play a vital role in delivering the ART's value.

Setting the Program Cadence and Launch Date

The next step is to establish the *cadence* of the program, including both the PI and iteration lengths. The recommended duration of a PI is 8 to 12 weeks, with a bias toward the shorter duration (10 weeks, for example). This allows the ART to have a predictable rhythm and velocity. The fixed cadence also allows people to schedule a full year of program events on their calendars.

Providing notice of the program events reduces travel and facility costs, and helps assure that most of the stakeholders will be able to participate. Once the program calendar is set, team events can also be scheduled, with each team defining the time and place for its daily meetings, iteration planning, review, and retrospective. Typically, all teams on the train should use the same iteration start and end dates, which facilitates management across the ART.

With the ART definition in hand, the next step is to set a date for the *first PI planning event*. This provides a 'date-certain' deadline for the launch, which will set the starting point and define the planning timeline.

SETTING THE DATE

Jennifer Fawcett, SAFe Fellow at Scaled Agile, Inc., discusses the importance of setting a date and using it as a 'forcing function':

Without a date for the first PI planning event, there is no deadline, no planning horizon, and no sense of urgency. It's super easy to keep procrastinating until everything is perfect. Instead, consider some of the factors that should drive the date by asking yourself the following questions:

- Is there a milestone that is driving the date (such as releasing or a market window)?
- What is the cost of delay (CoD) for the launch? (Is our platform seriously on fire?)
- How quickly can we develop the backlog refine it, socialize it, and get it in a 'ready state'?
- How many people and locations do we need to train, and how quickly can we mobilize around their training?

Training the ART Leaders and Stakeholders

Depending on the scope and timing of the rollout, there may be several ART stakeholders who haven't attended a 'Leading SAFe' training session. As a result, they may be unfamiliar with SAFe, its operating model, and the expectations of them. It's essential that leaders understand and support the new model, as well as their new responsibilities as part of it. SPCs can mitigate this problem by organizing a 'Leading SAFe' class to educate these stakeholders and motivate their participation.

This is often followed by a one-day 'implementation workshop,' where newly trained stakeholders and SPCs can develop the specifics of the launch plan. Essentially, this event marks the hand-off of primary responsibility for the change from the change agents to the stakeholders of the newly formed ART.

Organizing the Agile Teams

During the implementation workshop, questions will arise regarding how to organize the Agile teams around the system's purpose and architecture. Similar to organizing the ARTs themselves, there are two primary patterns for organizing Agile teams:

- *Feature teams.* Focused on user functionality, they're optimized for fast value delivery. This is the preferred approach, as each team is capable of delivering end-to-end user value.

- *Component teams.* These teams are optimized for architectural integrity, system robustness, and reuse of assets (e.g., code, components, services). They should be limited to significant reuse opportunities, areas of high technical specialization, and critical Nonfunctional Requirements (NFRs).

Most ARTs have a mix of features and components teams. Notably, ARTs should avoid organizing teams around architectural layers (e.g., UI, business logic, database), as doing so creates dependencies that can impede the flow of new features.

Forming the Agile Teams

The next step is to form the Agile teams that will be on the train. One innovative solution is to enable the people on the ART to self-organize into Agile teams with a set of *minimal constraints.*

> **SELF-ORGANIZING INTO AGILE TEAMS**
>
> Em Campbell-Pretty, SAFe Fellow at Pretty Agile Pty. Ltd., describes how to facilitate self-organizing an ART into Agile teams in her book *Tribal Unity: Getting from Teams to Tribes by Creating a One Team Culture*. Em notes, "Whether you already have teams or you are looking at creating teams, you need to be clear about their mission, and then ensure teams have the right set of skills to deliver on those missions, ideally autonomously. I would add that we want real teams, not just groups of people who work together." You can also read about team self-selection in her blog, "Adventures in Scaling Agile."[2]

---

2. http://www.prettyagile.com/2017/01/facilitating-team-self-selection-safe-art.html

In other cases, management makes initial team selections based on their objectives, knowledge of individual talents and aspirations, timing, and other factors. In most cases, this requires a bit of back and forth between the teams and management.

Prior to PI planning, all practitioners must be part of a cross-functional Agile team, and the initial roles of Scrum Master and Product Owner must also be established. The team roster template shown in Figure 20-2 is a simple tool that can help clarify and visualize the organization of each team.

Team #	Team name	Role	Team member name	Geographic location
1	Team A	Scrum Master	LastName, FirstName	City, Country
2	Team A	Product Owner	LastName, FirstName	City, Country
3	Team A	Developer		
4	Team A	Developer		
5	Team A	Developer		
6	Team A	Tester		
7	Team A	Tester		
8	Team A	<role>		
9	Team A	<role>		

Figure 20-2. An Agile team roster template

The simple act of filling out the roster can be quite informative, as it starts to make the more abstract concepts of Agile development real. Even the seemingly simple act of dedicating an individual to one Agile team can be an eye-opening experience—but there's no going back. The rules of Agile (one person–one team) are fairly clear.

The *geographic location* column is also helpful, as it defines the amount of collocation and distribution for each team. Collocation is better, of course. Sometimes, however, one or more individuals cannot be physically located with the others. That situation may change over time, but at least everyone understands where the current team members reside, so they can start thinking about Daily Stand-up (DSU) times and other team events.

Training Product Owner and Product Managers

Product Owners and Product Managers steer the train together. They have content authority over features and stories, respectively. These two roles are critical to the success of the ART, and the people fulfilling them must be well trained in the new way of working, must ensure collaboration, and must understand how to best accomplish their specific responsibilities. In addition, these roles will be responsible for building the initial program backlog, which is a crucial PI planning artifact.

The 'SAFe Product Owner/Product Manager' course teaches Product Owners and Product and Solution Managers how to drive the delivery of value in the SAFe enterprise.

Training the Scrum Masters

 Effective ARTs rely on the servant leadership of Scrum Masters and their ability to coach Agile team members to improve their performance. A Scrum Master is a specialty role that includes traditional Scrum leadership duties, as well as responsibilities to the larger team-of-Agile-teams that constitute the ART. In SAFe, Scrum Masters also play a critical part in PI planning and help coordinate value delivery through Scrum of Scrums meetings.

'SAFe Scrum Master' training teaches the fundamentals and explores the role of Scrum in the context of SAFe. This course prepares Scrum Masters to facilitate team iterations, successfully plan and execute the PI, participate in ART events, and measure and improve the flow of work through the system using Kanban.

Assessing and Evolving Launch Readiness

Training people in their new roles and responsibilities is a vital part of ART readiness, but it's just one element within a successful ART launch. PI planning is a significant event, and preparation for it is required. The SAFe article 'Prepare for ART Launch'[3] provides a set of checklists for that purpose.

Of course, given that SAFe is based on the empirical Plan–Do–Check–Adjust (PDCA) model, there is no such thing as perfect readiness for a launch. Trying to be too perfect up front will delay learning, postponing the transformation and realization of its benefits.

Preparing the Program Backlog

As previously mentioned, using the launch date as a 'forcing function' increases the urgency to determine the scope and vision of the PI. The scope of the PI, or 'what gets built,' is defined by the program backlog—the set of upcoming features, NFRs, and architectural work that outline the future behavior of the system. Consequently,

---

3. www.scaledagileframework.com/prepare-for-art-launch/

SPCs and LACE stakeholders often bring the ART stakeholders together to prepare a common backlog. This is often done through a series of backlog workshops and other related activities.

Step 8. Train Teams and Launch the ART

The Agile team members on the ART are the people who will actually build the systems the business needs. It's vital that they understand their part in the ART and gain the Lean and Agile skills needed to be effective. So, the next significant task is to train all the teams in the SAFe way of working.

Training the Teams

The 'SAFe for Teams' course is designed for this purpose. This team-building and training course features an introduction to Agile development, including an overview of the Agile Manifesto, core Scrum elements, and an exploration of the roles of Scrum Master and Product Owner. It also includes preparation for PI planning and building a Kanban board for tracking stories. In addition, teams prepare their backlog, which identifies the work needed for the upcoming PI planning event.

When approaching this training, keep in mind that it's likely many of the team members will have some degree of experience with Agile development and might feel that they are already equipped to work in SAFe. However, this team training is critically important for SAFe success, as it provides guidance that goes far beyond Scrum practices for team agility in the larger enterprise.

The Benefits of Big-Room Training

In some rollouts, training is performed team by team over time. However, we recommend a more accelerated approach, which includes training all the team members simultaneously. This practice has raised some eyebrows in the industry. Many picture 100-plus people in a room learning simultaneously, compare it to the intimate setting of a small team with a single instructor, and can't imagine that it delivers equivalent benefits. In reality, it delivers far more. But this is something you almost have to experience to grasp its full effect, as the following story describes.

Following are some of Mark's key insights:

- The Agile teams will be fully formed, at the same time
- Teams engage in collective learning
- The features for the PI will be ready
- Teams form their own identities

As different as it is, the 'all-in, big-room training' approach is one of SAFe's most cost-effective and valuable implementation strategies.

Launch the ART

There are many ways to start an ART successfully, and there's no specific timeline for the preparation activities we described. However, experience has shown that the easiest and fastest way to launch an ART is through the ART Quickstart approach, as illustrated in Figure 20-3.

The ART Quickstart approach begins after sufficient preparation. Then, the Agile teams are trained, and the first PI planning session is held in a single week. Although this may seem daunting, numerous SAFe adoptions show it is the easiest and most pragmatic way to help 100-plus people transition to the new way of working.

---

4. https://www.scaledagileframework.com/train-teams-and-launch-the-art/

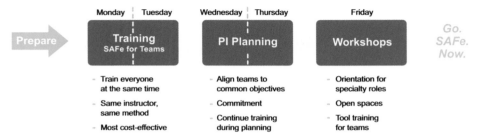

Figure 20-3. The one-week, all-in ART Quickstart approach

The First PI Planning Session

During the ART Quickstart, PI planning helps build team backlogs based on current priorities. It also reinforces the training team members have just received. Obviously, getting off to a good start with PI planning is essential to the success of the first PI. It demonstrates a commitment to the new way of working for all the teams and stakeholders. An effective first PI session will provide the following benefits:

- Build confidence and enthusiasm in the new way of working

- Start to establish the ART as a team-of-Agile-teams and the social network that it relies on

- Teach the teams how they can assume responsibility for planning and delivery

- Create full visibility into the mission and current context of the program

- Demonstrate the commitment of Lean-Agile Leaders to the SAFe transformation

To ensure a good outcome, an experienced SPC will typically co-facilitate the session.

Step 9. Coaching ART Execution

With the teams and stakeholders trained, and the new way of working now in effect, there's no going back. As you prepare to improve your practice of SAFe and evolve the organization, remember: Training people in Agile doesn't actually make them *agile*.

It's essential to actively coach the individuals who make up the ART and provide an environment that encourages learning and growth. Without this support, we would give up our responsibility as leaders and change agents. Instead, the Lean Enterprise

As a result, even the spread of good news to other value streams may not evoke an automatic embrace of SAFe across the enterprise. Many may think, 'What worked there may not work here.' So, in a sense, each new value stream represents the same challenge and opportunity to incorporate all the change management steps described so far. And each new value stream will need to go through the same series of steps that got you to this point, as illustrated in Figure 21-1.

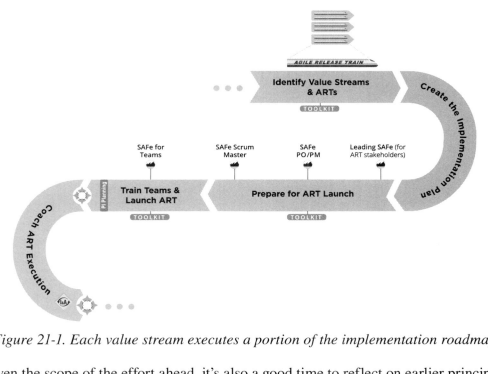

Figure 21-1. Each value stream executes a portion of the implementation roadmap

Given the scope of the effort ahead, it's also a good time to reflect on earlier principles and apply principle #6, 'Visualize and limit Work in Process (WIP), reduce batch sizes, and manage queue lengths.' We'll see these principles at work in the SAFe implementation railway, described next.

The SAFe Implementation Railway

A while ago, we had the opportunity to visit the folks at Northwestern Mutual Life Insurance & Financial Planning. We were so impressed by their Lean-Agile mindset, how they applied SAFe principles and practices, and the structured way they executed the implementation, that we asked if we could share their experience. One outcome was that Sarah Scott, SPC and Agile Lean Organization Coach at Northwestern Mutual, presented her company's work as a case study at the 2016 SAFe Summit. In turn, we've taken those insights and generalized their experience into guidance for what we now call the 'SAFe implementation railway.' The implementation railway metaphor is a fun and visual way to manage a large-scale transformation, as is described in the 'Launch more ARTs and value streams' article on the SAFe website.[2] For fun, now would be a good time to read this article!

With value streams and trains now running on a consistent basis, it's time to proceed to the next critical move in the SAFe implementation roadmap: extend to the portfolio.

Step 11. Extend to the Portfolio

 It's quite an accomplishment for an organization to have implemented SAFe across a set of value streams. The new way of working is well on its way to becoming second nature to everyone who had a role in the implementation. As a result, the effectiveness of the whole company starts to improve, and the broader goal is coming into sharper focus: a truly Lean-Agile enterprise with a fully implemented set of SAFe value streams.

This is a critical phase in the rollout: It tests the organization's commitment to transforming the business at all levels. Now is the time to expand the implementation across the entire portfolio to firmly anchor the new approach in the culture.

The success of these ARTs and value streams creates a buzz about the new and better way of working. At the same time, it tends to stimulate greater scrutiny of some of the higher-level business practices, which often reveals legacy, phase-gated processes and procedures that impede performance. Inevitably, that starts to put pressure on the portfolio and triggers the need for the additional changes that will be necessary to further improve the strategic flow across the portfolio. These issues typically include the following challenges:

- Too much demand versus capacity, which jeopardizes throughput and undermines strategy
- Project-based funding, cost-accounting friction, and overhead
- No understanding of how to capitalize expenses in an Agile business
- Overly detailed business cases based on speculative, lagging return on investment (ROI) projections

---

2. http://www.scaledagileframework.com/launch-more-arts-and-value-streams/

- Strangulation by the iron triangle (fixed scope, cost, and time projects)
- Traditional supplier management and coordination—focus on lowest cost, rather than highest life-cycle value
- Phase-gated approval processes that don't mitigate risk and actually discourage incremental delivery

Nowhere is Lean-Agile Leadership more important than in addressing these remaining legacy challenges. Without modernizing these approaches, the enterprise will not escape the inertia of its traditional legacy methods, causing the organization to revert to the old way of doing things. This inevitably leads to attempting Agile development with a non-Agile mindset, often referred to as 'Agile in name only.' The results can be severely compromised. But help is at hand. Figure 21-2 illustrates how these mindsets evolve with training and engagement while implementing SAFe.

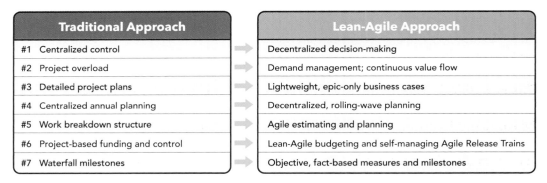

Traditional Approach		Lean-Agile Approach
#1 Centralized control	⇒	Decentralized decision-making
#2 Project overload	⇒	Demand management; continuous value flow
#3 Detailed project plans	⇒	Lightweight, epic-only business cases
#4 Centralized annual planning	⇒	Decentralized, rolling-wave planning
#5 Work breakdown structure	⇒	Agile estimating and planning
#6 Project-based funding and control	⇒	Lean-Agile budgeting and self-managing Agile Release Trains
#7 Waterfall milestones	⇒	Objective, fact-based measures and milestones

Figure 21-2. Evolving traditional mindsets to Lean-Agile thinking

Leading the Transformation

Many of these traditional mindsets exist throughout the organization and, left unchanged, can sabotage a fully realized implementation. To help the staff embrace the new way of working, we've described how SPCs and Lean-Agile leaders lead the transformation. Those leaders provide the knowledge needed to inspire an attitude that embraces the new mindset.

In many enterprises, however, Lean Portfolio Management (LPM) and Agile Program Management Office (PMO) personnel advance the need for change and provide the knowledge for the new way of working. They sponsor and participate in the LACE, support or encourage the development of the specialty communities of practice (CoPs) that focus on and advance the new roles, responsibilities, and behaviors. In so doing, they establish exemplary Lean-Agile principles, behaviors, and practices, as described in the following sections.

Align Value Streams to the Enterprise Strategy

Value streams exist for one reason: to meet the strategic goals of the portfolio. Implementing a process that establishes and communicates the strategic themes reinforces that result. This helps organize the portfolio into an integrated and unified solution offering. Strategic themes also inform value stream budgeting decisions, as described later.

Establish Enterprise Value Flow

Managing the flow of work from portfolio-level initiatives is an important step in the maturity cycle. This requires implementing the portfolio backlog and Kanban system, filling the role of Epic Owners by adopting the epics construct and Lean business case. Also, Enterprise Architects establish enabler epics—that is, common technological foundations support the broader use cases across the full portfolio.

Implement Lean Financial Management

As described in chapter 17, 'Lean Governance,' attempting to control the definition and cost of development via the 'project' construct only is problematic. As development proceeds using projects, the inevitable cost and schedule overruns cause personnel upheaval and financial churning. As we improve our methods and discover the long-lived nature of most work, we move to a more persistent flow-based, budgeting, and financial model. This new approach minimizes overhead, gives people a stronger sense of purpose, and facilitates the growth of institutional knowledge.

This is the larger purpose of the portfolio's value streams, funded by following SAFe strategy and investment funding practices.

Align Portfolio Demand to Capacity and Agile Forecasting

Lean thinking teaches us that any system operating in a state of overload will deliver far less than its potential capacity. This is certainly true for any development process in which excess work in process drives multiplexing (lowering productivity), unpredictability (lowering trust and engagement), and burnout (lowering everything).

22

Sustaining and Improving

"Excellent firms don't believe in excellence—only in constant improvement and constant change."

—Tom Peters

Introduction

In the previous chapters, we covered steps 1–11 of the implementation roadmap. In this chapter, we'll cover the last and most persistent step—step 12: sustain and improve.

Before we begin, we note that reaching this step is not the end, but rather the beginning of the new and larger journey of *relentless improvement*. The emerging Lean-Agile enterprise has started to build a new operating model and culture. Persistent progress is becoming the norm, but it can't be taken for granted. Sustaining and improving on the benefits gained requires dedication to basic and advanced practices, retrospection, and dedication to additional opportunities for improvement.

Here are some of the activities the enterprise can employ to ensure that the new practices become the new way of working and improving:

- Foster relentless improvement and the Lean-Agile mindset
- Implement Agile HR practices
- Advance program execution and servant leadership skills
- Measure and take action
- Improve Agile software engineering competencies

- Focus on Agile architecture
- Improve DevOps and continuous delivery capability
- Reduce time-to-market with value stream mapping

Each of these is described in the sections that follow.

Foster Relentless Improvement and the Lean-Agile Mindset

The effort continues right where it began—with leadership, relentless improvement, and the Lean-Agile mindset. Figure 22-1 illustrates the direct connection between leadership and relentless improvement.

Extending the benefits of SAFe requires that leaders set an example by providing a continuous sense of urgency for change. Activities include the following:

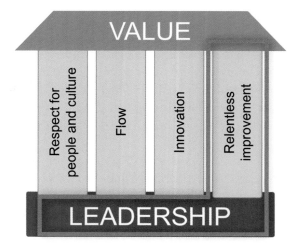

Leadership and relentless improvement are inseparable

"There is a constant sense of danger."

—*Toyota*

Figure 22-1. Lean leadership is the foundation for relentless improvement

- *Ongoing leadership training.* No matter how extensive the rollout training was, it most likely did not reach all the stakeholders who need to understand and embrace the new way of working. That includes individuals in the operations, human resources, legal, finance and accounting, sales, and marketing organizations, among others. If critical stakeholders don't understand or agree with the new culture, the enterprise will be applying a traditional, non-Agile governance model to a Lean-Agile development workforce. That doesn't scale; additional training is required.

- *Continuing role of the Lean-Agile Center of Excellence (LACE).* Earlier, we described the LACE as the engine of the 'sufficiently powerful coalition for change.' In the beginning, the primary role of the LACE is to implement the new way of working within the organization. After that, it often becomes a long-lived energy source inspiring continuous improvement.

- *Communities of Practice (CoPs).* Although it's influential, the LACE is just one part of the guiding coalition. To effectively sustain and improve the SAFe implementation, additional help is needed. As SAFe organizes people with different skills around a value stream, it may limit the opportunities to share knowledge and learn new skills with other people in the same role. As described in chapter 16, 'Agile Portfolio Operations,' CoPs help overcome this limitation by bringing people together around a subject domain, work roles, or other areas of common interest.

Implement Agile Human Resources Practices

Respect for people is a pillar of the SAFe House of Lean. After all, it's people who build these critical systems we all depend on. Given the importance of their contributions, management's challenge is to create an environment where workers can thrive and prosper.

Although Lean-Agile and SAFe provide many of the values and practices found within that environment, they also put extreme pressure on traditional human resources methods. To accommodate the modern knowledge worker, enterprises are compelled to embrace a new, Lean-Agile HR perspective. There are six major themes in this new point of view:

1. Embrace a modern talent contract, one that explicitly acknowledges the need for value, autonomy, and empowerment.

2. Foster continuous engagement with the business and technical missions.

3. Hire people for Agile attitude, team orientation, and cultural fit.

4. Eliminate annual performance reviews, replacing them with continuous, iterative performance feedback and evaluation.

5. Eliminate demotivating individual financial incentives. Take the issue of money off the table by paying employees enough to focus on the work, not the money.

6. Support meaningful, impactful, and continuous learning and growth.

For more on this topic, read the SAFe white paper, 'Agile HR with SAFe: Bringing People Operations into the 21st Century with Lean-Agile Values and Principles.'

Advance Program Execution and Servant Leadership Skills

Effective Agile teams and Agile Release Trains (ARTs) are the foundation of any SAFe implementation that produces substantial results. However, for facilitation and servant leadership, no roles are more important than those of the Scrum Master and Release Train Engineer (RTE). Once they become experienced with their responsibilities, these leaders will be ready to take the next step to help cultivate new skills and the performance of others. Additional training of these roles can include the following:

- *Advanced Scrum Master training.* The 'SAFe Advanced Scrum Master' (SASM) course prepares current Scrum Masters for their leadership role in enabling Agile team, program, and enterprise success. The course covers facilitating cross-team interactions to support program execution and relentless improvement. It enhances the Scrum paradigm with scalable engineering and DevOps practices, as well as the application of Kanban to facilitate the flow and support of interactions with Architects, Product Management, and other critical stakeholders.

-  *Release Train Engineer training.* Similarly, RTEs can improve their skills as Agile program managers, team coaches, and program-level facilitators. The 'SAFe Release Train Engineer' course with RTE certification is designed for this purpose. In this course, attendees gain an in-depth understanding of the role and responsibilities of an RTE. They learn how to facilitate and enable end-to-end value delivery through ARTs and value streams. Attendees also learn how to build a high-performing ART by becoming servant leaders and coaches, and how to plan and execute a PI planning event—the primary way to align all levels of a SAFe organization.

Measure and Take Action

Peter Drucker is credited with saying, "What's measured improves." In this section, we'll take a quick look at a few of the many opportunities to measure and act on the results.

Inspect and Adapt

The Inspect and Adapt (I&A) event is the cornerstone of program improvement. Unlike simpler forms of retrospectives, these events bring together the key stakeholders—the people who can change the systems in which everyone works—during a problem-solving workshop. They offer an objective demonstration, measurement, and structured root-cause analysis. *Leaders must actively encourage and participate in I&A problem-solving.* This closes the loop on the PI learning cycles and is the basis for continuously improving enterprise performance.

Lean Metrics

Lean metrics are agreed-upon measures that evaluate how well the organization is progressing toward the portfolio's, large solution's, program's, and team's business and technical objectives. Thanks to its work physics, timeboxes, and fast feedback, Lean-Agile development is inherently more measurable than prior methods. Chapter 17, 'Lean Governance,' and the metrics[1] article on the SAFe website provides many additional measures that enterprises can apply to objectively evaluate their progress toward better outcomes.

Enhance Performance with Self-Assessments

People don't like to be measured. After all, a person can be evaluated only by being compared to another person—and only the one at the top can feel good about that outcome. What's more, many measures traditionally applied to the development process and its workers are now obsolete. Instead, we suggest that teams self-assess themselves against agreed-to Agile values. SAFe provides a set of self-assessment worksheets for the team, program, large solution, and portfolio levels, with the results being presented in radar charts, as illustrated in Figure 22-2. See the metrics article on the SAFe website mentioned earlier to download the self-assessment spreadsheet.

---

1. www.scaledagileframework.com/metrics

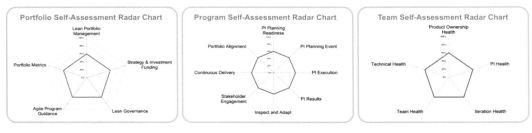

Figure 22-2. Example self-assessment radar charts

These assessments and others can be performed periodically to help teams, trains, and the portfolio advance their performance.

Improve Agile Software Engineering Practices

We've often observed that within the first year of adoption, teams can quickly reach an apparent velocity limit by implementing only the basic role and team project management practices. After that, further improvements in velocity and quality can occur through effective implementation of Agile technical practices.

Built-in quality software practices include continuous integration, test-first, test automation, and Behavior-Driven Development (BDD). Mastering these requires investing additional time and sharpening the team's focus, with the internal efforts typically augmented by outside experts who have applied these practices in other contexts. The Innovation and Planning (IP) iteration can often provide the dedicated time needed to master these new practices.

In addition, companies building really large and/or high-assurance systems need to focus on evolving the fixed and variable solution intent and maintaining architectural and other models that show how the system works. Implementing and advancing Model-Based Systems Engineering (MBSE) and Set-Based Design (SBD) can help develop and maintain these vital artifacts.

For teams building high-assurance systems—where the cost of error is simply unacceptable—these practices take place from verification through validation and compliance. Guidance for these practices are described in chapter 17, 'Lean Governance,' and the compliance[2] article on the SAFe website.

Focus on Agile Architecture

Whether the enterprise is Agile or not, it's impossible to build significant world-class systems without some degree of intentional architecture. However, the Big Design Up-Front (BDUF) practices of waterfall development are no longer relevant.

Instead, teams must evolve the solution architecture *while building the solution*. This includes creating the 'architectural runway' and practices for incrementally advancing legacy systems into the new platforms of choice. In other words, we have to change the engine while we're driving to the destination.

That's why it's effective to create an 'Agile architecture CoP.' This forum allows System, Solution, and Enterprise Architects to come together to define and learn the leaner and more incremental approaches to establishing and evolving solution architecture. It also permits them to advance their Agile architectural skills and craft. This CoP may address the following topics:

- Review and adopt the SAFe principles of Agile architecture
- Identify the enabler epics and capabilities necessary to evolve the solution architecture
- Identify methods of splitting architectural epics into enabler capabilities and features for incremental implementation
- Establish the decision-making framework and policies for architectural governance and capacity allocation
- Identify relevant Nonfunctional Requirements (NFRs)

In many enterprises, such CoP gatherings are run on the PI cadence, often aligned with the Innovation and Planning (IP) iteration. This conveniently supports the availability of development teams for fast feedback spikes to help establish the technical feasibility of design alternatives. The timing also supports the pressing need to prepare architectural concepts and models to review in the upcoming PI planning session.

---

2. www.scaledagileframework.com/compliance

Improve DevOps and Continuous Delivery

Once ARTs are launched, and value streams begin to operate better, the next set of bottlenecks and impediments becomes more visible. Often, improving the development cycle to be leaner just moves the bottleneck further down the value stream toward release and deployment. Some recommended practices to address this issue are described in chapter 9, 'Executing the Program Increment.' and the SAFe DevOps[3] and continuous delivery pipeline[4] articles on the SAFe website. Ultimately, achieving these goals requires shifting the company mindset and enabling the right environment. In turn, strong leadership is needed from managers and subject-matter experts who have the authority to create a continuous-value delivery culture. CoPs can also play a leading role.

Reduce Time-to-Market with Value Stream Mapping

Finally, there is another significant benefit to identifying the value streams and organizing release trains around them: Each value stream provides an identifiable and measurable flow of value to a customer. As such, 'value stream mapping' can be systematically applied to increase delivery velocity and quality. Value stream mapping involves five steps:

1. Map the current state by identifying all the steps, value-added times, hand-offs, and delays—from customer request to release.

2. Identify the most frequent sources of delays and hand-offs as the feature moves through the system.

3. Pick the biggest delay, and then perform root-cause analysis. Create improvement backlog items to reduce the delay. Reduce batch sizes wherever possible.

4. Implement the new improvement backlog items.

5. Measure again, and repeat the process.

ARTs apply value stream mapping to identify the steps and flow through the system. An example is illustrated in Figure 22-3. Teams quickly see that the amount of value-added touch time is a fraction of the time it takes to deliver the result. After all, it took them

---

3. http://www.scaledagileframework.com/devops/

4. http://www.scaledagileframework.com/continuous-delivery-pipeline

only 11 hours of work to create the new feature, yet it couldn't be delivered for 7 weeks! The majority of that time? Devoted to hand-offs and delays. The team has been working hard, and apparently efficiently from the touch time, but the flow through the system could not meet the demand. And don't expect that coding and testing faster will help. Instead, teams must adopt a system view and focus on delays. Reducing delays in the value stream is always the fastest way to reduce time-to-market. Using this procedure, the maturing Lean enterprise can systematically and continuously reduce time-to-market.

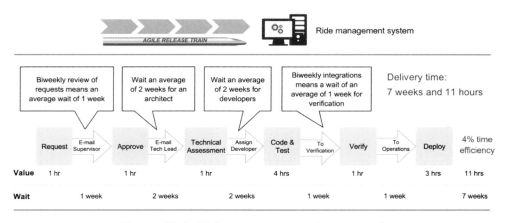

Figure 22-3. Value stream mapping example

Summary

Although it might appear so in the implementation roadmap, the sustain and improve step of the SAFe is not the last step in the transformation journey. Rather, it's the beginning of a new and larger journey of *relentless improvement*. The emerging Lean enterprise has started to build a new operating model and culture. Persistent progress is becoming the norm, but it can't be taken for granted. Sustaining and improving on the benefits gained requires dedication to basic and advanced practices, retrospection, and dedication to additional opportunities for improvement.

Conclusion and Moving Forward

"The rate of change is not going to slow down anytime soon. If anything, competition in most industries will probably speed up even more in the next few decades."
    —John P. Kotter

The marketplace is changing so rapidly that a paradigm shift is needed for how we support innovation to deliver increasingly valuable software and systems to the world. And yet, it seems that the bigger and more successful the company, the more difficult it is to change. Large enterprises can't innovate fast enough to keep pace with our increasingly digital world.

However, companies that effectively embrace innovative new development technologies and business models, and attack digital disruption head-on, can increase the value of existing products and services. No wonder 'disruption' is so powerful. It enables the emergence of new digital products, services, and businesses that upset the current market, triggering the need to reevaluate how enterprises innovate, operate, and adapt.

Fortunately, as we have discussed throughout this book, the last few decades have provided three bodies of knowledge that address these system-building challenges: Agile development, Lean product development, and systems thinking. SAFe unites these concepts—along with other industry trends—to bring new mindsets, thinking, and proven practices to answer this challenge. With SAFe, seemingly disparate practices—like Agile, Scaled Agile, Scrum, Kanban, Lean Startup, Lean UX, DevOps, and Continuously Delivery—need not be separate initiatives. Instead, they can be a continuum that helps enterprises deliver more innovative solutions at a velocity they could only imagine before. Also, SAFe is configurable and scalable. It meets the needs of small teams of teams, as well as the largest enterprise portfolios.

We can confidently say that nothing is more rewarding than creating an environment that inspires and motivates people to do their best and to meet each work day with joy and enthusiasm. The success of SAFe is a direct result of practicing what we preach. After all, we employ SAFe principles to run our entire business, not just product development. Our walls are plastered with Kanban boards, sticky notes, PI objectives, and backlogs. And we plan, iterate, and deliver using the same methods we recommend in SAFe. But most importantly, we embrace a learning mindset. We never assume that we have all the answers, and we do our best to listen as much to our detractors as we do to our enthusiasts. Indeed, we find motivations in both!

An organization that can unlock the intrinsic motivation of its people will perform at its highest level and fare significantly better in the marketplace than its less-inspired competitors. It will create a workplace that is rewarding, engaging, and fun. Mark Twain said it best: "Find a job you enjoy doing, and you will never have to work a day in your life."

However, we recognize that changing the way of working—both the habits and culture of a large development organization—is hard. Many enterprises report that implementing SAFe was simultaneously one of the toughest and, yet, most rewarding change initiatives they had ever experienced. We hope our book has inspired you to start or continue your learning journey to becoming a Lean Enterprise.

So, you may be asking yourself now, "where do I go next?" The last part of this book, 'Implementing SAFe,' provided a roadmap for the next steps on your journey. This roadmap functions as a guide that leads all who follow it to the road's ultimate destination—a Lean Enterprise. Here, winning is not a lucky random event, but a result of "the way we do things around here." This road will not always be easy to follow. Sometimes it may even seem to disappear. But remember to use SAFe's principles, values, and mindset to anchor and guide you, and you'll soon find your way forward.

Good luck on your journey, and we hope to see you in one of our classes or at one of the upcoming SAFe Summits!

Glossary

The Scaled Agile Framework (SAFe) glossary defines all of the terms on the Big Picture.

Agile Architecture
Agile architecture is a set of values and practices that support the active evolution of the design and architecture of a system while implementing new system capabilities.

Agile Release Train (ART)
The ART is a long-lived team of Agile teams, which, along with other stakeholders, develops and delivers solutions incrementally, using a series of fixed-length iterations within a Program Increment timebox. The ART aligns teams to a common business and technology mission.

Agile Team
The SAFe Agile team is a cross-functional group of 5 to 11 people who have the responsibility to define, build, and test, and where applicable deploy, some element of solution value—all in a short iteration timebox. Specifically, the SAFe Agile team incorporates the Dev Team, Scrum Master, and Product Owner roles.

Architectural Runway
The architectural runway consists of the existing code, components, and technical infrastructure needed to implement near-term features without excessive redesign and delay.

Built-In Quality
Built-in quality practices ensure that each solution element, at every increment, meets appropriate quality standards throughout development.

Business Owner
Business Owners are a small group of stakeholders who have the primary business and technical responsibility for governance, compliance, and return on investment for a solution developed by an Agile Release Train (ART). They are key stakeholders on the ART who must evaluate fitness for use and actively participate in certain ART events.

Capability
A capability is a higher-level solution behavior that typically spans multiple Agile Release Trains. Capabilities are sized and split into multiple features to facilitate their implementation within a single Program Increment.

Communities of Practice (CoPs)
CoPs are organized groups of people who have a common interest in a specific technical or business domain. They collaborate regularly to share information, improve their skills, and actively work on advancing the general knowledge of the domain.

Compliance
Compliance refers to a strategy and a set of activities and artifacts that allow teams to apply Lean-Agile development methods to build systems that have the highest possible quality, while simultaneously assuring they meet any regulatory, industry, or other relevant standards.

Continuous Delivery Pipeline
The continuous delivery pipeline represents the workflows, activities, and automation needed to provide a continuous release of value to the end user.

Continuous Deployment
Continuous deployment is the process that takes validated features from continuous integration and deploys them into the production environment, where they are tested and readied for release.

Continuous Exploration
Continuous exploration is the process of continually exploring the market and user needs and defining a vision, roadmap, and set of features that address those needs.

Continuous Integration
Continuous integration is the process of taking features from the program backlog and developing, testing, integrating, and validating them in a staging environment until they are ready for deployment and release.

Core Values
The four core values of alignment, built-in quality, transparency, and program execution represent the fundamental beliefs that are key to SAFe's effectiveness. These guiding principles help dictate behavior and action for everyone who participates in a SAFe portfolio.

Customer
Customers are the ultimate buyer of every solution. They are an integral part of the Lean-Agile development process and value stream and have specific responsibilities in SAFe.

Dev Team
The Dev Team is a subset of the Agile team. It consists of the dedicated professionals who can develop and test a story, feature, or component. The Dev Team typically includes software developers and testers, engineers, and other dedicated specialists required to complete a vertical slice of functionality.

Develop on Cadence
Develop on cadence is an essential method for managing the inherent variability of systems development in a flow-based system by making sure important events and activities occur on a regular, predictable schedule.

DevOps

DevOps is a mindset, a culture, and a set of technical practices. It provides communication, integration, automation, and close cooperation among all the people needed to plan, develop, test, deploy, release, and maintain a solution.

Economic Framework

The economic framework is a set of decision rules that align everyone to the financial objectives of the solution and guide the economic decision-making process. It contains four primary constructs: Lean budgets, epic funding and governance, decentralized decision-making, and job sequencing based on the Cost of Delay (CoD).

Enabler

Enablers support the activities needed to extend the architectural runway to provide future business functionality. These include exploration, infrastructure, compliance, and architecture development. Enablers are captured in the various backlogs and occur at all levels of the Framework.

Enterprise

The enterprise represents the business entity to which each SAFe portfolio belongs.

Enterprise Architect

The Enterprise Architect promotes adaptive design and engineering practices and drives architectural initiatives for the portfolio. The Enterprise Architect also facilitates the reuse of ideas, components, services, and proven patterns across various solutions in a portfolio.

Epic

An epic is a container for a solution development initiative large enough to require analysis, the definition of a minimum viable product, and financial approval prior to implementation. Implementation occurs over multiple Program Increments and follows the Lean startup 'build–measure–learn' cycle.

Epic Owner

Epic Owners are responsible for coordinating portfolio epics through the portfolio Kanban system. They define the epic, its minimum viable product, and Lean business case, and, when the epic is approved, facilitate its implementation.

Feature

A feature is a service that fulfills a stakeholder need. Each feature includes a benefit hypothesis and acceptance criteria, and is sized or split as necessary to be delivered by a single Agile Release Train in a Program Increment.

Foundation

The Foundation contains the supporting principles, values, mindset, implementation guidance, and leadership roles needed to deliver value successfully at scale.

Innovation and Planning (IP) Iteration

The IP iteration occurs every Program Increment (PI) and serves multiple purposes. It acts as an estimating buffer for meeting PI objectives and provides dedicated time for innovation, continuing education, PI Planning, and Inspect and Adapt events.

Inspect and Adapt (I&A)

The I&A event is held at the end of each Program Increment. During this significant event, the current state of the solution is demonstrated and evaluated by the train. Teams then reflect on and identify improvement backlog items via a structured, problem-solving workshop.

Iteration

Iterations are the basic building block of Agile development. Each iteration is a standard, fixed-length timebox, during which Agile teams deliver incremental value in the form of working, tested software and systems. The recommended duration of the timebox is two weeks. However, one to four weeks is acceptable, depending on the business context.

Iteration Execution

Iteration execution is how Agile teams manage their work throughout the iteration timebox, resulting in a high-quality, working, tested system increment.

Iteration Goal

Iteration goals are a high-level summary of the business and technical goals that the Agile team agrees to accomplish in an iteration. They are vital to coordinating an Agile Release Train as a self-organizing, self-managing team of teams.

Iteration Planning

Iteration planning is an event in which all team members determine how much of the team backlog they can commit to delivering during an upcoming iteration. The team summarizes the work as a set of committed iteration goals.

Iteration Retrospective

The iteration retrospective is a regular meeting where Agile team members discuss the results of the iteration, review their practices, and identify ways to improve.

Iteration Review

The iteration review is a cadence-based event in which each team inspects the increment at the end of every iteration to assess progress and then adjusts its backlog for the next iteration.

Large Solution Level

The large solution level contains the roles, artifacts, and processes needed to build large and complex solutions. This includes a stronger focus on capturing requirements in the solution intent, the coordination of multiple Agile Release Trains and suppliers, and the need to ensure compliance with regulations and standards.

Lean-Agile Leaders

Lean-Agile leaders are lifelong learners who are responsible for the successful adoption of SAFe and the results it delivers. They empower and help teams build better systems by learning, exhibiting, teaching and coaching SAFe's Lean-Agile principles and practices.

Lean-Agile Mindset

The Lean-Agile mindset is the combination of beliefs, assumptions, and actions of SAFe leaders and practitioners who embrace the concepts of the Agile Manifesto and Lean thinking. It serves as the personal, intellectual, and leadership foundation for adopting and applying SAFe principles and practices.

Lean Budgets

Lean budgets is a set of practices that minimize overhead by funding and empowering value streams rather than projects, while maintaining financial and fitness-for-use governance. This is achieved through objective evaluation of working systems, active management of epic investments, and dynamic budget adjustments.

Lean Portfolio Management (LPM)

The LPM function has the highest level of decision-making and financial accountability for the products and solutions in a SAFe portfolio.

Lean User Experience (Lean UX)

Lean UX is a mindset, a culture, and a process that embraces Lean-Agile methods. It implements functionality in minimum viable increments and determines success by measuring results against a benefit hypothesis.

Metric

Metrics are agreed-upon measures used to evaluate how well the organization is progressing toward the portfolio's, large solution's, program's, and team's business and technical objectives.

Milestone

Milestones are used to track progress toward a specific goal or event. There are three types of SAFe milestones: Program Increment, fixed-date, and learning milestones.

Model-Based Systems Engineering (MBSE)

MBSE is the practice of developing a set of related system models that help define, design, and document a system under development. These models provide an efficient way to explore, update, and communicate system aspects to stakeholders, while significantly reducing or eliminating dependence on traditional documents.

Nonfunctional Requirements (NFRs)

NFRs define system attributes such as security, reliability, performance, maintainability, scalability, and usability. They serve as constraints or restrictions on the design of the system across the different backlogs.

Portfolio Backlog

The portfolio backlog is the highest-level backlog in SAFe. It provides a holding area for upcoming business and enabler epics intended to create a comprehensive set of solutions, which provides the competitive differentiation and operational improvements needed to address the strategic themes and facilitate business success.

Portfolio Kanban

The portfolio Kanban is a method used to visualize, manage, and analyze the prioritization and flow of portfolio epics from ideation to implementation and completion.

Portfolio Level

The portfolio level contains the principles, practices, and roles needed to initiate and govern a set of development value streams. It is where strategy and investment funding are defined for value streams and their solutions. This level also provides Agile portfolio operations and Lean governance for the people and resources needed to deliver solutions.

Pre-and Post-PI Planning

Pre– and post–Program Increment (PI) planning events are used to prepare for, and follow up after, PI planning for Agile Release Trains and suppliers in a Solution Train.

Product Management

Product Management has content authority for the program backlog. These managers are responsible for identifying customer needs, prioritizing features, guiding the work through the program Kanban, and developing the program's vision and roadmap.

Product Owner

The Product Owner is a member of the Agile team responsible for defining stories and prioritizing the team backlog to streamline the execution of program priorities while maintaining the conceptual and technical integrity of the features or components for the team.

Program Backlog

The program backlog is the holding area for upcoming features, which are intended to address user needs and deliver business benefits for a single Agile Release Train. It also contains the enabler features necessary to build the architectural runway.

Program Increment (PI)

A program increment is a timebox during which an Agile Release Train delivers incremental value in the form of working, tested software and systems. PIs are typically 8–12 weeks long. The most common pattern for a PI is four development Iterations, followed by one Innovation and Planning iteration.

Program Increment (PI) Planning

PI planning is a cadence-based, face-to-face event that serves as the heartbeat of the Agile Release Train, aligning all the teams on the train to a shared mission and vision.

Program Kanban

The program and solution Kanban systems are a method to visualize and manage the flow of features and capabilities from ideation to analysis, implementation, and release through the continuous delivery pipeline.

Program Level

The program level contains the roles and activities needed to continuously deliver solutions via an Agile Release Train.

Release on Demand

Release on demand is the process by which features deployed into production are released incrementally or immediately to customers based on market demand.

Release Train Engineer (RTE)

The RTE is a servant leader and coach for the Agile Release Train (ART). The RTE's major responsibilities are to facilitate the ART events and processes and to assist the teams in delivering value. RTEs communicate with stakeholders, escalate impediments, help manage risk, and drive relentless improvement.

Roadmap

The roadmap is a schedule of events and milestones that communicate planned solution deliverables over a timeline. It includes commitments for the planned, upcoming Program Increment (PI) and offers visibility into the deliverables forecasted for the next few PIs.

SAFe Implementation Roadmap

The SAFe implementation roadmap consists of an overview graphic and a 12-article series that describes a strategy and an ordered set of activities that have proved effective in successfully implementing SAFe.

SAFe Program Consultant (SPC)

SAFe SPCs are change agents who combine their technical knowledge of SAFe with an intrinsic motivation to improve the company's software and systems development processes. They play a critical role in successfully implementing SAFe. SPCs come from numerous internal or external roles, including business and technology leaders, portfolio/program/project managers, process leads, architects, analysts, and consultants.

Scrum Master

Scrum Masters are servant leaders and coaches for an Agile team. They help educate the team in Scrum, Extreme Programming (XP), Kanban, and SAFe, ensuring that the agreed Agile process is being followed. They also help remove impediments and foster an environment for high-performing team dynamics, continuous flow, and relentless improvement.

ScrumXP

ScrumXP is a lightweight process to deliver value for cross-functional, self-organized teams within SAFe. It combines the power of Scrum project management practices with Extreme Programming (XP) practices.

Set-Based Design (SBD)

SBD is a practice that keeps requirements and design options flexible for as long as possible during the development process. Instead of choosing a single point solution up front, SBD identifies and simultaneously explores multiple options, eliminating poorer choices over time. It enhances flexibility in the design process by committing to technical solutions only after validating assumptions, which produces better economic results.

Shared Services
Shared Services represents the specialty roles, people, and services that are necessary for the success of an Agile Release Train or Solution Train but that cannot be dedicated to the train on a full-time basis.

Solution
Solutions are the products, services, or systems delivered to the customer, whether internal or external to the enterprise; they are produced by value streams.

Solution Architect/Engineer
The Solution Architect/Engineering role represents an individual or small team that defines a shared technical and architectural vision for the solution under development. Working closely with the Agile Release Train and Solution Train, this role participates in determining the system, subsystems, and interfaces; validates technology assumptions; and evaluates alternatives.

Solution Backlog
The solution backlog is the holding area for upcoming capabilities and enablers, each of which can span multiple ARTs and is intended to advance the solution and build its architectural runway.

Solution Context
The solution context identifies critical aspects of the operational environment for a solution. It provides an essential understanding of requirements, usage, installation, operation, and support of the solution itself. The solution context heavily influences opportunities and constraints for releasing on demand.

Solution Demo
The solution demo is the event in which the results of development efforts from the Solution Train are integrated, evaluated, and made visible to customers and other stakeholders.

Solution Management
Solution Management has content authority for the solution backlog. These managers work with customers to understand their needs, prioritize capabilities, create the solution vision and roadmap, define requirements, and guide work through the solution Kanban.

Solution Train
The Solution Train is the organizational construct used to build large and complex Solutions that require the coordination of multiple Agile Release Trains (ARTs), as well as the contributions of suppliers. It aligns ARTs with a shared business and technology mission using the solution vision, backlog, and roadmap, and an aligned Program Increment.

Spanning Palette
The Spanning Palette contains various roles and artifacts that may be applicable to a specific team, program, large solution, or portfolio context. A key element of SAFe's flexibility and configurability, the spanning palette permits organizations to apply only the elements needed for their configuration.

Spike

Spikes are a type of exploration enabler story in SAFe. Defined initially in Extreme Programming (XP), they represent activities such as research, design, investigation, exploration, and prototyping. Their purpose is to gain the knowledge necessary to reduce the risk of a technical approach, better understand a requirement, or increase the reliability of a story estimate.

Story

Stories are short descriptions of a small piece of desired functionality, written in the user's language. Agile teams implement small, vertical slices of system functionality and are sized so they can be completed in a single Iteration.

Supplier

A supplier is an internal or external organization that develops and delivers components, subsystems, or services that help Solution Trains provide solutions to their customers.

System Demo

The system demo is a significant event that provides an integrated view of new features for the most recent iteration delivered by all the teams in the Agile Release Train (ART). Each demo gives ART stakeholders an objective measure of the progress that occurred during a Program Increment.

System Team

The System Team is a specialized Agile team that assists in building and using the Agile development environment, including continuous integration, test automation, and continuous deployment. The System Team supports the integration of assets from Agile teams, performs end-to-end solution testing where necessary, and assists with deployment and release.

Team Backlog

The team backlog contains user and enabler stories that originate from the program backlog, as well as stories that arise locally from the team's local context. It may include other work items as well, representing all the things a team needs to do to advance its portion of the system.

Team Kanban

Team Kanban is a method that helps teams facilitate the flow of value by visualizing workflow, establishing Work in Process limits, measuring throughput, and continuously improving their process.

Team Level

The team level contains the roles, activities, events, and processes that Agile teams build and deliver value in the context of the Agile Release Train.

Test-First

Test-first is a built-in quality practice derived from Extreme Programming (XP) that recommends building tests before writing code to improve delivery by focusing on the intended results.

Value Stream

Value streams represent the series of steps that an organization uses to build solutions that provide a continuous flow of value to a customer. SAFe value streams are used to define and realize portfolio-level business objectives and organize Agile Release Trains to deliver value more rapidly.

Value Stream Coordination

Value stream coordination provides guidance to manage dependencies and exploit the opportunities in a portfolio.

Vision

The vision is a description of the future state of the solution under development. It reflects customer and stakeholder needs, as well as the features and capabilities proposed to meet those needs.

Weighted Shortest Job First (WSJF)

Weighted Shortest Job First (WSJF) is a prioritization model used to sequence jobs (e.g., features, capabilities, and epics) to produce maximum economic benefit. In SAFe, WSJF is estimated as the cost of delay divided by job size.

Index

Credits

Front cover: Scaled Agile, Inc.

Front cover: "SAFe has been a successful story for us...that has helped moved our team forward." Damian Brown, Sr. Director of Program Management Office, Fitbit

Back cover: Author photos by Stephen Collector

Preface: "SAFe Distilled is the book...as well as seasoned practitioners." Lee Cunningham, Sr. Director, Enterprise Agile Strategy at VersionOne, Inc.

Part I, Chapter 4: "If you can't describe what you are doing as a process, you don't know what you're doing." W. Edwards Deming

Chapter 1: "Every company is a technology...that shape our world." Stephenie Stone, Why Every Company Is A Technology Company Forbes Media, Jan 23, 2017. Published by Forbes.

Chapter 1: "Today, no company can make, deliver or market...into their production and service cycles." Stephenie Stone, Why Every Company Is a Technology Company Forbes Media, Jan 23, 2017. Published by Forbes.

Chapters 1, 4: "We are uncovering better ways of developing software by doing it, and helping others do it." Agile Manifesto

Chapters 1, 4: "A system must be managed. It will not manage itself...components toward the aim of the organization." The New Economics, William Edwards Deming, MIT Press, 2000.

Chapter 1: "All we are doing is looking...eliminating the non-value-added wastes." Taiichi Ohno,Toyota Production System, 01-Mar-1988, CRC Press.

Chapter 1: "The products we're developing are bigger...same product at the same time." Mike Eason, CIO, Commercial Banking, Capital One

Chapter 1: "Fostering a more engaged workforce...generate positive business results." SHRM Foundation Executive Briefing Employee Engagement: Your Competitive Advantage, https://www.shrm.org/resourcesandtools/business-solutions/documents/engagement%20briefing-final.pdf

Chapter 1: "With a proven framework...chance of success." Scaled Agile, Inc.

Part II: "The foundation for any successful change...principles and leadership." Richard Knaster, Dean Leffingwell

Chapter 3: "That is, while there...items on the left more", Jim Highsmith

Chapter 3: "Our highest priority is to satisfy...adjusts its behavior accordingly", Agile Manifesto

Chapter 3: "in the latter part...identifying the twelve principles." "The manifesto is a rallying...clear what is and isn't agile." Martin Fowler

Chapter 3: "This value is often put...PI Planning retro!" Scaled Agile, Inc.

Chapters 3, 4: "It is not enough that management...can change the system." W. Edwards Deming

Chapter 4: "The impression that 'our problems are different'...service are universal in nature." W. Edwards Deming, Out of the Crisis, August 11, 2000. Published by The MIT Press

Chapter 4: "A system must be managed", W. Edwards Deming

Chapter 4: "This can be an effective...suboptimal design", Marco Lansiti, "Shooting the Rapids: Managing Product Development in Turbulent Environments" (California Management Review 38, 1995)

Chapter 4: "While you may ignore economics, it won't ignore you", Donald Reinertsen, Principles of Product Development Flow, Celeritas Publishing

Chapter 4: "Generate alternative system-level...your most robust alternatives." Allen C. Ward, Lean Product and Process Development, Lean Enterprise Institute

Chapter 4: "The epiphany of integration...the project is in trouble", Dantar P. Oosterwal, The Lean Machine: How Harley-Davidson Drove Top-Line Growth and Profitability with Revolutionary Lean Product Development, AMACOM

Chapter 4: "process of converting...to knowledge", Dantar P. Oosterwal, The Lean Machine: How Harley-Davidson Drove Top-Line Growth and Profitability with Revolutionary Lean Product Development, AMACOM

Chapter 4: "There was, in fact...suggested the inverse might be true", Dantar P. Oosterwal, The Lean Machine: How Harley-Davidson Drove Top-Line Growth and Profitability with Revolutionary Lean Product Development, AMACOM

Chapter 4: "Operating a product development process near full utilization is an economic disaster", Donald Reinertsen, Principles of Product Development Flow, Celeritas Publishing

Chapter 4: "Cadence and synchronization limit the accumulation of variance", Donald Reinertsen

Chapter 4: "Future product development...react to the end results", Michael Kennedy, Product Development for the Lean Enterprise (Oaklea Press, 2003)

Chapter 4: "Knowledge workers are people...perform than their bosses", Peter F. Drucker, The Essential Drucker (Harper-Collins, 2001).

Chapter 4: "To effectively lead, the workers must be heard and respected." Peter Drucker

Chapter 4: "It appears that the performance...may be as basic as the others..." Daniel Pink, Drive: The Surprising Truth About What Motivates Us (Riverhead Books, 2011)

Chapter 4: "Autonomy is the desire to...goals to the company mission." Daniel Pink, Drive: The Surprising Truth About What Motivates Us (Riverhead Books, 2011)

Chapter 4: "our problems are not that different", W. Edwards Deming

Chapter 5: "Grow leaders who...philosophy, and teach it to others" The Toyota Way, Liker, Tata McGraw-Hill Education

Chapter 5: "Establish a sense … approaches in the culture", Leading Change, John P. Kotter, Harvard Business Publishing

Chapter 5: "Leader as expert … developer of people" David L. Bradford and Allan R. Cohen, Managing for Excellence (Wiley Publishing, 1997)

Chapter 5: "The Principle of Mission … minimal possible constraints." Donald Reinertsen, Principles of Product Development Flow, Celeritas Publishing

Chapter 5: "Listening. Listen to employees … within your organization" The Power of Servant-Leadership, Robert K. Greenleaf, Berrett-Koehler Publishers

Chapter 5: "Leaders switch roles … instead of financial rewards", Leadership's Online Labs, Byron Reeves, Thomas W. Malone and Tony O'Driscoll, Harvard Business Publishing

Part III: "Simplicity — the art of maximizing the amount of work not done — is essential", W. Edwards Deming

Chapter 6: "The more alignment you have, the more autonomy you can grant. The one enables the other", Stephen Bungay

Chapter 7: "Future product development … understand and react to the end results", Michael Kennedy, Product Development for the Lean Enterprise (Oaklea Press, 2003)

Chapter 7: "There is no magic in SAFe … except maybe for PI Planning." Scaled Agile, Inc.

Chapter 7: "I recall one PI planning event … team might take", Scaled Agile, Inc.

Chapter 7: "SAFe's use of PI objectives … expose these misunderstandings" Scaled Agile, Inc.

Chapter 7: "Staying ahead of PI preparation … alignment that PI planning fosters." Scaled Agile, Inc.

Chapter 7: "After the first day of … on the Big Picture." Scaled Agile, Inc.

Chapter 7: "During the confidence vote … everyone believed in." Scaled Agile, Inc.

Chapter 7: "I recently helped a European …" Scaled Agile, Inc.

Chapter 8: "Few ideas work on the first try. Iteration is key to innovation." Sebastian Thrun, chairman and co-founder of Udacity

Chapter 8: "Delivering full stories serially avoids the mini-waterfall", Scaled Agile, Inc.

Chapter 8: "Implementing stories in vertical slices", Scaled Agile, Inc.

Chapter 8: "A simple storyboard", Scaled Agile, Inc.

Chapter 8: "Continuous attention to technical excellence and good design enhances agility." Agile Manifesto

Chapter 8: "a disciplined technique for restructuring an existing body of code, altering its internal structure without changing its external behavior." Martin Fowler, Refactoring: Improving the Design of Existing Code (Addison-Wesley Professional, 1999).

Chapter 9: "Vision without execution is hallucination", Thomas Edison

Chapter 9: "Introducing the Continuous Delivery Pipeline", Scaled Agile, Inc.

Chapter 9: "A Surprising Discovery From Down Under: 'The team quickly made … what was running in production.'" Em Campbell-Pretty, SAFe Fellow and SPCT at Pretty Agile, Pty. Ltd

Chapter 9: "A Story From Facebook About Dark Launches: 'The secret for going from zero to seventy … UI lights have been turned on.'" Dark Launches, Gradual Ramps and Isolation: Testing the Scalability of New Features on your Web Site

Chapter 9: "Rehearse Failures With Chaos Monkey: 'Chaos Monkey is a service developed by Netflix … will be alert and able to respond.'" Netflix/SimianArmy Chaos Monkey

Chapter 10: "At regular intervals, the team reflects on how to become more effective, then tunes and adjusts its behavior accordingly." Agile Manifesto

Part IV: "No solution can ever be found by running in three separate directions." Scaled Agile, Inc.

Chapter 11: "Everything must be made as simple as possible. But not simpler", Scaled Agile, Inc.

Chapter 11: "While we use SAFe's solution intent to manage requirements … maintain over the life of the system." Harry Koehnemann, SAFe Fellow and SPCT at Scaled Agile

Chapter 12: "At its heart, engineering … a noble profession", Queen Elizabeth II

Chapter 12: "working software over comprehensive documentation", Jim Highsmith

Chapter 12: "Such early decisions … to waste and rework", Allen C. Ward and Durward Sobek, Lean Product and Process Development (Lean Enterprise Institute, 2014).

Chapter 13: "Principle of Alignment … with local excellence", Donald G. Reinertsen

Part V: "Being able to … but it is not easy", Geoffrey Moore

Part V: SAFe for Lean Enterprises, screenshot of Scaled Agile © Scaled Agile, Inc.

Chapter 14: "Most strategy dialogues … issues this abstract", Geoffrey Moore, Escape Velocity

Chapter 15: "Do our innovation … genuine competitive separation?:, Geoffrey Moore

Chapter 15: "The way to get … encourage strategy execution", Strategy Execution: Leadership to Align Your People to the Strategy

Chapter 15: "Robert Kaplan and David Norton … likely to support it", Strategy Execution: Leadership to Align Your People to the Strategy

Chapter 16: "The thing is … they're mutually reinforcing", Michael Porter, Harvard Business School professor

Chapter 16: "By documenting the … never-ending process", Standardized Work: The Foundation for Kaizen (1 Day Class)

Chapter 17: "A bad system will beat a good person every time." W. Edwards Deming

Chapter 17: "To address uncertainty … and increase learning", Joe Vallone, SPCT and Senior Consultant at Scaled Agile, Inc.

Chapter 17: "Innovation Accounting refers … within established companies", Definition of innovation accounting, lexicon

Chapter 17: "Inspection is too late. The quality good, or bad, is already in the product." W. Edwards Deming

Part VI: "Many leaders pride … the critical moves", Chip Heath and Dan Health, Switch: How To Change Things When Change Is Hard (Crown Business, 2010)

Part VI: "script the critical moves", Chip Heath and Dan Health, Switch: How To Change Things When Change Is Hard (Crown Business, 2010)

Chapter 18: "A strong guiding … and shared objective", Kotter, John P. Leading Change. Harvard Business Review Press

Chapter 18: "In a rapidly moving … under these circumstances", Kotter, John P. Leading Change. Harvard Business Review Press

Chapter 18: "vision for change", Kotter, John P. Leading Change. Harvard Business Review Press

Chapter 18: Implementing SAFe, screenshot of Scaled Agile © Scaled Agile, Inc.

Chapter 18: Leading SAFe, screenshot of Scaled Agile © Scaled Agile, Inc.

Chapter 18, Figure 18-2: screenshot of Scaled Agile © Scaled Agile, Inc.

Chapter 19: "Break down barriers between departments", W. Edwards Deming

Chapter 19, Figure 19-2: screenshot of Scaled Agile © Scaled Agile, Inc.

Chapter 19, Figure 19-3: screenshot of Scaled Agile © Scaled Agile, Inc.

Chapter 19, Figure 19-4: screenshot of Scaled Agile © Scaled Agile, Inc.

Chapter 19, Figure 19-5: screenshot of Scaled Agile © Scaled Agile, Inc.

Chapter 19, Figure 19-6: screenshot of Scaled Agile © Scaled Agile, Inc.

Chapter 19, Figure 19-7: screenshot of Scaled Agile © Scaled Agile, Inc.

Chapter 19, Figure 19-9: screenshot of Scaled Agile © Scaled Agile, Inc.

Chapter 19, Figure 19-10: screenshot of Scaled Agile © Scaled Agile, Inc.

Chapter 19, Figure 19-11: screenshot of Scaled Agile © Scaled Agile, Inc.

Chapter 19, Figure 19-13: screenshot of Scaled Agile © Scaled Agile, Inc.

Chapter 19: "Without a date for the first PI planning … everything is perfect." Jennifer Fawcett, SAFe Fellow at Scaled Agile, Inc.

Chapter 20: "Train everyone and launch trains", SAFe advice

Chapter 20: "Whether you already … who work together", Tribal Unity: Getting from Teams to Tribes by Creating a One Team Culture.

Chapter 20, Figure 20-1: screenshot of Scaled Agile © Scaled Agile, Inc.

Chapter 20: SAFe Product Owner/Product Manager, screenshot of Scaled Agile © Scaled Agile, Inc.

Chapter 20: SAFe Scrum Masters, screenshot of Scaled Agile © Scaled Agile, Inc.

Chapter 20: SAFe for Teams, screenshot of Scaled Agile © Scaled Agile, Inc.

Chapter 20, Figure 20-3: screenshot of Scaled Agile © Scaled Agile, Inc.

Chapter 21: "Consolidate gains and produce more change", Kotter, John P. Leading Change. Harvard Business Review Press, 1996

Chapter 22: "Excellent firms don't...and constant change", Tom Peters

Chapter 22, Figure 22-1: screenshot of Scaled Agile © Scaled Agile, Inc.

Chapter 22: SAFe Advanced Scrum Master, screenshot of Scaled Agile © Scaled Agile, Inc.

Chapter 22: SAFe Release Train Engineer, screenshot of Scaled Agile © Scaled Agile, Inc.

Chapter 22, Figure 22-2: screenshot of Scaled Agile © Scaled Agile, Inc.

Chapter 22, Figure 22-3: screenshot of Scaled Agile © Scaled Agile, Inc.

scaledagileframework.com

The world's leading framework for enterprise agility

- Freely available knowledge base of proven, integrated principles and practices for Lean, Agile, and DevOps
- Configurable and scalable for Teams, Programs, and Portfolios
- Role-based curriculum, worldwide Partner Network, and global community

---

SCALED AGILE®
LEARNING AND CERTIFICATION

scaledagile.com/learning

A comprehensive role-based curriculum for successfully implementing SAFe

- Actionable learning for every SAFe role
- Globally consistent courseware and certification
- Skills validation through professional certification

SCALED AGILE®
PARTNER NETWORK

scaledagile.com/partners

Worldwide SAFe expertise and support through 180+ Partners

- Training and coaching for all SAFe roles
- Implementation and consulting services across industries and disciplines
- Platforms for SAFe automation, visibility, and flow

SAFe®
COMMUNITY

scaledagile.com/community

Continuous learning, tools, and connections for SAFe professionals

- Network and learn with 200,000 SAFe professionals
- Advance your career with in-demand skills and certification
- Access tools, guidance, and role-based Communities of Practice

SAFe role-based curriculum

Scaled Agile offers a portfolio of professional credentials designed to meet the needs of Lean-Agile professionals. Each certification is supported by world-class courseware and value-added resources that prepare the individual to succeed as a key player in a SAFe enterprise.

SAFe courses and certifications include:

- **Implementing SAFe®**
  with SAFe® 4 Program Consultant certification

- **Leading SAFe®**
  with SAFe® 4 Agilist certification

- **SAFe® for Teams**
  with SAFe® 4 Practitioner certification

- **SAFe® Scrum Master**
  with SAFe® 4 Scrum Master certification

- **SAFe® Advanced Scrum Master**
  with SAFe® 4 Advanced Scrum Master certification

- **SAFe® Release Train Engineer**
  with SAFe® 4 Release Train Engineer certification

- **SAFe® Product Owner/Product Manager**
  with SAFe® 4 Product Owner/Product Manager certification

- **SAFe® DevOps**
  with SAFe® 4 DevOps Practitioner certification

- **More courses in development!**

FOR COURSE INFORMATION AND REGISTRATION, VISIT

scaledagile.com/**learning**

Register Your Product at informit.com/register
Access additional benefits and **save 35%** on your next purchase

- Automatically receive a coupon for 35% off your next purchase, valid for 30 days. Look for your code in your InformIT cart or the Manage Codes section of your account page.
- Download available product updates.
- Access bonus material if available.*
- Check the box to hear from us and receive exclusive offers on new editions and related products.

Registration benefits vary by product. Benefits will be listed on your account page under Registered Products.

InformIT.com—The Trusted Technology Learning Source

InformIT is the online home of information technology brands at Pearson, the world's foremost education company. At InformIT.com, you can:
- Shop our books, eBooks, software, and video training
- Take advantage of our special offers and promotions (informit.com/promotions)
- Sign up for special offers and content newsletter (informit.com/newsletters)
- Access thousands of free chapters and video lessons

Connect with InformIT—Visit informit.com/community

the trusted technology learning source

Addison-Wesley • Adobe Press • Cisco Press • Microsoft Press • Pearson IT Certification • Prentice Hall • Que • Sams • Peachpit Press

 Pearson